PASSENGER
STEAMERS
OF THE
RIVER
CONWY

Map of the River Conwy.

PASSENGER STEAMERS
OF THE
RIVER CONWY

SERVING THE FAMOUS
TREFRIW SPA

RICHARD CLAMMER

The
History
Press

First published 2014

The History Press
The Mill, Brimscombe Port
Stroud, Gloucestershire, GL5 2QG
www.thehistorypress.co.uk

© Richard Clammer, 2014

The right of Richard Clammer to be identified as the Author
of this work has been asserted in accordance with the
Copyright, Designs and Patents Act 1988.

British Library Cataloguing in Publication Data.
A catalogue record for this book is available from the British Library.

ISBN 978 0 7509 5902 5

Typesetting and origination by Thomas Bohm, User design
Printed in Great Britain

Contents

Author's Note

Acknowledgements

The greatest joy of researching and writing a book such as this is the new friendships and acquaintances which are made along the way. I have been tremendously grateful for the generosity, support and encouragement shown by a large number of friends, correspondents, organisations and institutions who have given freely of their time and knowledge, as well as allowing access to their collections and archives. Without them the book could not have been completed.

My interest in the Conwy steamers was first aroused in the 1980s by my good friend, the late Eric Payne of Ryde, Isle of Wight. A respected steamer historian, Eric was intrigued by some postcards he had obtained showing small paddle steamers moored at Trefriw Quay, a location which was then completely unknown to us both. Hearing that I was planning a holiday in North Wales during 1983, Eric asked me to investigate. Armed with copies of his cards, my family and I tracked down the location, penetrated the undergrowth on the overgrown quay and met Mrs Pritchard-Whykehurst, who was then living in the former Belle Vue Spa house. She showed us the Chalybeate water taps which still survived in the former veranda area and wittily pointed out the disadvantages of living in a house with only one living room but many, many bathrooms!

Initial reading revealed that, unlike many British pleasure steamers, the vessels which operated between Conwy and Trefriw had gone almost completely unrecorded, and that many maritime historians were unaware that they had ever existed. I decided to try to rectify the situation and a letter to the *North Wales Weekly News* led me to a number of valuable local contacts who had first-hand knowledge of the old steamers.

Pre-eminent amongst these was the late John R. Evans of Llandudno Junction, who had a deep and detailed knowledge of the area's maritime past. His father, Tom Evans, had served on board the river steamers for twenty-five years and John had spent much of his childhood sailing up and down the river. He had undertaken a great deal of research which he shared freely and his detailed letters and notes provided a superb reference point for my own investigations. He was a keen advocate of the publication of this history and it is a source of great regret that his death during 2009 prevented him from seeing it finished. In a similar vein, the late Doris Williams, daughter of Huw 'Black' Williams, the last engineer of the *King George*, Bill Edwards of Llandudno Junction, Kenneth Kay and Michael Meacher were all able to provide valuable, personal memories of the steamers.

Malcolm Fielding of the Inland Waterways Association, John Galvin, Stephen Gay, Geoffrey Hamer, Andy Heath, Brian Hillsdon (historian of the Steam Boat Association), Keith MacArthur, Ollie Pardo-Roques and Jane Salt of Sheffield Newspapers Ltd all provided valuable assistance with establishing the history of the *Princess Mary* after she left Conwy.

Crawford Alexander and Geoff Ellerton have provided all the information regarding the *Trefriw Belle*'s postal cachets, as well as giving me access to their photographic collections.

The Rt Rev. James Hannigan, Bishop of Menevia and Fr Quigley of St Mary's Church helped me to resolve the mystery of Fr Baron, the steamer-owning priest of Rhyl.

Two descendants of the Roberts family, Elsbeth Pears and Haydn Ward, have provided a wealth of information together with many priceless photographs from their extensive family archives, and ensured that my telling of the story of the generations of ship-owning captains is as accurate as possible.

In and around Conwy, Ken Hughes and Clifford Hughes have shared their extensive, practical knowledge of the passenger launches, mussel-gathering and river lore. Andrea Hughes from the harbour office has given much support, while respected local historian Llew Groom of Gyffin has provided much support and advice and tried to ensure that, as a non-native of the area, I do not make too many contextual blunders.

In Trefriw, Jim and Karen Black, Tony Ellis, Pat Rowley, Aneurin and Gladys Hughes and all the other members of the Trefriw Historical Society have been enormously supportive, sharing their knowledge and resources and encouraging my efforts, as an outsider, to record an aspect of their village. Custodian of the Trefriw Wells until its closure in 2011 and leading authority on the history of the site, Hilary Rogers-Jones, has read the relevant sections of the manuscript and given much valuable advice. Lindsay and Anne Gordon, proprietors of the Princes Arms Hotel, have allowed me access to their collection of items relating to the Victorian heyday of the Belle Vue.

Thanks are also due to Capt. Stephen Carter, the late Aled Eames, Andrew Gladwell of the Paddle Steamer Preservation Society Archives, Brian Jackson, Dr David Jenkins of the National Museum of Wales, Lewis Lloyd, Malcolm McRonald, Alan Sharp, Mike Tedstone, Ifor Williams and the members of the History of Deganwy Group for their advice and contributions.

I must record my thanks for the patient help and support given by the staff of the following archives and libraries:

Bangor Library
Bangor University Library
Bodleian Library, Oxford
Conwy Archives, Llandudno
Classic Boat Museum, Cowes
Gwynedd Archive, Caernarfon
Llandudno Library
Science Museum Library, London and Wroughton
Sheffield University Library
The National Archives, Kew (formerly the Public Record Office)
The National Library of Wales, Aberystwyth
National Maritime Museum Cornwall, Falmouth

Finally, I thank my wife Carol, who has accompanied me on all of my research trips to North Wales and spent endless hours immersed in various archives. Her patience, good humour, advice and encouragement have been beyond the call of duty!

A NOTE ON THE ILLUSTRATIONS

The author and publishers have made every effort to establish and acknowledge the provenance of each illustration used in the book and apologise if any copyright has been inadvertently infringed. Unless otherwise stated, all illustrations are from the author's collection.

Thanks are due to Alan Kittridge who drew the maps and gave considerable help with scanning and enhancing many of the photographs.

I

Setting the Scene

The River Conwy has its birth some 1,488ft (454m) above sea level, where it spills from the small lake called Llyn Conwy on the high, boggy peat moorlands overlooked by the mountains of Pen y Bedw, Eidda and Migneint. From there the infant stream tumbles its way north-eastwards across high, open country past Ysbyty Ifan to its confluence with the Afon Merddwr. Swinging sharply to the north-west, the river changes dramatically in character, cutting its way through deep, wooded gorges and ravines, over ledges and falls, past Foelas Hall and Padog to its confluence with the Afon Machno. Its augmented waters then descend over the tumbled rocks and tilted strata of the impressive Conwy Falls and through the famous Ffôs Noddyn or Fairy Glen before flowing onwards through a series of deep and beautiful pools to Betws-y-Coed.

Betws, lying as it does near the confluence of the Conwy, Lledr and Llugwy river valleys, has long been an important hub for travellers, a position consolidated by the decision to carry Telford's important Shrewsbury to Holyhead road across the Conwy at this point on a fine, cast-iron bridge known, from its 1815 opening date, as the Waterloo Bridge. The inns and shops which grew up to service the needs of those early travellers and subsequent Victorian tourists continue to serve the needs of the modern holiday-makers and Betws remains a bustling and popular town.

Below Betws-y-Coed the river enters the beautiful and tranquil Vale of Conwy. The valley gradually widens and the Conwy wanders gently across a flat and pastoral floodplain backed, especially to the west, by steep, wooded slopes rising to mountains beyond. At Llanrwst, on the eastern side of the valley, the river passes under the distinctive, three-arched bridge before crossing back to Trefriw on the western side of the valley where it is joined by the Afon Crafnant, which tumbles down from Llyn Crafnant, high in the hills above. This section of the Conwy, although placid in summer, is given to severe winter flooding, and extensive cobs or flood banks are apparent everywhere.

Below Trefriw Quay, which marked the former head of navigation, the river channel remains narrow and reed-fringed until, after passing Dolgarrog with its HEP station and former aluminium works, and Tal-y-Bont, it begins to widen appreciably and the influence of the tide become more apparent. After passing over the rocky outcrops known as The Arrows which make the river impassable at low tide and under Tal-y-Cafn Bridge, site of an ancient ferry and drovers' crossing, the true tidal estuary is reached. At high tide the river stretches like a wide, silver lake from shore to shore, but at low water reveals the extensive sand banks through which a braided channel picks its way down past Cwmryd Point to the west and Glan Conwy to the east, before making its dramatic entry past the magnificent medieval castle and under the three famous bridges into the ancient town and port of Conwy.

At Conwy itself the river has a rise and fall at spring tides of over 23ft (7m) and correspondingly swift tidal flows. The main channel runs between lines of moorings and extensive sandbanks for about 1½ miles down past Twthill Point before squeezing between the shingle spit of Conwy Morfa to the south and Deganwy to the north and disgorging its waters into the open sea of Conwy Bay, some 28 miles from the river's source.

Llanrwst.   The Bridge and Hotel.

The famous three-arched bridge at Llanrwst. On the opposite side of the bridge to the prominent hotel the road leads towards Gwydir Castle on the west bank of the Conwy and thence either south to Betws-y-Coed or north to Trefriw.

The River Conwy winding its way northwards towards the sea, viewed from high on the eastern bank above Tal-y-Cafn. This photograph was taken soon after a bridge replaced the ancient Tal-y-Cafn ferry in 1897.

A view taken from the hills above Glan Conwy looking north-westwards past the castle and the Conwy bridges towards the sea. The steamer landing stage at Conwy can be seen extending out from the shore between the castle and Bodlondeb woods on the hill behind. Deganwy stands on the point on the right, with St George's Harbour on the extreme right. West Shore, Llandudno, is located in the bay beyond Deganwy and in the far distance is the bulk of the Great Orme.

It is the 12 or so miles of navigable water between Deganwy, Conwy and Trefriw Quay which form the setting for this history, and the charming and picturesque village of Trefriw itself which provided the *raison d'être* for the development of a passenger steamer service on the river.

Nestling in a gentle arc against a steep hillside beneath the ridge of Cefn Cyfarwydd and overlooking the flat pastures of the floodplain, the village developed along and above the minor road which follows the western side of the Vale of Conwy at the point where the Crafnant and Geirionydd streams flow into the Conwy. Because of its position and aspect it is blessed with an agreeable microclimate, which played a major part in its development as a Victorian health resort. As early as 1879 Morris Jones[1] commented that:

> Regarding the village itself, its situation is such that germs cannot live there – every part of it is on a self-cleaning slope – its breeze is pure and balmy, and its beautiful surface receives the morning sun's most healthy greeting, so that it correctly deserves its title – the healthiest spot in Wales.

In addition to its topographical and climatic blessings, the village benefitted from the presence of a celebrated chalybeate well whose iron- and sulphur-rich waters were probably first discovered between AD 100 and 250 by soldiers of the 20th Roman Legion which was stationed at nearby Canovium (Caerhun). The mineral springs issue from a cave cut into the hillside at Cae Coch 1½ miles north of the village itself and as early as 1753 they were in regular use by local people and visitors. Sometime after that date, falling spoil and debris from the Cae Coch

'The healthiest place in Wales': The village of Trefriw nestling above the floodplain and beneath the mountains on the western bank of the River Conwy.

sulphur mine situated directly above closed the entrance to the cave and the wells lay abandoned and virtually forgotten until 1833 when they were excavated once again.

The beneficial qualities of the waters were claimed to offer a cure for anaemia, skin diseases, indigestion, rheumatism, palsies, nervous disorders, 'brain fag' and many other conditions and, as their fame spread, visitors began to flock to the area in search of health and amusement. At this time access to the caves was free and each morning small groups of visitors could be seen wending their way along the road from their accommodation in the lodging houses of Trefriw. Each armed with a wine glass or mug, a candle and a supply of matches, they would make their way into the three-branched cave to drink the waters or, if brave enough, to immerse themselves in the rock-hewn trough which served as the only bath. A later guidebook reflected that 'the lack of privacy, and the inconvenience occasioned thereby, rendered bathing not only a matter of considerable difficulty, but a most embarrassing ordeal'.[2]

The village also boasted a long and distinguished history. Llywelyn Fawr (Llywelyn the Great, *c.* 1173–1240) is said to have built a residence at Trefriw and later, to save his wife Joan the effort of walking up the steep mountainside to the old church at Llanrhychwyn, constructed the first church in the valley. At the end of the fifteenth century the powerful Wynn family purchased the Gwydir estate, which comprised vast tracts of land around Trefriw and Llanrwst, from Llywelyn's descendants and established their family seat on the site of the current Gwydir Castle. In their relentless pursuit of wealth and influence, subsequent generations of the Wynn family enlarged the estate, mined and quarried extensively in the hills for slate, lead and other minerals, felled timber from their forests and even improved the course of the River Conwy to allow larger vessels to reach their quay at Trefriw. Their influence on the industrial development of the area cannot be overstated and it is interesting to note that it was not until 1896 that their successors, the Barons Willoughby de Eresby and the Earls of Ancaster, gave up their ownership of the parish of Trefriw.

By the mid-1700s Trefriw was the site of Gwynedd's first printing press, where first the poet Dafydd Jones and later Ismael Davies and John Jones, produced poems, broadsheets, religious books and almanacs until 1825. The village was an early centre for the Nonconformist movement and by 1851 the census recorded that almost as many residents worshipped at the Calvanistic Methodist and Independent chapels as at the Anglican church of St Mary.

Trefriw's first fulling mill or pandy dated back to the fifteenth century, but it was during the first half of the nineteenth century that the water power available from the fast-flowing Crafnant stream was harnessed to better effect. A saw mill, slate-shaping mill and flour mill were established, soon to be joined by John William's iron foundry and forge, which manufactured iron goods, tools and mining equipment and, at its peak, employed twenty-five workers. In 1820 a new water-powered fulling mill replaced much of the village's previous cottage industry and, following its purchase in 1859 by Thomas Williams, developed into a major industry which survives to this day as the Trefriw Woollen Mill.

In an era when railways had yet to be built and the road carriage of heavy goods was both slow and difficult, it is easy to see why Trefriw Quay, situated at the head of navigation of the Conwy, close to the mineral and timber resources of the Gwydir estate and only 2½ miles by road from the important market town of Llanwrst, soon developed regional importance. It is not certain when the first quay was built at Trefriw, but a storehouse adjoining the quay was recorded in 1754. It would seem that the present structure, then under the ownership of the Gwydir estate, was constructed in about 1811, and that subsequent dredging and blasting of the river bed near Tal-y-Cafn soon made it accessible to seagoing vessels. In 1833 Samuel Lewis[3] recorded that:

> Vessels of 60 tons burden come up to this place bringing coal, lime and other heavy goods for Llanrwst and the neighbouring parishes, and conveying downwards the produce of the slate quarries of Trefriw and Llanrhychwyn. Lead ore and zinc exist in the parish and have lately been produced to a considerable extent.

By great good fortune, a number of the 'Trefriw Port Books' for the period 1826–76[4] have survived in local archives, enabling a detailed analysis to be made of the ships and cargoes which passed through the little port. Colin Thomas,[5] in his study of the period 1826–35, established that the quay handled between 350 and 450 vessels per year, divided into two clear groups. By far the largest number – 1,801 or 90 per cent – were river lighters (barges propelled by sail and sweeps) trading between Trefriw and Conwy where, it can be presumed, most of their cargo was transhipped into larger seagoing vessels for onward transport. The remainder were larger coastal sailing vessels known as flats, sloops or ketches, which were the heavy goods vehicles of their day and carried up to 35 tons, as compared with lighters' 4.9 tons, trading directly between Trefriw and Liverpool, Mostyn, Flint, Chester and a host of smaller ports and creeks along the North Wales coast.

Slate, which was quarried not only at Trefriw Quarry but also as far away as Cwm Penmachno and the slopes to the north of Blaenau Ffestiniog, absolutely dominated the export trade, accounting for as much as 81 per cent of the total tonnage handled at the quay. Almost all of this went downstream in lighters for transhipment at Conwy. Copper and lead ores and pyrites made up a further 11 per cent, most of which went direct to Liverpool, while timber, bark and a few small cargoes of hay, wool and salt made up the residue.

An early view looking upstream across the floodplain towards Llanwrst from the road above Trefriw Quay. On the right are the new Belle Vue Hotel and the road leading towards the first houses of Trefriw. The village itself is hidden in the trees beneath the mountain slopes in the middle distance. (Lindsay Gordon, Princes Arms Hotel)

Imports, although remarkably similar to exports in terms of tonnage, were of a completely different nature and reflected the agricultural and domestic requirements of both the Gwydir estate and the communities of the Vale. Limestone, which was burned and used to improve the soils on the upland and valley farms, made up 49 per cent and arrived exclusively in lighters from Conwy. Culm and coal accounted for a further 41 per cent, the latter being used to burn limestone and as the preferred domestic fuel for the wealthy, which arrived in seagoing vessels largely from Liverpool, Mostyn and Flint. The remaining 10 per cent of imports were made up of sawn timber, salt, grain, millstones and other 'sundry goods'.

Between the 1830s and '50s the trade continued to grow and many vessels, several of them locally owned, appeared regularly in the pages of the Port Books. In 1847, for example, the *Trefriw Trader*, *Britannia*, *Gwydir Castle*, *Marquis*, *Connovium* and *Phoebe* all called repeatedly. Some of their voyages also became more adventurous, with the *Trefriw Castle* and *Gwydir Castle* bringing coal from St Helens and the *Phoebe* venturing as far as Dublin and Newry with export cargoes of slate and oak bark.

By the late 1840s Trefriw was thus firmly established both as a developing but somewhat informal health resort and as a small but flourishing port serving Llanrwst, the upper vale and the Gwydir estate. It was in this context that the unique passenger steamship service which forms the subject of this history was to develop and flourish for almost a century.

Notes

1. Jones, Morris, *Gwyalchen o'r Cwm, 'Hanes Trefriw' / The History of Trefriw as it Used to be and as it is Now* (Llanrwyst, W.J. Roberts, 1879).(Translated by Tony Ellis and published by the Trefriw Historical Society, 2009).
2. 'Trefriw Chalybeate Wells, N. Wales, the Richest Iron Waters Known' (1908), in the collection of Trefriw Wells.
3. Lewis, S., *A Topographical Dictionary of Wales* (London, S. Lewis & Co., 1833) (later editions 1844 & 1849).
4. Bangor University Library, ref 26049 and 10390.
5. Colin Thomas, 'The Shipping Trade of the River Conway in the Early Nineteenth Century', in *Transactions of the Caernarvonshire Historical Society*, Vol.33 (1972), pp. 233–45.

2

The Packet Service – *Y Pacad Bach*, 1847–63

Navigation of the river above Conwy, although an everyday event which would have excited little comment at the time, required considerable skill and local knowledge, especially when a deep-laden, seagoing vessel was involved. Firstly the shifting and unmarked channel through the extensive sand and gravel banks between Conwy and Tal-y-Cafn had to be negotiated and then, once The Arrows ledge had been safely crossed, the vessel had to be worked up the ever-narrowing river to Trefriw. The motive power was sail, oar and possibly bow-hauling from the bank in the narrow upper reaches, assisted by the flow of the tide. Boats would go up river on the last few hours of the flood tide and return on an ebb, but the limited 'stand' of high water of just over an hour at Trefriw meant that return on the same tide was virtually impossible. Lighters would be forced to remain at the quay for at least one tide, while larger vessels often took several days to discharge and load their cargo before returning downstream.

Meanwhile, all around the British coast, change was afoot. Newfangled steamships, which had made their commercial debut on the Clyde with John Bell's famous *Comet* in 1812, were becoming more reliable and widely accepted. With their wooden hulls, clipper bows, huge paddle boxes, tremendously tall funnels and full sailing rig, they had established themselves on a number of regular coastal and cross-Channel packet routes and had first appeared on the North Wales coast in 1821 when the *Cambria* began operating from Liverpool to Bagillt on the River Dee. A year later the *Albion* established the first service to the Menai Strait, to be followed by other famous names such as the *Prince Llewelyn*, *Vale of Clwyd*, *Ormrod*, *Satellite*, *St David*, *Benledi*, *Erin-go-Bragh* and the ill-fated

Rothsay Castle, which was wrecked with great loss of life on the Dutchman's Bank in the entrance to the Menai Strait during August 1831. Many of these ships were owned by the dominant St George Steam Packet Company of Liverpool, Dublin and Cork (1821–43) and competition with other operators for the booming excursion trade to Rhyl, Bangor, Beaumaris and Menai Bridge became intense. On any summer's day during 1847 a watcher on the Great Orme would certainly have seen the *Cambria*, *Medina* or *Prince of Wales* en route from Liverpool to Menai Bridge, the *Mersey* or the new *Orion* heading for Caernarfon, or one of the Irish Packets belching smoke and sparks as she passed well offshore.

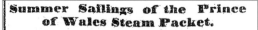

Summer Sailings of the Prince of Wales Steam Packet.

THE CITY OF DUBLIN COMPANY'S Splendid and Powerful NEW IRON STEAMER the

PRINCE OF WALES,

(Of 400 Tons Burthen, and 200 Horse power,

W. H. WARREN, R. N., Commander,

(Built expressly for the Station,)

HAS commenced her SUMMER SAILINGS, and will continue to leave MENAI BRIDGE on *MONDAYS, WEDNESDAYS, & FRIDAYS,* at Ten o'clock in the Morning; and from PRINCE's PIER HEAD, LIVERPOOL, on *TUESDAYS, THURSDAYS,* and *SATURDAYS,* at Eleven o'clock in the Morning.

Coaches for Holyhead, Carnarvon, & Amlwch, wait the arrival of the Prince of Wales, to convey Passengers forward, and return in the Morning in time to proceed to Liverpool.

Further particulars may be had on application to Mr. E. W. Timothy, or Mr. Henry Humphreys, Menai Bridge; Mr. John Jones, Ship-agent, Carnarvon; Mr. Robt. Pritchard, Post-master, Bangor; Mr. T. Byrne, Post-master, Beaumaris; or to Mr. J. K. Rounthwaite, at the Company's Office, 24 Water Street, Liverpool.

A newspaper advertisement, dated 8 May 1848, for the *Prince of Wales*, which was one of the regular steam packets engaged on the Liverpool–Menai Strait service. The generic woodblock illustration gives a good impression of a typical coastal steamer of the times.

Conwy itself received its own dedicated packet service in 1837 when the *Conway Castle*, commanded by John Jones, commenced sailing each Monday and Friday, returning from Liverpool each Wednesday and Saturday. Fares were 2s 6d on deck and 5s in the cabin. Her Conwy agent was one David Evans and passengers and luggage were landed free of charge in boats belonging to her owners. In addition, other coastal steamers would call in on special occasions, such as the

Prince of Wales' visit during an excursion via Conwy and Menai Bridge to Red Wharf Bay to witness a visit by the Royal Yacht in August 1847.

Thus, by 1847, the maritime fraternity of Conwy would have had over twenty years to become familiar with the coastal steamships and their ability to maintain a regular timetable on packet services and excursions, and would also have been aware of the imminent introduction of a steam ferry service across the Menai Strait from Bangor. It was therefore only a matter of time before someone considered the advantages of introducing a light-draught steamboat on a regular daily packet service between Conwy and Trefriw.

The result of these considerations was the *St Winifred*, a small paddle steamer which is said to have arrived on the river during 1847, although the first firm documentary evidence of her existence so far discovered dates from 1851. No picture of her has yet been discovered and her dimensions and details have gone unrecorded, though she is likely to have been in the order of 70ft long and capable of floating in a little over 1ft of water. Writing in the *North Wales Weekly News* in 1976, the late Ivor E. Davies[1] stated that:

> The only iron ship built [on the Conwy] was a paddle boat, one of those that plied up the river to Trefriw during the summer. It was built by John Williams, the versatile forge master whose forge was on the Crafnant stream behind the woollen factory at Trefriw. The plates were shaped at the forge but brought to be riveted together where the mussel purification tanks are today (at the mouth of the Gyffin stream near Conwy castle) where also the two railway tubes were fabricated.

Since the builders of all subsequent River Conwy passenger steamers are known, the steamer concerned must be *St Winifred*. Another reference,[2] however, suggests that she may have been built by Isaac Watt Boulton in Ashton-under-Lyme and either transported in sections for re-erection at Conwy, or floated through the inland waterways to Chester and thence along the coast. One is forced to wonder whether, in the 1840s, the expertise existed in the Conwy valley to design a steamer and construct her engines and boilers and, since Boulton is known to have constructed a number of small inland steamers at around that time, whether the Ashton-under-Lyme account is the more plausible. It is quite possible that elements of both stories are true and that Boulton designed the vessel and built her machinery, but sub-contracted either the construction or re-erection of her prefabricated hull to John Williams or other skilled iron workers. We know for certain that there was no shortage of the latter, since, between June 1846 and January 1849, the mouth of the Gyffin stream was the site of the prefabrication of the two vast, 1,300-ton iron tubes for Robert Stephenson's innovative iron bridge (which was to carry the Chester to Holyhead railway across the Conwy);

furthermore, experienced riveters and steam engineers were in ready supply. However, until definitive evidence comes to light, it is only possible to speculate.

What we do know is that the ship was named after St Winifrede, or Gwenfrewi, the seventh-century Welsh nun who, according to legend, was beheaded by Prince Caradoc after she had resisted his sexual advances. From the spot where her head fell, a spring of healing water broke forth which, now known as St Winifred's Well at Holywell, Flintshire, remains a place of pilgrimage to this day. St Winifred was resurrected after her head was reunited with her body by her uncle, the monk Beuno, and she went on to become Abbess of Gwytherin until her death around AD 650. The name was therefore a particularly appropriate and happy choice for a little steamer intended to voyage daily to the healing wells at Trefriw.

St Winifred was owned by the Inland Steam Navigation Company, more usually referred to as the Inland Company, and details of her sailings could be obtained from her master, Capt. W. Jones of Rose Hill, Conwy, or from Mr Edward Jones at the Blue Bell Inn, Conwy. She appears to have sailed from a berth in the mouth of the Gyffin stream at a point close to the present-day bowling greens and offered a year-round packet service to Trefriw, sailing every day of the week except Sunday, whenever the tide permitted.

A view looking downstream across the mouth of the Gyffin stream towards Conwy Castle and Stephenson's recently completed tubular bridge of 1848/9. Behind the tubes can be seen the shape of Telford's 1826 suspension bridge. The steamer entering the Gyffin should be the *St Winifred*, but it is clear that the engraver has exercised a high degree of artistic licence and has inserted a typical coastal packet of the period, whose tall masts would have precluded her from passing under the Conwy bridges.

A surviving timetable for October to December 1851 reveals fascinating detail of her schedule. The immutable cycle of the tides, which dictated that each successive high water is roughly half an hour later than the previous one, meant that her departure times changed continually. She would normally depart from Conwy approximately 2 hours before high water, take about 1¼ hours to sail upstream and spend between 15 minutes and 1¾ hours alongside alongside Trefriw Quay before returning on the first of the ebb tide. The length of her stay at Trefriw seemed to depend on the height of the tide. At spring tides, which ran faster and rose higher, she would make a faster passage upriver and be able to remain at Trefriw for longer while, conversely, neap tides meant less flow in the river, a slower passage, less rise of tide at Trefriw and therefore a shorter stay. In later years the river steamers were unable to reach Trefriw at all on small neap tides, but it is interesting to note that in the 1840s and '50s the river must have been deeper, since *St Winifred* was clearly able to make the passage throughout each month. The existence of a small lane in Llanrwst called Steam Packet Alley has led to speculation that *St Winifred* might have originally continued upstream to berth below Llanrwst Bridge, but since all contemporary accounts agree that Trefriw was the terminus, the name would appear to be more a result of local wishful thinking than of reality.

Sailings broadly kept to daylight hours although, in the dark, winter months recorded in the timetable, departures from Conwy as early as 5 a.m. and return sailings from Trefriw as late as 6.30 p.m. must have called for considerable skill on the part of Capt. Jones while navigating the winding river in pitch black. Just occasionally, if the tides were particularly early and late, it was possible to make two return trips in a day, as on Friday 3 October 1851 when *St Winifred* sailed from Conwy at 5 a.m., returned from Trefriw at 6.30 a.m., spent the low-water period lying on the mud in the Gyffin stream and then repeated her morning timings during the early evening.

Fares were 1s single, and it was noted that 'Cars [horse-drawn carriages] attend the steamer's arrival at Trefriw, and take passengers at very reasonable fares to Llanrwst, Betws y Coed, the springs, etc.'. Trefriw's first purpose-built hotel, the Belle Vue, had been erected on a terrace immediately above the quay during 1847 and it is clear that *St Winifred*'s owners had as much of an eye on the growing tourist market as on the their regular passengers and cargo trade. As early as July 1852 *Fraser's Magazine for Town & Country*[3] was commenting that 'a little steamer, not bigger than a jolly boat, plies between Trefriw, a couple of miles below Llanrwst, and Conway. The ride in this Lilliputian conveyance, at high tide, down the Conway, is perfectly lovely.'

Trade was clearly very encouraging, for, in 1852, the Inland Company added a second steamer to their fleet. Named *St George*, we know with absolute certainty that she was built in Staffordshire by Isaac Watt Boulton, who went on to found

THE STEAM PACKET
ST. WINIFRED,
IS INTENDED TO SAIL BETWEEN
CONWAY & TREFRIW,
DURING THE YEAR 1851, AS UNDER:—

	OCTOBER			NOVEMBER			DECEMBER		
		From CONWAY	From TREFRIW		From CONWAY	From TREFRIW		From CONWAY	From TREFRIW
SATURDAY		....	...	1	3 35 P.M.	5 10 P.M.		...	....
MONDAY		....	...	3	6 30 A.M.	7 45 A.M.	1	4 0 P.M.	5 30 P.M.
TUESDAY		....	...	4	7 0 ,,	8 20 ,,	2	5 0 A.M.	6 30 A.M.
WEDNESDAY	1	1 30 P.M.	4 0 P.M.	5	7 30 ,,	9 15 ,,	3	6 30 ,,	8 0 ,,
THURSDAY	2	3 0 "	5 0 "	6	8 0 ,,	10 0 ,,	4	7 0 ,,	8 30 ,,
FRIDAY	3	3 30	5 15	7	9 5 ,,	11 0 ,,	5	7 30 ,,	9 0 ,,
DITTO		5 0 A.M.	6 30 A.M.						
SATURDAY	4	5 0 P.M.	6 30 P.M.	8	9 45 ,,	12 0 ,,	6	8 0 ,,	9 30 ,,
MONDAY	6	7 15 A.M.	9 0 A.M.	10	10 0 ,,	1 0 P.M.	8	9 45 ,,	12 0 ,,
TUESDAY	7	8 0 A.M.	10 0 A.M.	11	10 30 ,,	1 30 ,,	9	9 45 ,,	12 30 P.M.
WEDNESDAY	8	9 0 "	10 30 "	12	11 35 ,,	2 0 ,,	10	10 0 ,,	1 0 ,,
THURSDAY	9	9 45 "	12 0 "	13	12 10 ,,	3 0 ,,	11	11 35 ,,	2 0 ,,
FRIDAY	10	9 45 "	12 30 P.M.	14	12 30 P.M.	3 30 ,,	12	12 0 P.M.	2 30 ,,
SATURDAY	11	10 0 "	1 0 "	15	1 0 ,,	4 0 ,,	13	12 30 ,,	3 0 ,,
MONDAY	13	11 35 "	2 0 "	17	4 30 ,,	6 0 ,,	15	2 50 ,,	4 30 ,,
TUESDAY	14	12 5 "	3 0 "	18	5 30 A.M.	6 45 A.M.	16	4 0 ,,	5 30 ,,
WEDNESDAY	15	12 5 P.M.	3 0 "	19	6 30 ,,	8 0 ,,	17	4 30 ,,	6 30 ,,
THURSDAY	16	12 10 "	3 45 "	20	7 15 ,,	9 0 ,,	18	6 0 A.M.	7 30 A.M.
FRIDAY	17	1 30 "	4 30 "	21	8 30 ,,	10 0 ,,	19	7 0 ,,	8 30 ,,
SATURDAY	18	3 30 "	5 0 "	22	9 0 ,,	10 30 ,,	20	7 15 ,,	9 30 ,,
MONDAY	20	5 30 A.M.	7 0 A.M.	24	9 45 ,,	1 0 P.M.	22	9 45 ,,	12 0 P.M.
TUESDAY	21	7 5 "	8 50 "	25	10 0 ,,	1 30 ,,	23	9 45 ,,	12 30 ,,
WEDNESDAY	22	7 30 "	9 13 "	26	11 35 ,,	2 30 ,,	24	10 0 ,,	1 0 ,,
THURSDAY	23	8 30 "	10 15 "	27	12 10 ,,	2 30 ,,	25		
FRIDAY	24	9 45 "	12 0 "	28	12 30 ,,	3 0 ,,	26	12 10 P.M.	2 30 ,,
SATURDAY	25	9 45	1 0 P.M.	29	1 30 P.M.	3 30 ,,	27	12 15 ,,	2 30 ,,
MONDAY	27	11 40 "	1 30 "		...	...	29	1 30 ,,	3 40 ,,
TUESDAY	28	12 15 P.M.	2 0 "		...	...	30	2 30 ,,	4 0 ,,
WEDNESDAY	29	12 30 "	2 30 "		...	...	31		
THURSDAY	30	1 0 "	3 0 "						
FRIDAY	31	1 30 "	4 0 "						

FARE, ONE SHILLING.

N.B.——Cars attend the Steamer's arrival at Trefriw, and take Passengers at very reasonable Fares to Llanrwst, Bettws y Coed, the Springs, &c.

Further information can be obtained by applying to Captain W. Jones, Rose Hill, or to Mr. Edward Jones, Blue Bell Inn, Conway.

H. JONES, PRINTER, STANLEY STREET, HOLYHEAD.

The first known sailing bill for *St Winifred*, covering the period October–December 1851.

A *North Wales Chronicle* advertisement for the river service, dated September 1852.

the famous Ashton-under-Lyme railway locomotive construction and hire company known as 'Boulton's Sidings'.

Born in 1823, Isaac was the son of Millwright John Boulton, who made and lost his fortune running horse-drawn passenger packet boats on the Peak Forest and other canals. Having served his apprenticeship with the works department of the Sheffield, Ashton & Manchester Railway, Isaac spent some years assisting his father in the management of the canal packet service before a combination of railway competition and the loss of 120 horses to the disease glanders led to its extinction in 1845. Isaac then set up as an engineer in his own right, built a steam coach, which he operated between Ashton and Manchester, and went on to construct a steamboat for the North Staffordshire Railway to operate on pleasure trips on Rudyard Lake, as well as with several other steam vessels of up to 75ft in length. He continued to run his own business until 1854 and it is during this period that *St George* was constructed. His biography[4] claims that steam vessels he built included 'the first tourist steamers to ply on the River Conway to Trefriw', and it is the use of the plural in this statement which gives rise to the suspicion that he may also have been responsible for *St Winifred*.

Having been completed at Isaac Watt Boulton's Ashton-under-Lyme works, *St George* was then partially dismantled and either brought in sections by rail or floated through the inland waterways to Chester where, on 28 July 1852, the *North Wales Weekly News* took up the story:

SUMMER AQUATIC EXCURSIONS – A pretty little steamer the *St George* has been lying at the Crane Wharf, Chester, this week which is intended to ply between Conway and Trefriw, in the Vale of Llanrwst. Trefriw is famed for its mineral springs and is annually resorted to by numbers of invalids who are greatly benefitted by the medicinal properties of the water. The village is very romantically situated in the most delightful vale in North Wales, and is within easy distances of Bettws-y-Coed, Capel Curig, Snowdon, Conway, Llanrwst, etc, etc. There are several beautiful waterfalls in the neighbourhood. The River Conway is a small but very picturesque stream and abounds with sport for anglers. The *St George* has been partially fitted up at Chester. She is of iron and was built in Staffordshire for the Inland Steam Navigation Company. By a novel and ingenious contrivance, the invention of Mr Gray the designer, the man who has the direction of the engine also guides the boat; a wire passing through the cabin from the rudder enabled the man standing at the paddle boxes to accomplish this. The *St George* is 20 horse power and draws only one foot of water. She is about 60 feet long, has a covered and an open cabin and will carry 120 passengers. She will leave Chester today.

A later copy of her registration documents, dated 14 October 1907, states that she was 72.3ft long, 10.2ft in the beam (plus paddle boxes) and had a depth of 4.07ft, measured from the side of her deck amidships to the bottom of the keel. Great care needs to be taken, however, when interpreting the stated depth of a vessel. Since we know that *St George* was able to float in a little over 1ft of water, this figure actually tells us that her freeboard, or distance of the deck above water, was a very modest 3ft, a fact that must have caused considerable anxiety to her crew during the coastal delivery passage from Chester to Conwy. An early photograph of the ship gives interesting detail of her layout. Her open foredeck, where any cargo would be stowed, was completely open and unadorned, with the ship's iron plates and frames clearly visible and forming the bulwarks. The wooden deck was placed right in the bottom of the hull and passengers sitting on the very basic wooden spar seating which was fitted along both sides would practically have been able to trail their fingers in the water as the ship steamed along.

Aft of the paddle boxes the deck was raised to the level of the top of the hull and surrounded by strong, wooden bulwarks which also extended out on to the aft sponsons. A few steps led down into a small saloon, where headroom and light was provided by a raised clerestory roof running down the ship's centre line. This also doubled as bench seating for passengers on the upper deck.

The ship was steered from between the large paddle boxes which, rather unusually, lacked the decorative, radial vents common in later steamers and simply bore the bold legend 'The Regular Steam Packet St George from Conway to Trefriw and back'. She had no mast, but had a tall thin funnel fitted to the top of the boiler, aft of the engines and paddle boxes. The register informs us that her engine was of a diagonal, direct-acting, surface-condensing design, that her engine room was 21.9ft long, and that she was capable of steaming at 8 knots. Since machinery of this type would have been rather sophisticated and unusual for the period, one is left to wonder whether *St George* was originally built with simpler oscillating or side-lever machinery and subsequently re-engined and lengthened at a time when we know that other modifications took place.

August 1852 was clearly blessed with some periods of calm weather as *St George* arrived safely in Conwy and by the beginning of September had joined *St Winifred* on the river. Newspaper adverts stated that 'One of the Inland Company's Steamers is intended to sail between Conway and the Vale of Llanrwst, 2 hours before high water daily' at a fare of 1s and referred would-be travellers

The earliest known photograph of a Conwy steamer shows the *St George*, as originally built, lying on the mud at low tide in her berth in the Gyffin stream between trips to Trefriw. Note her distinctly workaday appearance, with large, planked paddleboxes and rough, heavy bulwarks, well-suited to her early role as a year-round passenger and cargo packet. Her gangplank is resting on the paddle box and through the wire mesh railings the clerestory roof of her tiny and very basic aft cabin can be seen. The partially collapsed Bakehouse Tower of Conwy Castle was repaired in 1875 at the expense of the railway company in order to prevent any further falls of stone on to the railway line. (Elsbeth Pears/Haydn Ward)

to regular entries in the famous *Bradshaw's General Railway and Steam Navigation Guide*, which henceforth carried detailed monthly timetables.

With two steamers now available, the Inland Company was able to maintain a year-round service with no breaks for maintenance or repairs and, when demand was sufficient, to send two ships up-river in convoy on the same tide. It also seems highly probable that, when there was bulky or dirty cargo to be moved, one ship would be devoted to that task while the other carried the passengers. It would seem that Capt. Jones of Rose Hill moved to the new *St George* and passed command of the *St Winifred* to another Capt. William Jones, this time of Erskine Terrace, and that a Capt. Richard Roberts also occasionally took command. Contemporary accounts reveal that these masters were very happy to pick up or drop off passengers by request at any convenient point along the river bank. The steamer would be turned into the tide and either the bow or stern run into the reeds while the passengers jumped ashore and made their way home across the fields.

Although the seasonal tourists and 'invalids' in search of Trefriw's curative waters and climate were a small but significant part of the company's trade, during

CONWAY CASTLE, NORTH WALES.

An engraving from the *Illustrated Times* of 5 November 1859 showing passengers disembarking from one of the steamers at her berth in the mouth of the Gyffin stream, after the passage downstream from Trefriw. In the foreground two ladies have just engaged a porter to transport their luggage by hand barrow to their hotel or the railway station, while behind them a gentleman is assisting female passengers to descend the steep, narrow plank which is employed as a gangway. In the background a railway locomotive on the Chester & Holyhead Railway is passing under the impressive walls of Conwy Castle before entering the western portal of Stevenson's tubular bridge of 1848/9. The article accompanying the illustration sang the praises of Conwy, recommended the river trip and commented, 'The steamer itself, it is true, is a curious little boat and its appointments are not very splendid; and perhaps now and then you will hear it grating the bottom; and it may be that you will get aground and have to wait a quarter of an hour or so until the tide rises and lifts you off. But, if the weather be fine, all this is, of course, of no consequence in such scenery as this …'

the 1850s it was the daily packet service which formed the backbone and the Trefriw wharfage books enable us to build up a fascinating picture of this trade.

Frustratingly, these ledgers very rarely refer to the steamers by name, but refer only to 'The Packet' which, by the frequency and regularity of its arrivals and departures, must have been steam powered. It is reported that *St Winifred* was affectionately referred to locally as *Y Pacad Bach* and it can be presumed that the term was extended to include *St George* and therefore became the accepted term for whichever vessel happened to be in service.

Throughout the period 1855–63 one of the most regular and prolific users of the packet was one Ebenezer Faichney (sometimes spelt Fachney), a carrier of Little Bridge Street, Llanrwst. Faichney would import 'sundries' on a daily basis for onward distribution and sale using his carrier's wagons and it would appear that he rented a small warehouse on the quay for temporary storage.

THE CITY OF DUBLIN COMPANY'S
favourite Iron Steamer,
P R I N C E   O F   W A L E S,
(Of 400 tons burthen, and 200 horse power,—
THOMAS DAVIES, Commander),
Leaves MENAI BRIDGE, for LIVERPOOL, (calling off BAN-
GOR and at BEAUMARIS PIER.) every MONDAY, WEDNES-
DAY, and FRIDAY, at 10 a.m.; from PRINCE'S PIER HEAD,
LIVERPOOL, TUESDAYS, THURSDAYS, and SATURDAYS, at
11 a.m.
   The FAIRY Steamer has resumed the Carnarvon and Menai
Bridge Line, in conjunction with the PRINCE OF WALES.
   The Omnibus will leave the Bulkeley Arms, Menai Bridge, for
Llangefni, Llanerchymedd, and Amlwch, on the arrival of the
Packet; and will return from Amlwch with passengers intending
to go forward with the Steamer to Liverpool.
   For further particulars apply to Mr. E. W. TIMOTHY, Menai
Bridge; Mr. JOHN JONES, Carnarvon; or to Mr. J. K.
ROUNTHWAITE, 24, Water-street, Liverpool.
   City of Dublin Steam Packet Company's Office,
      Menai Bridge, 24th April, 1855.

BEAUMARIS, BANGOR, AND MENAI
BRIDGE.—The new Steamer
A N G L E S E A,
Capt. Hunter,
Leaves PRINCE'S PIER, LIVERPOOL, on
MONDAYS, WEDNESDAYS and FRIDAYS at Eleven o'clock Morn-
ing; and the MENAI BRIDGE on TUESDAYS, THURSDAYS,
and SATURDAYS, at Ten o'clock Morning.—Apply to
      PRICE & CASE, 16, Exchange Buildings, Liverpool.

CONWAY AND LLANRWST.

ONE of the Inland Company's Steamers
(weather and other causes permitting,) is
intended to sail between CONWAY and the
Mineral Springs in the Vale of (See Dr. O. O.
Roberts', Treatise on the Mineral Waters of
Trefriw,) LLANRWST, as under:—

	From Conway.	From Trefriw.
	H. M.	H. M.
JULY, 1855.		
28, Saturday	8 30 Morning	10 30 Morning.
30, Monday	9 40 Ditto	12 0 Ditto.
31, Tuesday	10 0 Ditto	1 0 Evening
AUGUST, 1855.		
1, Wednesday	11 45 Morning	2 0 Evening.
2, Thursday	12 15 Evening	2 30 Ditto.
3, Friday	12 30 Ditto	3 0 Ditto.
4, Saturday	2 15 Ditto	4 0 Ditto.
6, Monday	4 0 Ditto	5 30 Ditto.
7, Tuesday	5 0 Morning	6 30 Morning.
Ditto	5 45 Evening	7 0 Evening.
8, Wednesday	6 30 Morning	7 40 Morning.
Ditto	6 45 Evening	8 20 Evening.
9, Thursday	7 10 Morning	9 0 Morning.
Ditto	7 0 Evening	9 0 Evening.
10, Friday	8 0 Morning	10 0 Morning.
11, Saturday	9 5 Ditto	10 45 Ditto.
13, Monday	9 45 Ditto	11 40 Ditto.
14, Tuesday	10 0 Ditto	12 0 Ditto.
15, Wednesday	10 30 Ditto	1 0 Evening.
16, Thursday	11 45 Ditto	1 30 Ditto.
17, Friday	11 45 Ditto	2 0 Ditto.
18, Saturday	12 15 Ditto	2 40 Ditto.
20, Monday	12 30 Ditto	3 30 Ditto.
21, Tuesday	2 15 Ditto	4 0 Ditto.
22, Wednesday	3 35 Ditto	5 30 Ditto.
23, Thursday	5 0 Morning	6 20 Morning.
Ditto	5 30 Evening	7 0 Evening.
24, Friday	6 30 Morning	8 0 Morning.
Ditto	6 45 Evening	8 30 Evening.
25, Saturday	7 30 Morning	9 0 Morning.
27, Monday	9 45 Ditto	11 0 Ditto.
28, Tuesday	9 45 Ditto	11 40 Ditto.
29, Wednesday	9 45 Ditto	12 40 Evening.
30, Thursday	11 40 Ditto	1 15 Ditto.
31, Friday	11 40 Ditto	2 0 Ditto.

   FARES:—Cabin, 1s. 6d.; Fore End, 1s.
   The Steamer's intended time of sailing is published in Bradshaw's Guide, page 163.   Further information can be obtained by
applying to Capt. W. JONES, or to Mr. E. JONES, Blue Bell Inn,
Conway.

North Wales Chronicle advertisements for Saturday 28 July 1855 show the St Winifred's and St George's Trefriw sailings alongside those of the Liverpool–Dublin packet Prince of Wales and the new Liverpool–Beaumaris–Bangor–Menai Bridge steamer Anglesey.

The tonnages involved were quite substantial: during the 6 months from December 1855 to May 1856 he landed 213 tons 9cwt of goods which, at 4*d* per ton, attracted a wharfage charge of £3 12*s* 9½*d*. Over the next 12 months to May 1857 the tonnage had risen to 384 tons, giving an average monthly landing of 32 tons and a peak of 58 tons in April. The quantities went on increasing year on year until 1863, with the year ending May 1863 seeing no less than 817 tons 12cwt of sundries arriving at Trefriw, costing Faichney £13 12*s* 6*d* in wharfage.

The packet would typically carry about a ton of cargo per voyage, though this varied on a daily basis and sometimes approached 3 tons, as on the morning tide of 7 June 1858 when she arrived with 2 tons 18cwt.

Ebenezer Faichney's sundries were certainly not the only inward cargo to arrive by the packet at Trefriw Quay. John Williams, the Trefriw smith and forge master, imported iron moulds, at first only occasionally, but rising to three cargoes per month by 1856, as well as occasional loads of river sand. Other typical items carried by the packet also included:

June 1855	Flour
September 1856	Earthenware for Owen Owens of Trefriw
December 1856	Two casks of cement
January 1858	Cheese and butter for Morris Owen
February 1858	A quantity of butter for John Owens
June 1858	Slabs for Evan Jones and Sons
October 1858	Wheat for Evan Jones & Sons

The packet also carried considerable quantities of lead ore downstream on behalf of a number of mine owners, including John Roberts Esq., Messrs John George White and John Edwards of Rhaiadyrwst Mine, Mr Adam Eyton of Llanerch-y-Mor and the Pencraig Mine Company. These cargoes seem to have gone out at a rate of approximately one per month and were transhipped into larger vessels at Conwy Quay. In addition, iron moulds (used or damaged, perhaps?) left the quay at about the same frequency and there are occasional references to the packet arriving with another vessel in tow. With so much cargo passing to and fro and being transhipped at Conway, it is certain that, in addition to their overnight berth in the Gyffin stream, the steamers regularly used Conway Quay.

Throughout this period Trefriw Quay would have presented an animated and largely industrial appearance. Trade had continued to grow and in December 1857, for example, there were no less than forty arrivals. In addition to the river lighters, seagoing ships included the *Commerce* and *Friends* (which regularly brought cargoes of sand and clay for use at Trefriw forge), *Trefriw Trader*, *Martha*, *Machno*, *Hope*, *Marquis*, *Breeze*, *Vale*, *Eagle*, *Mary* and *Mary Elizabeth*, and once or twice a month a huge 'float' composed of up to 1,800ft of red pine timber baulks would be dispatched down river. The lower level of the quay was used for loading and unloading the cargoes described in the previous chapter, while a number of store houses were situated on the upper level and a wooden shipbuilding and repair yard was located near the entrance to the quay. Amidst all this bustle *Y Pacad Bach* was a familiar, daily sight as she landed her passengers at a flight of stone steps situated towards the downstream end of the quay.

The completion of the first tube of Stevenson's revolutionary bridge meant that, from 1 May 1848, passengers on the Chester & Holyhead Railway were able to reach Conwy and Bangor by train. The second tube opened to traffic in January 1849 and by March 1850 the magnificent Britannia Bridge across the Menai Strait had been completed and the route was fully open to its terminus at the port of Holyhead.

Although originally conceived to expedite the Irish mail service, the new line had a dramatic if unintended effect on the growth of tourism in North Wales. The regular steam packets and seasonal excursion steamers from Liverpool had

A Robert Fenton photograph of Trefriw Quay in about 1858, showing slate blocks and slabs awaiting export. The substantially built hand-operated crane would have been of great assistance in handling the heavy slate cargoes, which made up over 80 per cent of the export tonnage handled. The single-masted, sloop-rigged sailing vessel is typical of the coastal vessels which traded between North Wales and the Mersey, and has rigged a derrick to handle her own cargo. The view is taken looking upstream, with the village of Trefriw nestling at the foot of the hills behind the trees in the right background. (National Library of Wales)

already brought the Menai Strait within the reach of the more adventurous day tripper, but the new railway moved things on to a different level altogether. Conway was only 45 miles by rail from Chester, which, in the words of Black's *Picturesque Guide to North Wales*,[5] was a central terminus of several important railways, 'by means of which it has easy and expeditious communication with all parts of the United Kingdom'. London, for example, was now only 4 hours 30 minutes away and Birmingham a mere 2 hours 18 minutes via the London & North Western Railway, while the Great Western, Lancashire & Cheshire Junction, and Birkenhead & Chester railways offered efficient connections to other parts of the country.

This sudden increase in accessibility fed the Victorian fashion for visiting seaside watering places, gazing at picturesque ruins or marvelling at the sublime scenery of the mountains, all of which North Wales offered in abundance. Detailed guide-books became readily available and Bradshaw's monthly guide made it an easy matter for travellers to plan connections between railways, steamers and horse-drawn coaches which, taken together, provided a remarkably comprehensive and efficient network.

In addition, the routing of the railway along the north coast encouraged the growth of new resorts such as Llandudno (first established in 1850, Deganwy) Rhos-on-Sea, Rhyl, Abergele, and Penmaenmawr, whose summer populations would later swell the numbers visiting the Conway Valley and patronising the river steamers. As early as 1855 the *Llandudno Visitor's Handbook*[6] was noting that the picturesque scenery around Trefriw was unrivalled, and recommending the excursion up river by steamer, with a continuation by carriage to Llanrwst, Betws-y-Coed, Capel Curig or Rhaiadr Wennol.

Conwy itself, which had recently been noted for 'its poor, ill-built, neglected streets' and as 'likely to disappoint' now found itself described as 'one of the most romantic and interesting spots in Europe', while one observer opined:'I have seen no town where the military works of art are so happily blended with the pictur-esque features of nature; and no spot which the artist will at first sight view with greater rapture, or quit with greater reluctance.'[7] Attracted by these accolades, visitors began to arrive in greater numbers to tour the magnificent castle and town walls, explore the quaint streets and historic buildings and gaze in admira-tion at the parallel engineering wonders of Telford's 1825 suspension bridge and Stephenson's new tubular railway bridge.

The Inland Company naturally sought to take advantage of this situation, and subtly changed the emphasis of its advertising. From 1852 onwards its ser-vice appeared regularly in *Bradshaw* and a second surviving sailing bill, which is believed to date from July 1856, stresses the touristic appeal of the packet service by stating that 'The Steam Yacht St Winifred is intended to ply between Conway and the mineral springs of Trefriw, near Llanrwst, calling at intermediate places'.

An early photograph of Conwy, showing a number of local trading vessels beached at low tide. The view is taken looking downstream past the quay and town walls towards Bodlondeb Woods which crown the hilltop above Twthill Point. (Clifford Hughes)

The numbers travelling, although steadily growing, were still small. Between July and October 1860, for example, 396 passengers arrived at Trefriw and 316 departed, paying a landing fee of 1d each and yielding the quay's owners an income of £2 19s 6d.

Careful comparison of the 1860 wharfage book and *Bradshaw's Guide* provides us with some fascinating detail and a glimpse of how the steamers may have been deployed. The wharfage book states explicitly that there were no packet sailings between 29 February and 16 April, 18 May and 8 June, or 19 July and 2 August, and that there were only five sailings in total during August, which, at first sight, appears to be at direct odds with *Bradshaw* where the timings of daily trips throughout the year are confirmed. In fact, the explanation may be straightforward: it would seem likely that during the periods when the packet did not operate there were insufficient bulky cargoes to justify the use of two ships and that *St Winifred*, which the wharfage book clearly regards as the 'packet' was laid up, leaving *St George* to cope easily with the modest number of local passengers, tourists and Ebenezer Faichney's daily deliveries of 'sundries'. This impression is reinforced by the fact that *Bradshaw's Guide*'s usual reference to 'The Inland Company's Steamers' is temporarily replaced by 'The Inland Company's regular packet *St George*' between September and December 1860. It would seem that the newer steamer was regarded as most suitable for the passenger trade while the older *St Winifred* was relegated to cargo work and relief sailings when demand was sufficient.

A tantalising entry in the wharfage book for March 1860 stated that 'the packet is at Liverpool repairing'. For either of the tiny steamers to have undertaken such a long and potentially perilous coastal voyage during stormy spring weather, the repairs must have been of a major nature and too extensive to be carried out locally. Since the vessel involved was not identified by name, one can only speculate whether it was *St Winifred*, which had become unreliable with age and heavy use, or *St George*, which had been sent for major modifications. We do know that, at some stage during the late 1850s or early 1860s, *St George's* appearance was altered when her heavy wooden bulwarks were replaced with light metal railings and her paddle boxes were modified. It is possible that, at the same time, she was lengthened and her machinery modified.

During the summer of 1860 the Inland Company faced competition on the river when a steamer called *Victoria*, commanded by a Capt. Davis, began to operate from Llandudno to Trefriw, calling at Conwy en route. Her first sailing took place on 16 July and continued in service until 5 October, during which period she carried 305 passengers up river and 266 down. Since it is unlikely that she would have rounded the Great Orme each day, it seems probable that she embarked her Llandudno passengers from boats off the West Shore. The passenger figures do not indicate what proportion of passengers came from Llandudno and how many were collected at Conwy, but it is significant that, after only 10 years of growth, the infant resort was felt large enough to justify its own steamer.

At some stage during the late 1850s or early 1860s *St George* was modified to make her better suited to the developing tourist trade on the river. Her heavy wooden bulwarks were replaced by light metal railings covered with a fine wire mesh, and her paddleboxes adorned with elegant radial vents, a central crest and the legend 'St George between Conway and Trefriw'. She is seen here at her berth in the Gyffin stream shortly after the alterations were made. (Elsbeth Pears/Haydn Ward)

Since *Victoria* did not reappear in 1861 one can assume that the experiment was a little ahead of its time and not a financial success. However, as we shall see in later chapters, the idea of running a steamer direct from Llandudno to Trefriw was very far from dead.

While the appearance of *Victoria* on the river must have rattled the owners of the Inland Company, there were other developments afoot which must have concerned them far more profoundly. Since 1846 a number of schemes had been proposed to build standard or narrow-gauge railways up either the west or east bank of the Conwy, and these had finally crystallised on 23 July 1860 when a Parliamentary Bill for the construction of the Conway & Llanrwst Railway received royal assent.

The route of the new, standard-gauge line was from Llandudno Junction (already an interchange between the Chester & Holyhead main line and the St George's Harbour & Railway Company's branch to Deganwy and Llandudno) to Llanrwst, with intermediate stations at Llansaintffraid (Glan Conwy) and Tal-y-Cafn. The first sod was cut on 25 August 1860 and the construction was driven ahead by the powerful London & North Western Railway which, by that time, had absorbed the Chester & Holyhead Company. A special train reached Llanrwst from Llandudno Junction at 1.30 p.m. on Tuesday 16 June 1863 amid great celebrations, and a public service with three trains each way on weekdays began on the following morning. The line was subsequently extended to Betws-y-Coed in 1868 and to Blaenau Ffestiniog in 1879.

Commentators immediately praised the scenic beauties of the new line, which provided a fast and attractive alternative to the steamers for tourists wishing to visit the upper vale. Freed from the constraints of the river's tides, visitors could now spend a full day in the area before returning by the evening train.

Of even more concern was the fact that Llanrwst station was provided with sidings and an extensive goods yard and quickly began to steal trade away from Trefriw Quay, where tonnages reached their all-time peak of 16,532 tons in 1862 and then began to decline sharply. The traditional imports and exports continued, but in far smaller quantities, and the wharfage books began to include regular accounts for 'loads from the quay to the station' and 'cartage to the station'. Significant quantities of slate and other outgoing goods were now being brought to the quay for storage before being shipped out by rail.

Ebenezer Faichney evidently found it more convenient to have his daily deliveries taken straight to Llanrwst and from 22 June 1863 no more 'sundries' arrived at the quay. The writing was clearly on the wall for the daily steam packet, which did not sail at all between July and September except for two outward cargoes of iron moulds on 21 and 25 September. The end finally arrived on 17 October 1863 when, in bold red ink, the wharfage book bore the entry 'Packet stopped running'.

CUTTING THE FIRST SOD OF T E CONWAY AND LLANRWST RAILWAY.—SEE PAGE 253.

The ceremony to celebrate the cutting of the first sod of the railway from Llandudno Junction to Llanrwst on 25 August 1860. The opening of the line to passenger and goods traffic 3 years later effectively marked the end of both the packet service and Trefriw as a commercial port.

Bradshaw's Guide confirms that the winter service ceased with the end of the packet, and from 1864 onwards the familiar entry for 'The Inland Company's Steam Packets' was replaced by the wording 'The Inland Company's Steamer St George'. It is therefore certain that the winter of 1863–64 saw the end of *St Winifred*'s regular service on the river. Her fate is not recorded but there is evidence that she may have lingered on until 1869, undertaking very occasional cargo runs with laths, poles or iron moulds, and towing floats of timber baulks downsteam to Conwy.

Notes

1. Davies, Ivor E., 'The floating traders of oak and iron', in *North Wales Weekly News*, 16 December 1976.
2. Bennett, A.R., *The Chronicles of Boulton's Sidings* (Locomotive Pub. Co., 1927).
3. *Frazer's Magazine for Town & Country*, Vol. 46, No. 271, July 1852.
4. Bennett, A.R., op. cit.
5. Black, Adam and Charles, *Black's Picturesque Guide to North Wales* (5th edition) (Edinburgh, Adam & Charles Black: Chester, Catherall & Pritchard, 1874).
6. Parry, R., *The Llandudno Visitor's Handbook with Historical notices of the Neighbourhood* (Llandudno, 1855).
7. Black, Adam and Charles, op. cit.

3

The Trefriw Wells, the Roberts Family and the St George's Steamship Company, 1864–72

Following the demise of the year-round packet service between Conwy and Trefriw, the *St George* settled into a regular, seasonal pattern of operation. Her first sailings were usually at around the time of the Whitsun holidays in early June, and she continued daily until mid or late September, when she was laid up for the winter.

With the completion of the railway to Llanrwst, there were now four alternative routes up the Conwy valley. Running parallel to the railway on the east or Denbighshire bank was the Conway to Betws-y-Coed turnpike road which, like the railway, offered spectacular views across the river and meadows towards the mountains which rose, tier on tier, on the opposite bank. This road (the present-day A470) passed through Llansanffraid Glan Conwy, close beneath Bodnant Hall on its wooded hillside, onwards past Tal-y-Cafn and Lord Newborough's magnificent home, constructed amongst the ruins of the former Maenan Abbey, to Llanrwst. On the western or Caernarfonshire bank ran the third alternative in the form of the smaller turnpike road (now the B5106) from Conwy to Trefriw, Gwydir Castle and Betws via Ty'n-y-Groes, Tal-y-Bont and Dolgarrog. Tucked in at the foot of the mountain slopes, this road offered fewer picturesque views but felt more intimate and, more importantly, gave ready access to the numerous waterfalls, so beloved of Victorian tourists, which tumbled down from the mountains above. Both roads were well served by scheduled horse-drawn carriages, or 'cars' as they were known locally. The fourth and final alternative was, of course, the steamer service on the river.

The guidebooks which proliferated at this period offered the prospective tourist much advice on how to make the best use of these alternative modes of

Vale of Conway from Trefriw.

The view looking seawards along the Vale of Conwy, taken from the hillside above the northern extremity of Trefriw village. The turnpike road (today the B5106) led past Trefriw Wells, some half a mile distant, and thence to Conwy.

transport. While the return steamer trip remained as popular as ever, it was now possible, given a willingness to take a 'car' or walk the 2½ miles from Trefriw to Llanrwst station, to travel in one direction by steamer, explore the district, and return by train or vice versa. Regular carriage services on both roads provided an alternative to the railway, circular tours via Betws-y-Coed and Capel Curig were readily available. Private cars plying for hire from both quay and station added further to flexibility to the mix.

Most of the guidebooks, however, agreed that by far the best way to appreciate the beauties of the valley was to travel in at least one direction by the *St George*, and offered detailed descriptions of the trip.

Black's Picturesque Guide to North Wales,[1] for example, stated that:

A small steamer plies daily between Conway and Trefriw. The hours of departure from Conway vary according to the tide, but the steamer waits little more than half-an-hour at Trefriw, which is within 2½ miles of Llanrwst. The sail is a pleasant one of about 10 miles, and the scenery is varied and beautiful …

An 1872 guide to Trefriw and district[2] concurred, adding that: 'The fare is one shilling, and a more advantageous investment of that coin can scarcely be conceived. You have the leisure and opportunity on board the tiny *St George* to contemplate the magnificent scenery presented to view on both sides, whilst gliding smoothly along the winding stream.'

The author of *A Handbook for Travellers in North Wales*,[3] having possibly encountered *St George*'s limited facilities on a wet day, restricted himself to lukewarm comment that: 'A primitive little steamer sails from Conway 'weather permitting', as far as Trefriw, 2½ miles short of Llanrwst; and if the traveller can spare a morning, it by no means an unpleasant way of viewing the scenery on both sides of the river.'

Richard Richards, writing in 1868,[4] was positively effusive about his trip up river and, in addition to giving a vivid description of the passing scenery, provided much useful detail about the handling of the steamer herself:

> We started precisely to the minute advertised, for the worthy captain was the very soul of punctuality, which is said to be the very soul of business. The steamer at once dashed out right valiantly into the middle of the stream, for the tide was running in very strongly … The river is whimsically winding and circuitous in many parts of it; and by reason of the numerous sandbanks which often occur in the very middle of the stream, the navigation is extremely difficult, and even dangerous.; and, indeed, it can only be accomplished successfully by a steady and skilful hand, which Captain Jones, on this occasion, proved himself to be. I cannot seriously affirm that we ever 'did' a figure of 8 in these tortuous meanderings; but we were often at sixes and sevens! So that the passengers were afforded ample opportunity of leisurely inspecting the varied views on each side of the river, and from nearly every point of the compass.

Having described in detail the beauties of Benarth, the buildings of Llansaintffraid Glan Conwy, the pastoral delights of the floodplain where 'there were harvest men employed in reaping and carting', Bodnant Hall, Lord Newborough's 'Abbey' and the 'impetuous cataracts' plunging down from the western hills, he continued:

> The Vale, in its entire length, is a gem of lovely picturesqueness and wooded-hilly scenery, and was quite a relief and a treat to many of those on board who probably for months before had been immured in smokey towns, or had seen of Wales nothing save sandy beaches, bleak, bare hills or the ever-moaning sea. … There was a rich, gorgeous beauty about these woody slopes that was quite refreshing, and which was well calculated to remind the visitors from far-off England of some of the most prized of his native haunts on the Avon or the Trent. The man who can look upon such a scene as is to be witnessed in this lovely Welsh valley without a feeling of grateful thankfulness to the Great Author of our being for creating a world so beautiful and so pleasing, ought to be banished for life to the steppes of Russia, or to the arid deserts of Asia or Africa.

On arrival at Trefriw, Richards was less than impressed by the quay which, some 6 years after the peak of its trade, was still handling and storing significant amount of cargo, and would certainly have had the air of a primarily industrial facility in steady decline. He commented:

> We had now reached the end of our little voyage of pleasure, having made the nominal nine miles in about one hour – not so bad in a little steamer up a narrow river. There is what is by courtesy called a 'landing pier' at Trefriw; but it certainly is not a convenience of which the village has much to boast or be proud about, for it is scarcely an accommodation at all.

He was more impressed with Trefriw itself, which he judged to be:

> A neat little village; and by reason of its beauty and salubrity is much frequented in summer by pleasure seekers and invalids from all parts of the country, including Wales itself. In addition to the Hotel, the place contains two or three decent inns, and several pretty residences in the cottage-villa style of architecture. The parish church, which is situated near the centre of the village, is a respectable edifice … Not far from the church on the side of the road to Llanrwst, is one of the most picturesque and rustic water-mills which I ever remember to have met with in the country … The village is built mainly on the side of the hill, on ledge-like terraces, and is viewed as a whole to the greatest advantage from the other side of the river, near to the 'Abbey'.

Trefriw's appeal to 'pleasure-seekers and invalids' had been boosted significantly in 1863 when Lord Willoughby de Eresby of Gwydir Castle constructed, at his own expense, a small but massively built stone bath house just below the entrance to the caves at 'Trefriw Spa' from which the famous mineral waters issued. The bath house had two doorways, leading into separate men's and women's rooms where a variety of slate and other baths were fed by water piped from the caves above. Within the caves themselves, the left-hand tunnel, which had previously been used as a bath, was fitted with a waist-high dam in order to combine its waters with those from the long reservoir in the central tunnel. A third tunnel curved away to the right, terminating in a circular well where patients wishing to drink the waters continued to take their own dosages.

The chalybeate water, rich in the easily absorbed protosulphate of iron and sulphates of alumina, magnesia, lime and other elements, was crystal-clear and sulphurous-tasting whilst underground, but quickly took on a yellowish tint when exposed to daylight and became undrinkable. For this reason, visitors continued to take their regulated doses – never more than a small wine glass full twice per day – by candlelight in the caves, whilst light was excluded as far as possible from the bath house.

High tide at Trefriw. On the left of the photo one of the local trading vessels is unloading her cargo into a cart while, at the landing steps at the far end of the quay, an empty *St George* awaits her passengers, who are doubtless making the most of their brief time ashore in the Belle Vue Hotel and immediate surroundings before embarking for the return trip to Conwy. (Karen Black/Trefriw Historical Society)

St George at Trefriw, showing the range of agricultural and industrial buildings which continued to occupy the quay for several years after the cessation of the packet service in 1863. In the centre of the picture is the Belle Vue Hotel and, to its left and situated opposite the entrance to the quay, the Store House – the home of Capt. Robert Roberts and his family. The master, engineer and deckhand are posing for the photographer.

Fairy Falls, Trefriw.

The water-powered Trefriw Flannel Mill (later the Trefriw Woollen Mill) stands beside the picturesque Fairy Falls where the Crafnant stream tumbles its way into the centre of Trefriw Village.

The massively built stone bath house constructed at Trefriw Wells in 1863 by Lord Willoughby de Eresby.

The interior of the caves.

Access to both the drinking water and the baths remained free of charge for a further 10 years and the fame of the site – now variously referred to as the 'The Vale of Conway Spa', 'Trefriw Spa' or 'The Cae Coch sulphur springs' – was boosted by the appearance of various articles in the medical press which analysed the waters and praised their efficacy. One such article, published in the *British Journal of Homeopathy* for 1864,[5] chronicled (in revolting detail) the author's experiments with different courses of internal and external treatment, made recommendations on appropriate dosages, compared the Trefriw waters with other British chalybeate spas and concluded that it:

> … is easily accessible, abundant and uniform in quantity, and certain and uniform in composition and effects. It is therefore the best of the sulphate chalybeate waters of this country; and as sulphate chalybeates are the best of all chalybeates, the Trefriw Spa is the finest chalybeate water of Great Britain. Now, it is a great boon to the inhabitant of the northern and midland counties to have the finest chalybeate of the country near at hand, cheap and easily to be got at, and situated in one of most beautiful spots in the kingdom, the scenery of which has both the grand majesty of the Caernarfonshire mountains, and the calm quiet of a lovely valley bisected by a beautiful winding river, the air of which is not only pure and mild in the valley, and light, sharp and invigorating in the mountains, and tempered by sea-breezes.

Because the *St George* service was now targeted chiefly at the steadily increasing numbers of tourists and health-seekers who were visiting North Wales, the 'crack of dawn' departure times of the packet service days were abandoned in favour of slightly more civilised hours. This, however, was all relative, as Victorian tourists still seemed willing to be on board for 6.30 a.m. on a summer morning! On evening tides the steamer was usually back in Conwy before night-fall, and several writers waxed eloquent on the romance of returning downstream in the dusk. One naturalist who had spent his day searching for freshwater pearls in the river above Llanrwst[6] embarked at Trefriw for his homeward trip and wrote:

> … I took the little steamer at Trefriw, at the height of the tide, for Conway; passed many pretty towns on the river, one pleasing spot being Rhiw, the site of Roman Conovium. It was dusk as we approached Conway; the darkly wooded hills and the castle to the left, the bridge in front, the rounded rocks of Diganwy and the Great Orme's Head to the right, composed one of those scenes which one occasionally sees, not soon to forget.

Fares during the 1860s were 1*s* 6*d* single for the after end (which benefitted from a spartan saloon below decks and a canvas awning which could be spread over a frame to protect passengers from the rain or sunshine), or 1*s* for the foredeck. Return tickets were 2*s* 6*d* and 2*s* respectively.

At some stage during the late 1860s, the *St George* passed into the ownership of a Trefriw family called Roberts. The precise date has yet to be established, but there are a number of indications that the transfer took place between 1866 and 1870: the last reference to 'The Inland Company's steamer St George' in *Bradshaw's Monthly Guide* appeared at the end of the 1865 season, to be replaced in 1866 by the simple heading 'The St George'; the Trefriw wharfage books record that from 1867 to 1869 the *St George* came up to Trefriw during the winter months 'to repair' and from 1870 to 1876 (the last entry in the ledger) contained an annual account for the 'winterage of the *St George*', indicating that the vessel had spent the closed season laid up at Trefriw. Both of these facts would make most sense if the ship was, by then, owned in Trefriw.

The wharfage books also reveal that Capt. Jones remained in command of the ship at least until the end of the 1870 season. *St George* commenced her 1868 season on 6 June, and her 1869 season on 14 June. 'The Packet' (presumably the old *St Winifred*), also commanded by a Capt. Jones, is recorded as making one trip in each of July, August and September 1867 with 'poles to Conway'. It reappeared on 16 and 17 July 1868 carrying laths inwards and iron moulds outwards, and seems to have enjoyed a final fling between 13 and 19 March 1869 when she made four journeys towing floats of baulks and one carrying boards and towing

A crowded *St George* arriving at Trefriw. (Doris Williams)

a sailing vessel called *Heather Belle*. After that she disappears from the records, presumably either broken up or sold away from the river.

St George faced some opposition on the river when, on 6 June 1868, a steamer named *Deganwy*, commanded by a Capt. Owen, made her first appearance at Trefriw with twelve passengers on board. No other trips were recorded in that year but she returned during 1869, running trips 'to and from Deganwy with passengers' on 14, 19 and 26 June and 5 and 7 July. Although little else is known about the ship, she can claim the distinction of making the first recorded direct sailings from Deganwy to Trefriw, a service which was to prove of immense importance in years to come. On 17 August 1870 the wharfage book also contained a single and intriguing entry, 'Steamboat *Waterwich* up first'.

The generation of the Roberts family which took over the *St George* had been long established in Trefriw and were the children of Robert Roberts (1786–1879), a farmer of Bryn Pyll, and his wife Gwen Jones (1794–1838) formerly of Dolwyddelan. The couple had seven children: William (1818–73), John (1821–76), Robert (1824–86), Anne (1827–77), Mary (1830–88), Thomas (1833–91) and David (1835–90). John, who lived with his family at Coed Gwydir, Trefriw, followed his father into farming and neither he nor his two sisters seem to have had any direct connection with the *St George*. William, the eldest son, moved away to Liverpool where he became firstly a draper and later a ship owner in partnership with Messrs Taylor and Bethell and with connections to the famous Black Ball Line of clipper ships. He died a wealthy man and may well have injected capital into the acquisition of steamboat service.

The remaining three brothers, Robert, Thomas and David, all went to sea in coastal and ocean-going sailing ships, qualified as master mariners, and seem to have been involved in the acquisition and operation of the *St George*.

Robert, who married Elizabeth Owen and had three children named Elinor, Gwen and Robert Owen (who will appear later in this history), lived at The Store House which was located directly opposite the entrance to Trefriw Quay. In addition to being a master mariner, he was a farmer, timber merchant and ship owner. Among the vessels he was involved with was a small steamship called the *Temple* which was built and launched at Trefriw on 20 March 1874, and floated downstream to Conway on 15 April 'to take in her engine'. She was apparently built near the lime kilns at Trefriw and was able to carry 120 tons of cargo. He had shares in the ocean-going *North Star* and the 280ft steamer *Empire*, which was designed for the Indian and American trade and was christened by his daughter in September 1881. He owned several coastal sailing ships including the *Esther*, *Jenny*, two successive *Trefriw Traders* (which were lost in 1847 and 1849 respectively), and the *Martha Ann* which foundered off Ireland.

David (known locally as Dafydd Bryn Pyll) was a colourful character about whom many family legends developed. He is remembered as a handsome, courteous, rather aloof man with an aristocratic bearing and a distinct twinkle in his eye. He was widely read in comparative religions and caused a local scandal by rejecting the Calvinistic beliefs of the rest of his family and, during one of his spells at home from the sea, daring to discuss his radical and alternative thinking with a Sunday school class with which he had been entrusted. Banned by the chapel elders, he simply transferred his classes on board an old hulk which he kept moored alongside Trefriw Quay. His classes prospered and the Sunday schools emptied, until social pressure brought the insubordinate youth of Trefriw back to the chapel and David returned to sea! At some stage during his youth he dallied with training as a draper and, while doing so, married his boss's daughter, Elizabeth Mulholland, with whom he returned to Trefriw. Tiring of her expensive tastes and lack of intellectual interests he returned to the sea and, while he was away, bigamously married another woman, Eliza Davies. Liable to be arrested if he returned home, David disappeared until Elizabeth died. He then returned to Eliza, who bore him five children, before the urge for adventure struck him once again and he went back to the sea, eventually dying in Australia at the age of 55.

For all of his alternative views and the legends which surround him, David was a much-respected seaman and a good businessman. His skills must have been central in the setting up of the new steamboat company and he apparently returned to help out several times during the years ahead. At one stage he was skipper of the family's 35-ton flat *Jenny*. One of his relatives recalls him, probably in 1884 or 1885 after he had returned to live with Eliza, living on board a yacht on the moorings off Conwy Quay.:

Captain Robert Roberts (1824–86) of The Store House, Trefriw, with his three children, Elinor, Robert Owen and Gwen. (Elsbeth Pears)

One of Robert Roberts' fleet of coastal cargo vessels, the *Esther*, beached at low tide on the foreshore between Conwy quay and castle.

I can recall him vividly. He was striking to look at; tall and spare, with strong features, a big chiselled nose, with reddish hair and a short curly reddish beard. He had the family look about him. He shewed [sic] us his deck garden with pride, the pride of initiative no doubt. Cabbages and lettuces grew in grocer's boxes. He got out deck chairs for us and brought up an accordion from down below to show us how he could attract fish to the ship's side. To me, here was something to beat the Arabian Nights. He made tea in the saloon and talked of the beauties of perfect peace. No domestic instructions, no unwelcome visitors, no friction and plenty of time to read. 'And if I'm dunned for rates and taxes I can up sticks and jow' he said, turning to me. I appointed him there and then my special hero. The cabin settee was littered with passengers' tickets for the little steamers, and I suppose the yacht was a handy headquarters for Deganwy.

The third brother, Thomas, was also a self-educated man who went to sea at an early age in vessels trading between Conwy and Liverpool and, having gained wide experience, his Master's qualification and sufficient capital, took over the *St George* along with his brothers. He later moved to 4 Llewelyn Terrace, Conwy, where he lived with his wife Jane and had five children, two of whom, Robert and William, went on to form the next generation of steamer captains and managers. He prospered in business and, in addition to running the steamboat company, went into partnership with Capt. Griffith Jones to set up the successful firm of Roberts & Jones, ship brokers and owners, on Conwy Quay. He was an active member of the Welsh Congregational Church at Conwy and, during the family's time in charge, the river steamers never ran on Sundays. When they put to sea on longer voyages, however, it was said that the brothers 'left their religion on the perch' (the tall post with a basket on top which marked the channel into Conwy) ready to collect again on their return!

Having acquired the *St George*, the three brothers named their new enterprise the St George's Steamship Company. There has been much speculation over their choice of name. Duckworth and Langmuir[7] asserted that the Roberts had:

> … a curious association with the St George Steam Packet Company, famous in the early days of steam navigation. It appears that the latter had an idea of running a packet service from Deganwy, where the St George's Quay was built. Nothing further was done; but from this quay (though they did not use it) the owners of the Conway river steamers adopted their name.

Since the packet company had ceased to exist in 1843 and the quay was not constructed until 1868, this theory seems somewhat unlikely. However, the area is peppered with St George references – Llandudno itself was almost named

St George's Harbour when Lord Mostyn considered creating a packet port there; the branch line railway to the town was known as the St George's line; and the new harbour at Deganwy was indeed named after the saint. Any one of these, or a combination of all, could have given rise to the Roberts' choice of their company name, or it may simply have been that they decided to name it after the little paddle steamer which they had purchased.

The change of ownership had little outward effect on the river service. The *St George* continued to ply her seasonal trade, her departure times governed by the time of high water each day, and patronised by ever-increasing numbers of passengers. It has been discovered that, en route between Conwy and Trefriw, the steamer would frequently put into the bank to pick up or drop off local people and their light goods at points convenient to their farms or homes. In addition, there was a tiny landing stage just upstream of Trefriw Wells, alongside which the tiny *St George* would sometimes squeeze herself to collect passengers who had been taking the waters.

Considering the healthy climate, extreme beauty and bucolic charms of Trefriw and its environs, it is scarcely surprising that they also became a magnet for artists. An art movement, popularised by David Cox, had begun in Betws-y-Coed during the 1850s but had been driven out by the arrival of the railway and mass tourism. In search of a quieter location within the valley the artists moved to Trefriw and were to remain there until the turn of the century when the increasing popularity and bustle of the village caused them to move on again. The surviving paintings of the 'Trefriw School' provide us with superb visual records of the area during the second half of the nineteenth century.

Writers too recorded their impressions of the valley in poetry and prose, and many sampled the delights of the river trip. The atmosphere of a voyage during the early days of the Roberts' St George's Steamship Company was captured wonderfully in an article entitled 'The Narrative of an Uneventful Voyage', which appeared in the Victorian periodical literary magazine *All the Year Round: A Weekly Journal*,[8] founded and edited by Charles Dickens and contributed to by many writers, usually anonymously. Upon his death in 1870 it was taken over by his eldest son, Charles Dickens Jnr, who would have written or edited the following contribution. Lengthy though it is, it is quoted in full for its sharp observation, its humour and for the wonderful detail it gives of a typical voyage on board the *St George* in the summer of 1875. Both spelling and punctuation have been left unaltered:

> The St George steamship, ten feet in the beam, and forty feet from stem to stern, with a pair of paddle-wheels a size too large for it, and a thin chimney painted in black and red bands, plies between Conway and Treffriw. She makes, once a day, an insignificant little trip on the Conway river, hurrying up on the bosom of the tide, and back again as fast as she can dip the blades of her over-grown

paddles, as though she were afraid of a premature ebb. Farther than Treffriw, even she cannot poke her smoky nose up the beautiful valley; and for this small favour she is a tide-and-time server of the most pronounced type, to the endless vexation of would-be passengers. You arrange a nice little excursion, with trains and everything to match; rain intervenes to upset the plan; and the next day the St George sails an hour later, to suit the tide; and in that interval you are cast upon the streets of Conway. This at least was the fate of Mens, Corpus and myself, three indolent tourists – neither artists, nor antiquarians, nor botanists, nor pedestrians, nor of such as go about 'seeing places', nor afflicted with a passion for ferns, or churches, or mountains, nor even health-seekers – but merely lazy units enjoying lazy weeks in Wales.

A fillip in the early morning gives a tone of one sort or another to the whole day. Today the necessary stimulus was supplied by Corpus, who, having experienced a shock of mild delight in the main street of Conway, felt and exhaled its serene influence throughout the day. Corpus's delight was due to an exquisite appreciation of retributive justice. Harmless and incapable of revenge himself, he felt a keen enjoyment in the vengeance of fate. Not many days before, he and Mens, waiting for the train at Conway, and idling in a hungry mood through its streets and byways, came upon an eating establishment – 'The Original Conway Refreshment Room'. Proprietor Mr William Williams. In the window was a bowl of mushrooms, flanked by two mutton chops, with a few buns occupying commanding positions on jam-pots in the back-ground. Imposing itself obtrusively on the pavement was a bill of fare, announcing that chops, steaks, tea and

Conway River.

A fleet of coastal trading vessels drying their sails on a still day at Conwy while a larger, square-rigged vessel lies alongside the quay. Although taken after 1888, when the steamer landing stage was constructed beside the town wall, the photograph gives a fine impression of type of vessels which served the river during the first half of the nineteenth century.

coffee were always ready, and that there was an ordinary at one o'clock – hot roast joint and vegetables, one shilling. Thrusting himself even more obtrusively into the street, and eyeing Mens and Corpus with a meaning smile, stood Mr William Williams. With a glib tongue he extolled his viands, his low prices, his wife's cookery, above all his hot, roast joint. Hunger blinded the better judgement, and opened the eyes and ears. There was time, before the train left, to partake of Mr William Williams's ordinary. There was also time to repent.

The staircase leading to the upper room was narrow and sticky. Greasy bodies had rubbed against the wall on one side; greasy hands had handled the banister on the other; spots of grease made the stairs slippery. The narrow passage which ended in the upper room was dark, and the walls were stained. The room itself was lit with a dismal sheen from black horsehair. Horsehair covered the seats and the backs of the chairs; horsehair draped the sofa from head to foot; the two armchairs were horsehair boxes, on legs, with the lids propped up and the fronts knocked out. The blind was half drawn down; the window was fast closed and fly-blown. Neither Mens to Corpus, nor Corpus to Mens, would confess irresolution; but courage and hunger were fast ebbing away, and the house was pervaded by a small of roast mutton. In five minutes the ring of the bell brought up a servant girl, and the cloth, not a clean one, was unfolded, and stroked down on the table. Then followed, in slow succession, knives, forks, and glasses; and Mens smiled faintly, and heaved the last sigh of an expiring appetite. The door closed again, and all signs of the approaching ordinary died away. Presently, with a silent turn of the little brass handle, entered, like mutes, two females in black – mother and daughter – faded, both of them, and very pale, but the daughter the paler and ghastlier of the two. These subsided into two deep hollows in the sofa, raising a horsehair billow between them, and produced, one her work, the other and discoloured volume of neutral tint. Their entrance disturbed the air currents, and the room was alive with strange and undefined odours. Presently the door was opened, the smell of mutton again prevailed, and the dingy maid laid plates for four. Mens turned to corpus with a smile, cheerful to the last. Corpus, careless whether he was audible or inaudible, blurted out – 'I can't dine with those women'; and threaded passage and staircase into the street. Mens, following with more deliberation, met 'dinner' on the staircase, and Mrs William Williams at the foot, storming at her departing guests. From a safe distance, two men that day pronounced a curse on 'The Original Conway Refreshment Room'.

This happened a few days ago; now, once more in the main street of Conway, Corpus hugged himself with visible delight. Mens, less demonstrative, drank in the scene with quiet enjoyment. The shutters of 'The Original Conway Refreshment Room' were closed; the premises were 'to let'; Mr William Williams had betaken himself, his wife, his shilling ordinary, and his whole redolent surroundings elsewhere. 'But what,' asked Corpus, 'can have become of the ghoulish females?' We left this monument of the justice of fate for the deck of the St George.

The St George is moored, or tied with a bit of cord, to a mud bank below the castle, with the tide rising up in brown swirls around her. On the beach the women are measuring mussels by basketfuls, and stowing them away in sacks; the beach itself is composed chiefly of brickbats and mussel-shells. A mud bank close at hand is well stirred into slime by the tide, not inodorously; on the left is a timber yard; in front the railway, skirting the castle wall.

But who are these, so withered, and so anything but wild in their attire? To Corpus's immense glee they are the ghoulish females, paler than ever, and seated very close to the side of the boat. The mother wears a pair of netted gloves; the daughter's are of black kid, worn white at the finger tips, and in need of extensive repairs. Altogether, the mother and daughter have a seedy aspect; perhaps they have been someway involved in the fate of Mr William Williams. From time to time they afford Corpus much ill-suppressed amusement, and even Mens chuckles at intervals in his quiet way.

A graphite sketch by Frank Lewis Emanuel, showing *St George* at her landing stage in the Gyffin stream where Dickens' protagonists embarked. The buildings to the left of the picture are clearly recognisable today. Emanuel was born in London and studied at both the Slade School of Art and the Acadamie Julian in Paris. From the early 1880s he began to show his work at the Royal Academy, the Paris Salon and many other prestigious galleries. He exhibited at the Royal Academy every year for over 40 years and several of his works are in the collection of the Tate Gallery.

The skipper has come on board in his shirt-sleeves; argal, though the clouds are low, we shall have a fine day. A man of blackish hue succeeds in hiding himself up to his middle among the machinery, and pokes about out of sight, as if here killing a rat. In this place of comparative concealment he combines the offices of engineer and stoker. A third man, whose prevailing tint is brown, and who is more genuinely dirty than the engineer, we call 'the crew'. The whistle fails to bring any more passengers on board, the tide is flowing strongly, and 'the crew' bringing his brown body to bear on the boat-hook, pushes off. The mussel-packers on the beach stand up and stretch themselves, a few railway hands lounge over the embankment-wall, whilst the overhanging castle-tower makes a final threat of tumbling on to them. There comes a farewell whiff of mud and shell-fish, and we puff away up river.

Including the funereal women and our three selves, we passengers number thirty-two. 'The crew' having satisfied himself on this point, and imparted the information to the skipper, retreats into the lee of a paddle-box, and falls asleep with his head in a bucket of ashes. As we advance the mountains grow up one behind the other, range beyond range; the banks approach us; we are leaving the open water for the intricacies of the narrow channel.

Meanwhile the skipper becomes conversational, to the extent of naming a few mountains wrongly, and telling us a variety of obvious untruths with Welsh indifference, but from our comfortable seats on the paddle-boxes we forget to be angry with him, in our enjoyment of one of the most worshipful valleys in Wales. On the left a wooded hill-side; on the right a higher and gentler slope, pierced out into fields, and flecked with cottages; rising above all on the right, and in front, mountains that we recognised afar off – old friends seen from Bettws and Nant Gwynant. Close at hand low meadows, ending abruptly in little clay cliffs three feet high, visibly eaten away by the current, and topped with overhanging and treacherous turf. Little black cattle grazing in these meadows, sheep, and leisurely horses of a rough, ill-fed breed. Around them and amongst them and bearing down on to them in distant flocks, and flapping over their heads, and skimming along the ground, and running jerkily from tuft to tuft, are the pewits; dull, restless little bodies on the ground, glorifying the air with their white fans when on the wing. Several cormorants in their summer plumage stop fishing as we approach and follow us over head. Gulls, peering downwards with their clever faces, recognise, so Corpus thinks, the funereal women as old friends; and when 'the crew' awakes, and lowers overboard his bucket of cinders, and brings it up again full of dirty water for the stoker-engineer, they settle down astern, and we lose sight of them as we turn into the next reach. Passing a little marsh-isolated landing stage, communicating with the hillside by a rusty tramway, the bank is fringed for a mile or more with flags and bulrushes. The fussy little wave from our exaggerated paddle-wheels ruffles the equanimity of these; they are taken vastly by surprise, and bow themselves more hastily than gracefully. But before we are many yards ahead they recover their dignity, and wave slow and measured salutes. A heron, who has been dozing among them, lowers his high shoulders, flaps his wings, and trails his long pair of legs over a hedge and out of sight.

'The crew' has not been long wake when he is called to take the wheel, and elbows through the passengers, treading on their toes. The skipper produces from an unexpected cavity in his shirt a bundle of dirty tickets, and goes round for his fares. We notice that the elder of the funereal women is in difficulties for change, and at last has to make it up with a postage stamp. The skipper resumes the wheel, and presently turns the St George's bow directly towards the feet of two men standing on the clay bank, with portmanteau, guns and fishing rods.

Every moment we expect to go end-on into the bank; but the boat answers her helm smartly, whisks round within a few feet of the bank, and presents her stern to the two men, who throw their luggage in before them, and jump on board. Presently, by a similar manoeuvre, we land an old farmer, in silk knee-britches, blue hose and shoes. He has chosen to be disembarked on swampy ground, half a mile from road or habitation, and before we are out of sight he is over his shoes in mud and water.

Some passengers are attempting to extract from the skipper the names of the waterfalls. He is probably telling them wrong; and, even if he is right, it would be impossible for them to reproduce the inarticulate noises he makes. Near one of the waterfalls is a sulphur spring, and close by a sulphur-ore mine. And whilst we, wondering vaguely what sulphur-ore is like, and which was discovered first, the mine or the spring, and whether the spring will fail when the mine fails, and who in the name of fortune is the better for drinking rotten-egg water, despair of enlightenment on any of these points, the St George has quietly sidled up to the miniature quay at Treffriw.

Here we disembark; and Corpus, urged thereto by divers twinges of conscience, offers his hand to the funereal women, who are both of them entangled, as to the legs, in long black dresses. The middle-aged daughter extends a very large hand, and places it on Corpus's arm, but the elderly mother declines, possibly remembering Corpus's behaviour at Mr. William Williams's ordinary.

The St George, we have been told, lies three-quarters of an hour at Treffriw quay, and then scuttles down on the tide without a minute to spare. Mens, Corpus and I betake ourselves to a wood overlooking the quay, to smoke our cigars. But first I get the three-quarters of an hour confirmed from the skipper's lips, and at the waterside I find the women in black lingering where we have left them, and asking feeble questions of a stolid native. As I turn away, the elder of the two, impelled by the younger, places herself in my path. I make an effort to escape, and the younger woman says, 'Now, mamma, ask him.'

Upon that, the elder, with a faint smile, and a movement in side her loosely hanging clothes between a bow and a crooked curtsey, say: 'If you please, sir, we were wanting to know if that gentleman was Mr. Corpus.' Oh, horror! And I can think of nothing to say but the truth.

'Ye-es, the name of one of those gentlemen is Corpus.'

'The stout one, I presume.'

'Ye-es,' I reply, 'the stout one.'

'Is he going back on the steamer this afternoon?'

Here again I can think of nothing but the truth and answer 'Yes'.

Mens and Corpus are eyeing the encounter from a safe distance; and the road being clear in their direction, I bow, and make my escape.

Corpus is dumbfounded at the news I bring. Visions of a summons taken out by Mr. William Williams on account of an untasted ordinary, with the ghoulish females in the witness box, float into his ken; only to be succeeded by the still more frightful fancy of a tender passion inspired in the breast of the daughter, whom he helped from the boat on to the quay. He is young and life is before him, but he feels he will be haunted by those beings in decayed mourning. Mens and I cannot help him in his distress. We smoke on in silence, and are inclined to be amused.

To dissipate his humours I recommend to Corpus's notice the sherry-flask; and, disentombing it from his pocket, Corpus discovers with it a letter, found that morning at the Penmaenmawr post-office, and stowed away for after reading.

He takes a pull at the flask, and begins reading. What is it, in that innocent sheet of note-paper, that makes him work his face in an agony? The edges of it are fair and white, unstained by the fatal colour. Can it be a long-forgotten tailor's bill, which Corpus fondly hoped had been sent to somebody else? Can it be a summons home on important business – that holiday cut-throat? No, it is something worse; a communication crossed and recrossed by the maternal pen, concerning an elderly aunt of Corpus's and her single elderly daughter, to whom, by a series of testamentary eccentricities, has come all the family money. 'I am told', the letter runs, 'that they always dress in black, and live very quietly. They were lately lodging at Mr. William Williams's, High Street, Conway; but are now at Mr. Jones ApJones's in the same street. I heard from your Aunt Frummety this morning; she thinks she has seen you, has recognised you by your photograph, and hopes you will call. 'Do, my dear George,' pleads Mrs. Corpus, 'make them out. They are leaving Wales in a few days, and perhaps you could persuade them to come to us for a week, and could bring them home with you. It would be a good opportunity of making their acquaint-ance; we have been separated too long.' Corpus reads, and we listen, and the St George begins an angry whistle below us.

'My boy', say Mens, taking up the letter from the grass, where Corpus had thrown it, 'here is another postscript. It is thirty years since I saw your Aunt Frummety; she was then a fine young woman. Perhaps her daughter takes after her.'

Corpus groans and smokes viciously.

The St George continues whistling; only five minutes remain of its five-and-forty.

Mens and I consult apart, then Mens speaks. 'Corpus, my boy, if they go by the boat, we will walk.'

Corpus clasps us each by the hand; and now the whistle stops, and an impatient little bell, rung by the skipper himself, fills idle Treffriw with a sense of importance.

From our seat we can watch the passengers and cargo going on board. A gamekeeper, with a couple of spaniels in leash; a market woman; two or three quarrymen; a couple of coops of fowls, given into special charge of 'the crew', and assigned to a warm place on the boiler; a partly of tourists, who cover a seat with shawls, and open their maps. Nothing in black is visible, neither up the road towards Llanrwst, nor down the road, as far as we can see it, towards Conway. Time's up. The bell ceases. 'Cast off', cries the skipper; while Treffriw crowds the quay with hands in pockets. 'The crew' makes ready with his boathook; but, instead of pushing off, he has for a moment, to hold on. We come dashing out of the underwood with a 'whoop', and jump on board.

Passengers, crew and staff from the Belle Vue Hotel pose for the photographer on board *St George* at Trefriw around 1875, the year in which Charles Dickens Jnr published his account of a voyage on board. Note the lettering on the paddlebox which reads 'St George between Conway & Trefriw'. (National Library of Wales)

Now that we are fairly under weigh, how bright and cheerful everything seems. The sun did not touch us in the wood; here it is pouring its full strength on the boat, on the stream, on the broad valley.

We have not half so many passengers as on the up voyage, and the tide runs faster. There never was a merrier craft than the St George, with its chimney striped as gaily as a wasp. We don't at all object to the brown fleece of smoke trailing away astern, which the sky is perpetually combing off. If the spirits of the air want to spin a yarn up the Bettws Valley, they are welcome to the St George's funnel as a distaff.

Corpus is in the best spirits of us all.

A trouble, not of clouds, or sweeping rain,
Nor of the setting sun's pathetic light
Engendered,

Has blown over him and passed away. He dare not yet ask the skipper about the two ladies in black, for fear the worthy should notice their absence and put back. But he leans against the paddle box and sings: 'A maiden who dwelt in the forest of Arcady, where the sun is gold, and the moonlight silvery.'

'Ease her!' cries the skipper, and stoker-engineer bestirs himself and moves a lever or two.

'What are we stopping for?'

We are not stopping; we are making a steep turn into a side channel, running out of the main stream, as it seems, into a primaeval forest of bulrushes. The bulrushes look as if they will brush our paddle-boxes on each side.

'Where are you going?' asks Corpus of the skipper.

'Take up two ladies at the sulphur springs.'

'Two ladies in black?'

'Aye, aye,' says the skipper, lending a hand to 'the crew', who has put the helm hard a-port.

Poor Corpus! We eye him narrowly. He steps to where he can get an uninterrupted view across the steamer's bow.

We can just see over the level top of the bulrush forest, and far away across it is a semblance of a jetty just under the hill. Towards this the channel we have entered appears to be winding. On the jetty, side by side, stand two black figures. We are nearly half a mile off, but there is no mistaking them.

'Captain, I will give you five shillings to keep your old course,' whispers Corpus, touching the skipper's arm.

A few bulrushes jump up from under the paddle-box, and sweep their wet heads sternwards along the bulwarks. 'Hard a-head a few strokes,' says the skipper.

'I will give you ten shillings,' says corpus.

The skipper looks Corpus in the face, and for a moment lets go the wheel.

'A sovereign to keep your course,' and Corpus presses the coin into the man's palm.

'Hard astern', cries the skipper, and we slowly work our passage backwards between the now doubly-agitated bulrushes. The St George's nose is soon pointing downstream again. On the jetty across the bulrushes the black figures exercise a sort of shadow-dance, a quadrille of forlorn ghosts, forgotten by the old ferry-man. As we pass on there is a sad sound as if the shades had their obols ready, and were abusing Charon bitterly. But the skipper's back is in the direction of these black portents; he smokes one of corpus's cigars, and calls the mountains by their wrong names.

As we edge alongside the mud bank at Conway, and the plank is run out for us to walk ashore, the Irish Mail comes booming through Stephenson's bridge and thundering under the castle walls. The train which we are to follow, does not start for half an hour. 'We have just time to call on dear Aunt Frummety,' remarks Corpus and we trudge off, pass the deserted abode of Mr William Williams, and the blank shutters of the Original Conway Refreshment Room, in search of Mr Jones ApJones's residence. Mr Jones ApJones is in the same line of business as the late Mr William Williams, if he has not taken over that individuals plant and stock in trade. Mr ApJones owns the Conway Castle Refreshment rooms. He too provides a frugal ordinary at one o'clock, though by this time in the afternoon there is nothing left of it, but the faint odour of cooking, and a tepid shoulder of mutton agape in its own gravy.

'Mrs and Miss Frummety at home?' asks Corpus.

'Indeed, Sir, they are away in the steamer to Treffriw. But they'll be back any minute, and I'm just gone about taking their dinners in.'

Mrs Corpus heard in due time that the Frummetys were unfortunately out when George called, and that George was coming home at once by way of Barmouth and South Wales.

Notes

1. Black, Adam and Charles, op. cit.
2. *A Guide to Trefriw, Llanrwst and Bettws-y-Coed*, Cambrian Series (Caenarfon, Rees & Evans, Herald Office: June 1872).
3. *A Handbook for Travellers in North Wales* (3rd edition) (London: John Murray: 1868).
4. Richards, R., 'Up the River Conway to Llanrwst', an article from *Miscellaneous Poems and Pen-and-Ink Sketches* (Bangor: North Wales Chronicle Office, 1868).
5. Hayward, John W., MD, MRCS, LSA, 'The Vale of Conway Spa', in *The British Journal of Homeopathy*, vol. 23 (1867).
6. Garner, Robert, *Holiday Excursions of a Naturalist* (London, 1867).
7. Duckworth, C.L.D. and Langmuir, G.E., *West Coast Steamers* (T. Stephenson & Sons; Prescot, 1953 & 1956).
8. Dickens, C. (ed.), 'The Narrative of an Uneventful Voyage', in *All the Year Round: A Weekly Journal*, vol. 13 (1875).

4

The Growth of Trefriw, the Limited Company and Fleet Expansion, 1873–93

Throughout the 1870s the little *St George* continued to ply her quiet summer trade along the beautiful Conwy valley, which the guidebooks were beginning to refer to as 'The Welsh Rhine'. Boosted by the steady growth of Llandudno, the other coastal resorts and the tourist trade to North Wales in general, both the Trefriw waters and the steamer service grew steadily in popularity, but complaints began to be voiced that the potential for expansion was being hindered by the lack of facilities offered in the village of Trefriw itself. The Belle Vue, standing on its terrace above the quay, was the village's only quality hotel, and one observer, writing in the late 1860s, had been moved to remark that:

> Since the waters have been brought into notice the demand for accommoda-
> tion has been regularly increasing, and from the want of such accommodations
> scores upon scores of individuals who, by their residence, would have greatly
> benefitted themselves and materially promoted the prosperity of everyone
> interested in that part of the country, were obliged to return disappointed or
> seek relief at some other spa.[1]

The next 20 years, however, saw this defect remedied, as Trefriw was provided with a range of excellent facilities to serve the seasonal tourists and health-seekers. These would, in their turn, lead to significant developments in the steamer service.

A major, and arguably pivotal, influence in the transformation of the village was Rev. John Gower, who was appointed rector to the parish in 1869. Born on

The Belle Vue Hotel in its original form, *c.* 1875. (National Library of Wales)

A wonderful portrait, *c.* 1875, of 'Jo Belle Vue', one of the porters who would have carried visitors' luggage between the steamer and the hotel. (National Library of Wales)

29 October 1831 at Pistyllbach, Pembrey, near Llanelli in Carmarthenshire, Gower came to Trefriw from Queen's College Birmingham and took up residence in the impressive rectory located on School Bank Hill where he remained for the next 44 years, until his death in 1913. Throughout that period Gower cleverly combined his spiritual role with that of businessman and entrepreneur and maintained a guiding and financial interest in almost every aspect of Trefriw's development.

Rev. John Gower pictured at one of his three weddings. In November 1884 he married Elizabeth Twigg, who died in May 1889. His second marriage was to Edith Ada Chipperfield in May 1884, but she too died less than 2 years later. Finally, in November 1907 he married Harriett Anne Campling, who outlived him by some 20 years. (Gladys Hughes)

The first major project was the construction of a new and greatly improved pump room at Trefriw Wells by the grandly titled Trefriw Chalybeate Wells & Baths Company Ltd which, having already signed a 45-year lease with Baroness Willoughby de Eresby for a parcel of land including the original caves and bath house at Cae Coch at a rent of £10 per annum, was incorporated on 26 May 1873. By 30 November 1874, 314 of the £4 shares had been taken up. The list of initial shareholders makes fascinating reading:

Thomas Jones	Llanrwst	Physician	80
Samuel Rees	Trefriw	Gentleman	50
John Gower	The Rectory, Trefriw	Clerk in Holy Orders	40
John Jones	Millhouse, Trefriw	Merchant	40
Robert Roberts	Store house, Trefriw	Merchant	25
John Taylor	Bethesda, Bangor	Gentleman	30
Richard Jones	Trefriw	Merchant	5
Humphrey Lewis	Llanrwst	Merchant	10
Thomas Roberts	Glamdwr, Trefriw	Captain	4
John Rees	Caernarfon	Gentleman	20
Anne Jones	Trefriw		10

It is interesting to note that the largest shareholder, Thomas Jones, was a local medical man, and that both Rev. Gower and two members of the steamer-owning Roberts family were represented. In the years ahead, as more capital was raised by the issue of additional shares, the relative size of shareholdings remained largely unaltered, although Gower increased his to 63¾ and Robert Roberts reduced his to 7½.

The new company immediately set about constructing an elegant new pump and bath house on a flat area of land between the original 1863 bath house and the road. Constructed in the Tudor style of grey stone with stepped gables, it was an imposing building and offered greatly enhanced facilities to its visitors. The old caves on the hillside above were closed to the public and the waters were instead piped directly to the pump room where the health-seekers could purchase their recommended doses from the bars in the first- or second-class drinking rooms, at 2*d* or 1*d* a glass respectively.

At about the same time as the construction of the new spa, Baroness Willoughby de Eresby and her son Lord Aveland decided to grant, on favourable financial terms, a large number of other leases in Trefriw, which stimulated something of a building boom. It is possible that their decision may have been influenced by discussions between their agent, Mr McIntyre and Rev. Gower, for in 1880 Gower formed the Trefriw Improvement Committee with the aim of improving facilities for visitors and thereby stimulating the commercial development of the village. One of the committee's first actions was to provide bench seats along the road between the village and the spa in May 1881. The committee seems to have gradually transmogrified into an improvement company, suggesting that its members' motives were not entirely philanthropic.

By 1881 a guidebook,[2] which had previously been somewhat critical of Trefriw's facilities, was able to report:

> Since our former edition and especially in the last two years, the means and facilities of access to the village have been greatly increased. The village itself has been much enlarged and improved and its sanitary condition which was always good has been further provided for by an ample and special water supply and system of drainage and an excellent, well-situated cemetery. Many new houses have been built and several new shops opened … new places of worship erected … and numerous and picturesque walks laid out.

The most popular short walk was to the Fairy Falls, which lay within a few minutes of the village centre. Formed by the Afon Crafnant tumbling down the hillside from the mountains above, the falls lay within a narrow ravine whose damp rocks were carpeted with ferns and mosses and which was overhung with the drooping branches of close-growing trees. Paths and steps had been cut into the sides of the valley and an ornamental iron bridge was constructed to allow tourists to cross high above the foaming waters. At the foot of the falls, and completing the quintessentially romantic Victorian scene, stood the famous Vale of Conway Flannel Mills, whose huge waterwheel was turned by the stream. The mills were a major attraction in themselves and visitors were able to 'buy excellent woollen stocking and homespuns, which have the merit of being pretty as well as being good'.[3]

For the more energetic, paths led up the steep hillside behind the village to the twin mountain lakes of Llyn Crafnant and Llyn Geirionydd – the former famed for its trout fishing and cottage tea room, and the latter for its monument to the poet Taliesin. A circular walk to either lake was about 5 miles in length, but the guidebooks recommended extensions to Capel Curig (another 3 miles) and onwards to Betws-y-Coed:

> It is a pleasant and an easy walk of five and half miles from here to Bettws-y-Coed, down hill all the way … we pass the Swallow Falls and certainly should turn aside for a few minutes to look at them. A mile or so further on we turn again into the woods to see the celebrated Miner's Bridge. And from Bettwys, if we have had enough of walking, we may return to Llanrwst by train, congratulating ourselves upon a delightful day's excursion.[4]

Llyn Crafnant, one of the two dramatic lakes in the mountains above Trefriw which were popular destinations on walks from the village. The cottage provided refreshments and boats could be hired for fishing or rowing on the lake. (Crawford Alexander)

The journey from the railway station at Llanrwst to Trefriw was a scenic but round-about route of about 2½ miles, crossing the river by the ancient Llanrwst Bridge and thence via Gwydir and along the western side of the valley. In 1881 Rev. Gower, backed no doubt by his improvement company, decided to shorten this journey by constructing a direct route between Trefriw and the station. The road, known as Gower's Road or the New Road, left Trefriw High Street opposite the Flannel Mill and, raised above flood level on a slight embankment, ran in a straight line across the floodplain to cross the river on a substantial timber bridge and emerge almost opposite the station. The road was built of a suitable width to take carriages, and a toll of 1*d* for pedestrians and 2*d* for vehicles was collected at a toll house known as Gower's House. Carriages awaited the arrival of every train and the new road proved an immediate success.

It is interesting to note that in 1890 a proposal was made to turn the New Road into an electric tramway. In 1895 Gower and his associate Mr Jones of Trefriw approached the Llanrwst Guardians to request that they swap a piece of land alongside their workhouse for another piece in Gower's ownership, in order that the construction of the tramway could proceed. The matter was deferred but the scheme rumbled on until 1920 when a local government board inspector expressed his opposition to the proposed route and the matter was finally allowed to drop.

A horse-drawn trap taking visitors from Trefriw to join the train at Llanrwst railway station crosses the bridge over the Conwy on the New Road or Gower's Road of 1881. Out of sight behind the photographer is the toll house known as Gower's House, where a collector will be waiting to extract 2*d* from the driver.

The Trefriw Improvement Company Ltd, meanwhile, was busy negotiating the purchase of a piece of land beside the New Road and close to the village centre, upon which they planned to create a recreation ground. Opened in 1888, the new facility was sometimes referred to as the 'Pleasure Ground' or 'Tennis Ground', and boasted two or three croquet lawns, several tennis courts, bowling and quoiting greens and various shelters, pavilions and cloakrooms. All necessary equipment could be hired on site while, for those disinclined to take part in the sports, the carefully landscaped grounds, with their fine views across the flood-plain to the hills beyond, provided a pleasant location to sit and relax. A major tennis tournament was held each August which attracted many first-class players, and during tournament week dances and concerts were held as well as a carnival procession which, at its peak, attracted over 1,000 participants.

The building of many new, villa-style residences greatly increased the supply of lodging houses in the village and guidebooks insisted that:

> The intending visitor to Trefriw has little cause to apprehend being obliged to retrace his weary steps to Llanrwst for a night's rest as was the case with hundreds in former years. He will now find the good folk of Trefriw quite prepared to meet all his requirements and to lodge him in a comfortable manner.[5]

Trefriw recreation ground, which opened in 1888, was one of Trefriw's major attractions. The more energetic visitors could indulge in tennis, croquet or bowls while others simply chose to sit and relax. (Vera Clegg)

Trefriw village high street, showing some of the Victorian villas constructed from 1873 onwards, which helped provide visitors with a far better range and quality of accommodation.

The Belle Vue, located at the northern end of the village and close to the steamer quay, remained the premier hotel and was warmly recommended in the guide-books. An 1872 edition reported that, 'it had been much enlarged of late, has excellent coffee rooms, some good sitting rooms and between 20 and 30 bed-rooms. An omnibus meets the early, late and midday trains at Llanrwst and goes to the Hotel.'[6] In 1875 the hotel was let by Peter Lewis to Owen Jones, who remained the proprietor for the next 10 years and made further improvements, including the introduction of regular concerts.

One regular performer was the famous blind harpist, David Francis. Born in 1865 in a humble cottage near the Llechwedd slate mines in Blaenau Ffestiniog, he was famed under his Welsh bardic name of Y Telynor Dall o Feirion (meaning The Blind Harpist of Merioneth) and was part of a long tradition of blind harpists, many of whom made a living by busking in taverns. From 1881 onwards he was employed by the hotel to spend the summer months entertaining guests. Owen Jones may well have needed to look to his laurels at this time since, in addition to the popular Ship Inn on the High Street, a new hotel called the Geirionydd had just opened in the very centre of the village, opposite the Fairy Falls and next to the recreation ground, and threatened to be a formidable rival.

In 1885 the Belle Vue was taken over by the popular Tommy Dutton, who had moved to the area with his wife Mary and their three children because he found Trefriw more suitable for his wife's delicate chest than the neighbourhood of London. The Duttons also had interests in the Castle Hotel in Conwy, and used their considerable charm and skill to further increase the popularity of the hotel. Regular balls held throughout the winter months were popular with local

The Blind Harpist of Bettws-y-Coed.

David Francis, the famous blind harpist who, from 1881 onwards, was a regular performer at the Belle Vue Hotel and the Trefriw Wells. (Conwy Archive Service)

residents and hotel guests alike. Concerts and theatrical entertainments were also a regular feature, and David Francis continued to be employed during the summer season. Passengers from the river steamers flocked ashore in search of refreshments during their brief stay at the quay and the hotel became a popular venue for lunch after church on Sundays. Excellent trout and salmon fishing was available in the nearby river and advertisements emphasised the hotel's unique position as what today would be referred to as a transport hub. Not only was it conveniently placed midway between the village and the wells, but the river steamers were moored within a stone's throw, the four-horse coaches from Llandudno and Betws-y-Coed stopped outside and Llanrwst railway station was only 1½ miles away by road.

By the late 1880s, therefore, Trefriw had equipped itself with everything necessary to attract, entertain and accommodate visitors, without in any way detracting from its inherent atmosphere of calm and beauty. Its efforts were crowned with success, for the visitors came in ever-increasing numbers. The hotels were filled with the wealthy, many of whom would take up residence for up to 10 weeks at a time to 'take the cure' at the wells and benefit from Trefriw's famous climate; the middle classes occupied the many lodging houses which had sprung up in the

A selection of dance cards from popular balls held at the Belle Vue Hotel during the late 1880s when Tommy Dutton was proprietor. (Lindsay Gordon, Princes Arms Hotel)

village; and the village became a popular holiday haunt for Welsh Nonconformist ministers. A.G. Bradley[7] wrote:

> One is given to regarding this kind of place as the haunt of jaded sybarites from the cities, but the simple preacher from the Welsh hills would drink one of these men under the table in the matter of sulphur or alum and go on his way rejoicing [and would enjoy] a gentle toddle backwards and forwards to the Wells in conversation with people of his own sort.

Some people came to fish or go walking, others to paint or take part in the sports at the recreation ground. In addition, day trippers from the coast would arrive

"Belle Vue Hotel," Trefriw.

BEAUTIFULLY SITUATED. One and a-Half Miles from Llanrwst and Trefriw Station. On the banks of the River Conway. Near the Lake District, Chalybeate Wells and Fairy Falls.

Tennis, Good Salmon & Trout Fishing, Boating, &c.

A Steamer plies daily between Conway and the Hotel.

FAIRY FALLS, TREFRIW.

Four=horse Coaches leave Every Morning for the most beautiful Tours in Wales.

T. DUTTON, *PROPRIETOR.*

POSTAL ADDRESS :
Carnarvonshire, R.S.O.

An advertisement for the Belle Vue Hotel, from the *Caernarfon & Anglesey Postal Directory*, 1886.

by coach, train and, of course, by the ever-popular *St George* which continued to land her 'daily hordes of sufferers' at the quay.

Indeed, the tiny steamer was now so popular that she struggled to cope with the demand of and frequently left queues of disappointed passengers on the quayside at Conwy. The quay itself had become a source for concern and, since 1885, had been in urgent need of repairs and re-gravelling. Accumulating mud and rubbish made it unsafe for ships to take the ground at low tide and there were frequent complaints that the timber merchants Messrs P.& H. Lewis, whose premises were on the quay, were constantly obstructing the pathways with piles of timber.

It was clear that immediate steps had to be taken to improve the boarding arrangements for the *St George's* passengers and, in the longer term, to purchasing a second steamer. For the Roberts family, however, the timing was not ideal. Of the three brothers involved with the steamer business Robert Roberts of the Store House, Trefriw, had died in 1886 and David, the wayward sibling, having spent three or four seasons in command of *St George* between 1882 and 1885, had gone to live in New Zealand and, while returning home once again, died in Sydney, Australia in 1890.

This left Capt. Thomas Roberts, now resident at 4 Llewelyn Terrace, Conway, as the sole remaining founder member of the company. Thomas had three sons: Robert (1860–67 February 1939), Thomas 'Tommy' (1867–12 July 1891) and William (1862–26 January 1927), all of whom became masters in sail. Robert and William, together with their cousin Robert Owen (1863–12 July 1924, the son of Robert Roberts of the Store House) were to form the next generation of steamer managers and skippers.

For the moment, however, Capt. Thomas Roberts did not allow the grass to grow under his feet. In the summer of 1888 Conwy Council had decided to let the tenancy of an area of land on the foreshore to the highest bidder. Known as the Wing Gate Yard, this land consisted of two plots extending in total for 120ft eastwards from the point where the town wall ran down into the sea, and was ideally suited to development as a boatyard or shipping business. Thomas put in a bid of £8 per annum for one plot on a 21-year lease 'for the purpose of making a landing stage for the steamers plying between Deganwy, Conway and Trefriw, and also to lay them up during the winter months',[8] and submitted detailed plans for enclosing the area with a fence. After driving up the price by playing one bidder against another, the council let both plots to Thomas for a total of £22 plus rates, while a ship's chandler called Richard Thomas was allocated an adjoining 18yd strip. By April 1889, the Harbour Committee minutes recorded that the land had actually been let to 'Messrs. Roberts & Lewis', indicating that Capt. Roberts had entered into some sort of formal financial agreement with P.& H. Lewis the timber merchants, a fact that was to have great significance in later developments.

Firmly aground at low tide, *St George* lies on the mud at Conwy quay, showing her shallow, flat-bottomed hull to perfection. Until her new dedicated landing stage was constructed in 1888 the ship generally departed from her berth in the Gyffin stream, but sometimes ran from the quay as well as coming there to take on coal. During the nineteenth century many of Conwy's essential goods passed across the quay, which was served by regular steam and sailing coasters from Liverpool and elsewhere. Among the cluster of quay-side buildings is the transit shed belonging to the Manchester, Liverpool & North Wales Steam Ship Company. (Courtesy of the Bridge Inn, Conwy)

The Wing Gate Yard was to be the hub of the St George's Steamship Company's operation for the rest of its existence. Captain Roberts immediately set about constructing a stout timber pier tight against the town wall and directly opposite the current Nos 17 and 18 Lower Gate Street. A horizontal walkway crossed the beach and connected to a hinged section that led down to the floating pier head, which consisted of the hull of a redundant sailing flat called the *Cemaes*. This hulk doubled as a storage space for ship's gear and initially for the supplies of coal, which had to be carried on board the steamer every few days in wheelbarrows or wicker baskets and tipped into her coal bunkers.

In subsequent years the company constructed two large timber sheds on the site immediately adjoining the landing stage. Each was fitted with a patent slipway, allowing the smaller vessels to be drawn out of the water for refit and repair during the winter months, safe from the worst of the wind and weather. The coal for the steamers was stored in the ground floor of the medieval Porth Isaf Tower, a little further along the town walls at the point where Lower Gate Street opens on to the quay, and an office (later shared with Crossfields boatyard) was established in the old customs house by Porth Bach, which today serves as the harbourmaster's office.

An aerial view of Conwy. On the extreme left is the Gyffin stream from where the Trefriw steamers originally departed. The centre left is dominated by Conwy Castle and the magnificent bridges linking Conwy to The Cobb (or Embankment). Conwy Quay is clearly visible in the centre of the picture while, slightly downstream to its right, the town wall can be seen running down on to the beach. On the upstream side of the walls, nearest the camera, are the double-roofed black sheds, landing stage and slipways at the St George's Steamship Company's Wing Gate Yard, developed from 1888 onwards. On the far side of the wall is Crossfield's boatyard, which was established in 1906.

Captain Roberts had already constructed a floating landing stage at Deganwy on the opposite side of the estuary. Situated on the branch line from Llandudno Junction to Llandudno, the town had received its own railway station in 1868, and was rapidly developing into a resort in its own right. The landing stage was situated conveniently close to Deganwy station, enabling the large numbers of visitors who patronised Llandudno during the summer months to take a very short train journey before alighting and joining the steamer for a trip to Conwy and Trefriw.

Thus, from May 1889 onwards a new pattern was established which would last for the rest of the company's history. Having prepared for her day's sailings along-side the company's new stage at Conwy, the steamer would cross to Deganwy to pick up passengers from Llandudno and the surrounding area before cross-ing back to Conwy to collect more passengers and proceed up river to Trefriw. Although those intending to embark at Conwy were delighted that a new land-ing stage had replaced the inconvenience of the town's timber-strewn quay, they were irritated that, more and more frequently, the *St George* would be full before she left Deganwy and that they could do nothing but swallow their disappoint-ment as she steamed by.

The solution, of course, was to build a second steamer. The cost, however, was more than Capt. Roberts and his youthful sons and nephew could generate from within the family, so it was decided to form a limited company and raise the capital required by selling shares to the public. The St George's Steamship Company Ltd was incorporated during 1889 with Capt. Thomas Roberts as its first managing director. Unfortunately no list of shareholders has yet been discovered, but it seems probable that the Roberts family would have retained a majority interest while other shares were taken up by local businessmen, people with an inter-est in the success of the river trade, such as Rev. Gower and the members of the Trefriw Improvement Company and, almost certainly, some of the family's wealthy ship-owning contacts in Liverpool. There were three Conwy men who were almost certainly major shareholders. The first was Capt. Griffith Jones, who, for several years, had been a partner of Capt. Thomas Roberts in their successful ship-owning and broking firm of Roberts & Jones and was, for a period during the 1890s, master of the *St George*. The others were Messrs P. & H. Lewis, the timber merchants based on Conwy Quay.

The order for the new steamer was placed with the yard of William Thomas & Sons of Amlwch on nearby Anglesey. Curiously, the order was not placed by the St George's Steamship Company, but in the name of Messrs P. & H. Lewis. At first sight one might suspect that the timber merchants were attempting to build and run their own steamer in opposition to the established company but, given their partnership with Thomas Roberts in the Wing Gate Yard and their shares in the St George's Company, it seems more likely that some internal financial arrangement

THE   🚢   STEAMER

"ST, GEORGE,"

(Weather and other causes permitting) is intended
to run on one of the most beautiful rivers
in Wales, between

DEGANWY, CONWAY, AND TREFRIW,

And the Mineral Springs in the Vale of Llanrwst.
as under :

SEPT. 1892.		From Deganwy		From Conway.		Ret. from Trefriw.	
1	Thursday ...	4 15	p.m	4 30	p.m	6 15	p.m†
2	Friday	5 45	—	6 0	—	7 40	— †
5	Monday ...	8 32	a.m	8 48	a.m	10 36	a.m
6	Tuesday ...	8 50	—	9 5	—	11 20	—
7	Wednesday	9 45	—	9 50	—	12 0	noon
8	Thursday ...	10 8	—	10 22	—	12 42	p.m
9	Friday	10 35	—	10 50	—	1 20	—
10	Saturday ...	11 20	—	11 35	—	2 0	—
12	Monday ...	1 10	p.m	1 24	p.m	3 20	—
13	Tuesday ...	2 0	—	2 15	—	4 0	—
14	Wednesday	3 20	—	3 25	—	5 0	—†
15	Thursday ..	4 35	—	4 50	—	6 30	—†
16	Friday	6 10	—	6 25	—	8 5	—†
19	Monday ...	8 45	a.m	8 50	a.m	10 50	a.m
20	Tuesday ...	8 55	—	9 10	—	11 30	—
21	Wednesday	9 45	—	9 50	—	12 5	p.m
22	Thursday ...	10 8	—	10 22	—	12 35	—
23	Friday ...	10 25	—	10 40	—	1 5	—
24	Saturday ...	11 12	—	11 20	—	1 30	—
26	Monday ...	12 10	p.m	12 25	p.m	2 22	—
27	Tuesday ...	12 50	—	1 5	—	2 50	—
28	Wednesday	1 40	—	1 50	—	3 20	—†
29	Thursday	2 10	—	2 26	—	4 10	—†

On return will proceed as far as Deganwy, except *
† Doubtful if Steamer will reach Trefriw.

FARES :

Fore End, 1/-; Cabin and Deck, 1/6; Return, 2/6.

*For the convenience of passengers, Refreshments
will be ready daily on arrival at the* BELLE VUE
HOTEL, TREFRIW.

A newspaper advertisement showing *St George*'s timetable for September 1892.

was taking place. It is possible that the shares in the limited company had not sold sufficiently quickly to generate the capital to place a firm order with the shipbuilders, and that P. & H. Lewis had advanced some additional funds, or that they were the largest single shareholders and therefore named as managing owners.

Whatever the case, the building of Yard No. 22 went on apace and, named *Prince George*, the ship was launched amid the usual celebrations on 8 March 1890. She was built of steel, weighed 23.53 gross tons and measured 72.2ft by 12.15ft by 3.71ft. Her official number was 120788 and she was registered at Beaumaris.

On 25 March the finished hull was towed to Caernarfon where she was to be fitted with her engine and boiler by De Winton & Company, the famous railway locomotive and marine engineers. The engine was of a compound diagonal, surface-condensing design, the two cylinders having a diameter of 11in and 20in and a stroke of 24in. The engine room was 22.4ft long and she was fitted with a single, steel, multi-tubular boiler with a working pressure of 85psi.

At this point something of a mystery develops. Having reported the launch in glowing terms, the *North Wales Weekly News & Visitors Chronicle* made no further mention of the new ship until June 1893 when she appeared for the first time in the St George's Steamship Company's weekly sailing advertisements. The newspaper normally reported anything positive relating to the steamer company to such an extent that one is forced to suspect that the editor and the company

Prince George of 1890 about to pass under the Conwy bridges on her way upstream to Trefriw on a rising tide. Note her distinctive, diamond-patterned railings and the fact that, because it is a fine day, the awning over her aft deck has been rolled up on to its framework.

management were linked either by friendship or finance. Now, however, there was complete silence. The weekly adverts and accounts of the *St George's* trips continued to appear, but never a mention of *Prince George*, leaving one groping for an explanation for the intervening years.

A number of possibilities suggest themselves. Firstly, it is just conceivable that P. & H. Lewis had indeed purchased the vessel on their own account and were operating in opposition to the *St George* and that the newspaper, as was the case when later competitors appeared on the river, chose to ignore them completely and refuse to carry their adverts. This, however, seems most unlikely for the reasons given above. Secondly, it is possible that some serious problem arose with the De Winton engines preventing the ship's entry into service and leading to a legal dispute. Even if this was the case, however, one would have expected the problem to be resolved by the start of the 1892 season and some hint of the difficulties to have appeared in the press or the company records. Neither happened, and the 'missing years' of the *Prince George* must remain a mystery for the time being.

The year 1891 was to prove a sad and pivotal one for the Roberts family. At 8.45 p.m. on the evening of 12 March Capt. Roberts' youngest son Tommy set out for Conwy in command of Roberts & Jones' flat *Agnes* to make the passage upstream to Trefriw. When about 1½ miles into her journey the *Agnes* touched bottom and came to a sudden halt. The flooding tide caught the rudder, forced it violently to one side, and Tommy was swept overboard by the tiller. His crewman was unable to locate him in the darkness and his body was recovered by a search party next morning.

CaptainRobert's funeral was held on 13 March, the chief mourners being his brothers Robert and William. His father was too ill to attend, having been laid low with a serious asthmatic cold since the winter. The tragic death of his youngest son must have been the final straw, for on 12 July 1891, at the age of 58, he too passed away. In recording his funeral, the local press recalled that Capt. Thomas Roberts had received little formal education and had been entirely self-taught. He had gone to sea at a tender age, risen to command sailing vessels in the Liverpool to Conwy trade and developed into a successful ship owner, steamboat proprietor, partner with Capt. Griffith Jones in their successful ship-broking firm, and a local 'man of means'. He had been an active member of the Welsh Congregational Church at Conwy and both he and Tommy were interred in the local cemetery. Ironically, only a few days after his funeral the new 160-ton, 80ft ketch *Conovium*, which had been built to the order of Roberts & Jones by Thomas Lewis of Bangor, was launched at Conwy, the last sailing ship to built in the port.

With their father and eldest brother dead, it fell to the surviving brothers, Robert and William Roberts, together with their cousin Robert Owen Roberts, to take over the reins of the steamboat business. At the relatively tender ages of 31, 29 and 28 years respectively, all three had spent their lives at sea, were qualified masters in sail and were intimate with the trade of the river. Between them they owned and skippered a number of local sailing vessels.

Robert was skipper/owner of the *Pilgrim* and, along with his partner Capt. Griffith Jones, owned the recently launched *Conovium*. When he came ashore to manage the steamers he passed command of the *Pilgrim* to Capt. Robert Hughes and became the local agent for the steamship *W.S. Caine*, which maintained a regular cargo service between Conwy Quay and Liverpool.

William also traded extensively under sail, skippered the *Pilgrim* from time to time and, following the upheaval of 1891, commanded all of the company's river steamers. He went on to become Conwy harbourmaster from 1902, company manager from 1907 and managing director from 1911.

Robert Owen, who later married Alice Roberts, had spent his early life circling the globe in deep-sea sailing ships and had spent some time in New Zealand, returning home in 1891. He divided his time between the St George's Steamship Company and his own trading vessels, the *Colonel Gamble* (105 tons of cargo) and the small, cutter-rigged *Gladys*. From 1903 Capt. Robert Hughes was employed as skipper of the *Colonel Gamble* until he purchased her outright in 1912.

A number of other vessels including the *Tryfan* were owned within the family and the three young Captains Roberts must have had a busy and demanding few years learning to balance the demands of their existing coastal sailing ship trade with that of an expanding seasonal steamer service. All three acted as skippers of the paddle steamers but continued to go to sea in their sailing ships as required. From 1893 to 1901 Capt. Griffith Jones was in command of *St George*, which suggests that two of the Roberts must have had commitments which took them away from the river.

A portrait of Robert Owen Roberts taken in Australia shortly before his return to Conwy in 1891 to assist with the running of the steamer company. (Elsbeth Pears)

The Roberts' small, sloop-rigged trading vessel *Gladys*, seen here at Trefriw Quay, was one of Robert Owen Roberts' many commands. (Elsbeth Pears)

In September 1891 the Conwy valley experienced one of its regular, serious floods. A period of heavy rain had ensured that the river and its tributaries were already in spate when a large spring tide combined with a northerly gale prevented the floodwaters from escaping to the sea. Parts of Trefriw were inundated and on the floodplain only the tops of hedgerows were visible. Whether or not the steamer service was suspended is not recorded, but *St George* made her last sailing of the season on 26 September and was laid up for the winter.

Newspaper advertisements for the 1892 season referred only to the *St George*, but in June 1893 the company's new steamer finally made her appearance. As if to add to the mystery of the 'disappearance' of the *Prince George* between 1890 and 1893 the new ship was referred to consistently in advertisements and newspaper articles until 1906 as the *New St George* and even bore the name emblazoned on her paddle boxes. This, of course, has provided a rich vein of confusion for historians, many of whom have assumed that the new ship was christened

New St George and renamed *Prince George* in 1907, or that there might even have been two sister ships, one of each name.

In actual fact, the explanation was far simpler. The new ship was actually launched and registered as *Prince George*, a name which she always bore in small lettering on her bows and stern. However, since the name *St George* was synonymous with the river trip to Trefriw, the company chose to benefit from what today would be called 'brand recognition' and advertise the newcomer as *New St George*.

Prince George (as she will henceforth be referred to) was an exceptionally handsome little steamer. Unlike *St George* with her open forward well-deck and short sponsons, *Prince George*'s upper deck ran continuously from bow to stern and was carried out to the full width of the ship over her elongated sponsons to provide a greatly increased seating area. She was fitted with extremely distinctive diamond-patterned metal deck rails with a short, solid section immediately above her upright stem. Her well-raked funnel, whose lower portion was braced by metal struts, was positioned just abaft the paddle boxes and hinged a little over a third of the way up to allow her to pass under the Conwy bridges at high tide. Forward of the funnel was a small, raised deck bearing the ship's wheel and engine control levers and surrounded by rails on which lifebelts were hung. From this position the skipper or helmsman could steer and control the ship whilst communicating

THE ⛵ STEAMERS

"ST. GEORGE," and the "NEW ST. GEORGE,"

Weather and other causes permitting, are intended to run one of the most beautiful rivers in Wales between

DEGANWY, CONWAY AND TREFRIW,

And the Mineral Springs in the Vale of Llanrwst, as under :—

JUNE		Leaves Deganwy.		Leaves Conway.		Ret. from Trefriw.
1 Thursday	...	10 20 a. m.	... 10 35 a.m.	.	12 40 p.m
2 Friday	..	11 10 —	... 11 22 —	...	1 15 —
3 Saturday	...	11 30 —	... 11 45 —	...	1 45 —
5 Monday	...	1 0 p.m.	... 1 15 p.m.	..	2 56 —
6 Tuesday	...	1 50 —	... 2 5 —	...	3 48 —*
7 Wednesday	.	3 15 —	... 3 20 —		4 50 —*
8 Thursday	...	4 5 —	... 4 20 —		6 0 —*

Fares, Fore end, 1/-; Cabin & Deck, 1/6; Return, 2 6.
The steamers will start from the Landing Stage at the North end of Conway Quay, and on their return will proceed as far as Deganwy. * Doubtful if Steamers will reach Trefriw. Fares according to distance.

Dated 1 June 1893, this is the first known newspaper advertisement to show both *St George* and *New St George* (*Prince George*) in operation on the river.

Conway River and Mountains.

Prince George speeds upstream towards Tal-y-Cafn.

verbally with the engineer/stoker in the engine room just below. Fore-end passengers paid 1s single and 2s return whilst those at the after end of the ship, who benefitted from a large awning and a small but cosy cabin below decks, paid 1s 6d and 2s 6d respectively. With a large passenger capacity of 200, a speed in excess of 10 knots, a very shallow draft and a racy profile she quickly proved herself ideal for the river and became a firm favourite with skippers and passengers alike.

Notes

1. Quoted in *A Guide to Trefriw, Llanrwst and Bettws-y-Coed*, Cambrian Series (Caernarfon: Rees & Evans, Herald Office, June 1872).
2. *Guide to Trefriw and the Vale of Conway Spa* (3rd edition) (J.W. Hayward MD, 1881).
3. *Trefriw, a Guide Book* (London & Manchester, Abel Heywood & Sons: 1904) (published under the auspices of the Trefriw Improvement Committee, price 1d).
4. Ibid.
5. Ibid.
6. *A Guide to Trefriw and the Vale of Conway Spa* (2nd edition) (J.W. Hayward MD, 1872).
7. Bradley, A.G., *Highways and Byways in North Wales* (London, 1898).
8. Conway Harbour Committee minutes, 1884–92, Conway Archives, XB2/149.

At slack high water on a perfectly still summer day, *Prince George* rests above her own reflection while her passengers take refreshments in the Belle Vue Hotel, *c.* 1900.

An animated scene as *Prince George* and *St George* embark a full load of passengers at the company's Deganwy landing stage, *c.* 1900. The rival *Queen of the Conway*, which arrived on the river in 1899, can be seen in the background.

5

Competition and a Challenging Decade, 1894–1903

The two steamers would spend the winter months drawn up on their covered slipways at the company's Wing Gate Yard beside the town walls at Conwy where routine maintenance, painting and any necessary repairs would be carried out. They were normally launched again in early May to undergo boiler testing and inspection by the Board of Trade surveyor from Liverpool, before the season commenced in late May – an annual ritual described affectionately by the *North Wales Weekly News* on 18 May 1906:

> There can be no surer indication of the advent of summer than the appearance of the steamboats on the river. Smartly painted and thoroughly overhauled, the 'St. George' and 'New St George' have, during the present week, been disporting themselves here and there, making trial manoeuvres of all sorts, preparatory to the opening of the regular service between Deganwy and Trefriw. And when a closer view has been obtained there can be no two opinions as to the way in which these toy liners are renovated for another year's work. Every bolt has been tested, and the gay appearance they now present is the result of many weeks hard and patient toil. Those who wish to see the surrounding coast before the boats become too crowded should make the trip early.

It became the norm for the larger and newer *Prince George* to run the longest season, joined by *St George* in the peak months or whenever demand was sufficient, and the residents of Trefriw quickly became used to the sight of the two little paddle steamers arriving in convoy at the quay. Just upstream from the wells themselves, the original tiny landing stage had been replaced by a slightly larger one adjacent to the wharf where the inclined plane carrying the tramway from the Cae Coch sulphur mine reached the main river, but in all other respects the service continued in its familiar and comforting manner, as described by a Julia Dorr, writing in 1895:[1]

> The thing we had come to Conway to see was the castle. But on the principle of leaving the best till the last, we saw everything else first, keeping it and gloating over it as a child gloats over his sugar-plums, though it was always in our thoughts as in our sight, – the one dominant feature in the landscape, ruling it as a mountain rules the valley.
>
> 'Be sure to go up the river to Trefriw,' our friend of the carnations had said, as a parting injunction. The next morning was hot, and the cool breeze from the river was delicious. 'What time could be better than the present?'
>
> So to the dock we went, and for an hour awaited the arrival of the small steamer; the Conway being a tidal river, and completely ruled by the caprices of the lady moon.
>
> But we were off at last, like a parcel of children playing at seagoing, in a toy boat on a toy river. Nothing more enjoyable can well be conceived. All was so sweet, so still, so serene, that it was like moving in a happy dream.

The Beach. Conway.

Prince George and *St George* alongside the St George's Steamship Company's Wing Gate Yard. The two large boatsheds and slipways are hidden behind the town wall, but the heavily built landing stage is clearly visible. *Prince George* (left) is lying alongside the hulk of the *Cemaes* which formed the floating pier head, while *St George* is moored to some large piles which were installed to accommodate the second steamer and act as a winter lay-up berth. (Clifford Hughes)

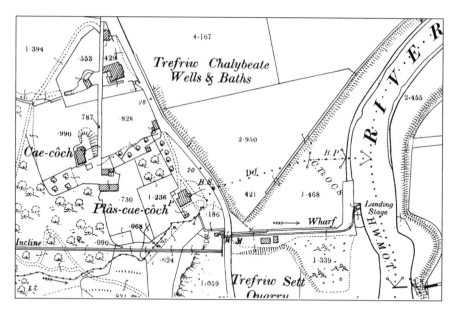

A 1900 revision of the 25ft Ordnance Survey map shows the location of Trefriw Wells relative to the river, landing stage and inclined plane. The Cae Coch Sulphur Mine was further up the hillside at the top of the incline.

The softly rounded hills, cultivated, and clothed to their summits with all imaginable shades of green and olive; the lovely stone cottages, picturesque on the outside at least, springing up in all sorts of out-of-the-way places, – now clinging to some sharply defined point far up the hillsides, now nestling deep in sheltered valleys, but all alike mantled with ivy and bright with roses; the fern-clad banks of the stream; the arched bridges; the ancestral farmhouses, gray with age; and here and there the stately splendour of hall or castle, made a series of pictures never-to-be-forgotten.

Our captain was very accommodating, and helped to carry out the illusion that it was all play. If he saw a would-be passenger strolling leisurely over the fields towards the river, he quietly turned his prow to the shore, and waited till the new-comer leaped on board. If a woman wanted to land where there was no dock, that she might shorten the distance homewards by going 'cross lots', she had only to suggest it, and she was put ashore forthwith, sometimes, as it seemed, at the imminent risk of an overturn.

At Trefriw, which certainly had very little to show for itself except its ferns and its long ranks of pink and purple foxgloves, there was time for luncheon, if anybody wanted it. Beyond this point the river is not navigable, and we were soon on our return voyage, 'going out with the tide'.

This tranquillity, however, was severely ruffled during 1894 when a vigorous debate broke out over the proposal to build a new bridge at Tal-y-Cafn,

A group of fashionably attired passengers enjoy the scenery from the deck of *Prince George* as she steams up the river towards Trefriw. The lady on the left seems less impressed with the experience and puts one in mind of the fictional Aunt Frummety who appears in Dickens' entertaining account of the voyage featured in Chapter 2! At the wheel, a very smartly dressed Capt. Robert Owen Roberts concentrates on the navigation. (Elsbeth Pears)

replacing the ferry which had served the crossing since the early fourteenth century. The dispute hinged on the width and height of the central navigation arch which, in the Act that had been placed before parliament earlier in the year, was given as 113ft wide with an air draught (clearance) of 'not less than 14ft and not exceeding 18ft' at high water spring tides, 'as shall be agreed between the Engineer of the Corporation and the Engineer of the Bridge Company'. A meeting had been held at the bridge site between the two engineers, accompanied by Capt. Griffith Jones and Capt. Roberts on behalf of the St George's Steamship Company and other parties interested in ensuring that the navigation of the river up to Trefriw was not impeded. All parties allegedly agreed that the central span should be 150ft wide and that the height above normal high water springs should be 16ft, the same as that under the Conwy suspension bridge. This agreement was not, however, committed to writing and when the Tal-y-Cafn Bridge Bill came before the House of Lords on 8 May 1894 the Conwy Corporation decided to oppose it, insisting (against the recommendations of their own Borough Engineer) that a clause be inserted increasing the span to 225ft and the clearance to 26ft.

Deadlock ensued. On 20 April 1895 a public meeting was held to air both sides of the argument and seek a way forward. The Corporation insisted that it was acting to protect the river users and although neither Capt. Roberts nor Capt. Griffith Jones (who was an alderman himself and possibly subject to conflict of interests) chose to speak at the meeting it is clear from other sources that, unsurprisingly, they were very much in favour of the higher arch.

Supporters of the bridge, which included most of the population of Eglwysbach, Tal-y-Cafn, Tal-y-bont, Rowen and surrounding districts, expressed their fury at Conwy Corporation's actions, pointing out that, while the Act provided for objections to be submitted within a period of 21 days from the publication of the plans, the Corporation had taken more than 10 weeks to express their disapproval. Furthermore, when the Corporation sought the support of the Board of Trade, the latter had been quick to point out that they had already approved the original plans and that any attempt to make alterations would be contrary to the Act and outside their powers.

Tal-y-Cafn ferry. In addition to the rowing boat in the foreground, a larger, barge-like craft, which can be seen moored at the far slipway, was available to transport carriages and livestock over the ancient crossing which was located on the line of the old roman road from Chester to Bwlch-y-Ddeufaen.

The Corporation had been seeking to take the matter to arbitration, which would, of course, have led to further delays and prevented the Bridge Company from commencing work for many more months. The chair of the meeting, having listened to the opinions of all present, expressed his dismay at the situation and appealed for a faster and fairer solution to be found, concluding that:

> Even granted that the bridge, built as proposed by the company, would cause some slight inconvenience and delay to the comparatively few small craft that now sail up the river, what is that compared with the great inconvenience (not to say constant danger) to which the inhabitants of the whole district are subjected by the present state of things at Tal-y-Cafn. Surely, in a matter of this kind the larger interests of the vastly greater number should carry most weight?

It would appear that the meeting did indeed break the deadlock and that, faced with the weight of public opinion, Conwy Corporation withdrew its objections. Work commenced on the new bridge during May 1895 and it was eventually completed during 1897, with the original planned clearance of 16ft. Although the construction works and the finished bridge undoubtedly altered the river flow and added an additional navigational challenge to the steamer skippers, no untoward incidents were recorded and, with their funnels hinged down, the two paddlers were able to pass carefully beneath the central span in all but the most exceptional conditions. The skippers made careful notes of visual clues to the clearances at each bridge on the river, and one of Capt. R.O. Roberts' notebooks records that, in 1914, Tal-y-Cafn Bridge had a clearance of 21ft on a 16ft tide, and 24ft when four courses of stonework on the bridge piers were showing above water. *Prince George* measured precisely 13ft 10in from the top of her flag staff to the waterline.

In Trefriw itself the familiar pattern of summer tennis and croquet at the recreation ground, balls at the Belle Vue, concerts at both the wells and hotel and, of course, the central business of 'taking the waters' continued as before. Some observers, however, noted that in comparison with the initial vigour of the 1880s, a certain ennui seemed to have set in, possibly a case of familiarity leading to a degree of apathy. The popularity of the annual tennis tournament declined sharply and in 1894 the Wells Company, finding itself in some difficulties, underwent a change of ownership, with the freehold passing to Rev. Gower.

During 1896 a new character appeared on the village stage. Charles Fruen, a 46-year-old surveyor and architect who had previously been involved in property development in London, arrived in Trefriw with the stated aim of revitalising the village. How Rev. Gower and the Improvement Committee reacted is not recorded!

Talycafn Bridge.

The new bridge at Tal-y-Cafn which replaced the ferry in 1897 was warmly welcomed by most local people but unsuccessfully opposed by the three Captains Roberts, who regarded it as an impediment to safe navigation. Henceforth the steamers had to lower their funnels to pass safely underneath the bridge.

Fruen proceeded to purchase 100 acres of land in the Crafnant and Conwy valleys for the sum of £6,800. High on the slopes of the Crafnant valley he laid out a golf course, which a later commentator described as 'a Gibraltar of bunkers and hazards and holes and greens, a links over which a herd of mountain goats might delight to clamber – one of the most "sporting" in the kingdom, but small'.[2] During the following year, 1897, he purchased the Belle Vue Hotel from Tommy Dutton for £5,500 and the steamer quay in front of the hotel for a further £1,800. He formed a syndicate with two gentlemen named Tewson and Burfield to develop these properties and proceeded to spend almost £10,000 on improvements.

An 1897 guidebook noted that the Belle Vue was now 'under entirely new management ... Great additions and structural alterations have been effected ... distinguished by a degree of artistic luxury and refinement not elsewhere obtainable in Wales.' There were two luxury fitted bathrooms, constant hot water, ladies' lavatories and 'sanitary arrangements entirely reconstructed on the most advanced and approved principles. In place of the old fashioned small windows, a beautiful, large bay window has been added.'[3] A new wing was added to the northern side of the building in about 1899 and Fruen immediately let the hotel to a Miss Wade, who was to hold the lease until 1905.

No major alterations were made to the quay, although it was tidied up and the last vestiges of its former industrial use were gradually swept away.

TREFRIW

TENNIS, &C., GROUNDS.

These Grounds were formed in 1888, by the

Trefriw Improvement Co., Limited.

....

They are beautifully kept, are in a lovely situation, and are situate within a few minutes walk of the Village.

....

The Grounds contain fine TENNIS COURTS, large BOWLING GREEN, CROQUET & QUOITING GREENS, and comfortable CLOAK ROOMS and SHELTER.

....

The Grounds are well patronized by residents and Visitors.

....

The OPEN TENNIS TOURNAMENT takes place in August, and BOWLING and CROQUET MATCHES are arranged for throughout the Season.

....

For further particulars apply to

Miss KING, Hon. Sec.,

2, Rhiwlas Villas, Trefriw.

An advertisement for the Trefriw Recreation Grounds, from T.E. Jones' 1897 guidebook.

CHALYBEATE WELLS,

TREFRIW.

(UNDER NEW MANAGEMENT.)

This Chalybeate is the best and one of the strongest in Europe, the supply is abundant, and its properties invaluable. Leading medical men from all parts of the Country have borne testimony to the curative and beneficent nature of the waters.

Admission to Grounds, 1d., (including one dose of Water).
Water sold in Bottles 2d. a dose.
12 Doses sent for 3s., carriage paid to any address.

BATHS.

COLD: 1st class, 1s. 6d.; 2nd class, 1s.; 3rd, class 6d.
HOT: 1st class, 2s.; 2nd class, 1s. 6d; 3rd class, 1s.
Admission to Old Roman Cave, 1d.

APARTMENTS.

REFRESHMENTS.

Teas from 6d. upwards. Picnics and Private Parties can be arranged on the Grounds.
Mineral Waters. Cigars. Tobaccos. &c.

SELECTION OF MUSIC BY

BLIND HARPIST

And other amusements. Comfortable shelter and every accommodation.

For further particulars, apply to

WILLIAMS BROS.

An advertisement for the Trefriw Wells from T.E. Jones' 1897 guidebook.

The Belle Vue Hotel showing the new bay windows and other structural alterations undertaken in 1897 by Charles Fruen and his associates. Shortly after this engraving was published a new long wing was added to the north side of the hotel.

Fruen also seems to have acquired ownership of the Ship Inn and interests in both the wells and the recreation ground, although, as later developments were to prove, his financial affairs were anything but transparent.

On the river, meanwhile, *St George* and *Prince George* continued their seasonal trade unopposed until, in July 1898, an article in the *North Wales Weekly News* gave the first indication of challenges ahead. Entitled 'Employees' Annual Trip', it read:

> On Saturday [16 July] the employees of Messrs. Thomas Lewis & Co, City Steam Mills, Bangor, had their annual trip. Mr T. Lewis of Gartherwen placed at their disposal the paddle steamer '*Queen of the Conway*'. The large party comprising the employees and some of their friends, left Bangor pier at 7 o'clock in the morning and sailed up the River Conway as far as the new bridge at Tal-y-Cafn and back to Deganwy, where they disembarked. A most enjoyable day was spent at Llandudno. The party arrived safely back at Bangor at about half past eight in the evening.

The Thomas Lewis in question was a prominent citizen and captain of industry, with interests in many aspects of Bangor's commercial life. Having served his apprenticeship as a druggist, he went on to become a prominent Liberal politician, Justice of the Peace, Mayor of Bangor from 1886 to 1887 (following a bizarre

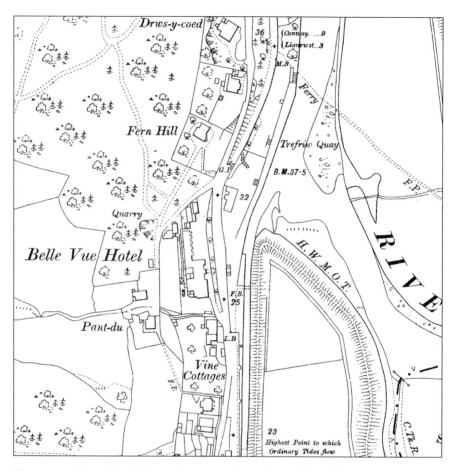

The 1900 revision of the Ordnance Survey map clearly showed the Belle Vue Hotel
with its new wing and extensive outbuildings, separated from the quay by the Conwy
to Betws-y-Coed road.

and acrimonious dispute which went as far as the House of Lords) and a High
Sheriff of Caernarfonshire from 1901. In addition to his career as a flour merchant
and owner of the City Steam Mills, he was a ship builder and ship owner, with
a particular interest in steam power. He acquired his first ship in 1880, a little
schooner-rigged steam coaster called *Medway* which traded between Beaumaris
and the Mersey with grain and food stuffs, and went on to order two new steamers, the 67-ton *St Seiriol* and the 107-ton *St Tudwal* in 1886 and 1895 respectively.
Lewis owned his own jetty and warehouse at Garth, the lane leading to it being
known to this day as Medway Road.

Lewis also had financial interests in the fast-developing resort of Llandudno
and sometime in 1897 had obtained at least partial ownership of Trefriw Quay.
The precise arrangement remains obscure, but it seems likely that he may have
injected some finance into Charles Fruen's new consortium. It was at this point

Prince George at Trefriw Quay, *c.* 1900. The new, white-painted wing of the Belle Vue Hotel stands out clearly against the ivy-clad original building. On the quay itself, which still looks extremely rough underfoot, all but two of the original industrial buildings have been swept away and the wall between the upper and lower levels repaired.

that it struck Lewis 'how anomalous a state of things it was that there should be no direct water communication between Llandudno and Trefriw' and he set about forming a steamship company to rectify the situation.

The Llandudno & Trefriw Steamship Company Ltd (L&TSS Company) was duly floated. Thomas Lewis's fellow directors were Stephen Dunphy, W. Ellis Jones and E. Shaw Thewlis, all of Llandudno, who promptly set about acquiring a suitable ship and putting the necessary infrastructure in place.

The vessel chosen was the *Queen of the Tees*, a 76.93-ton, double-ended paddle steamer measuring 85ft in length, with a beam of 14.15ft and a depth of 5.7ft. She had been built by J.P. Rennoldson & Sons of South Shields during 1891 and was fitted with a 20nhp (105ihp) surface-condensing, side-lever engine with a single cylinder (diameter 22in and stroke 40in) of a type much-favoured in the paddle tugs of the era. Her single steel boiler was built by J. Eltringham & Company of South Shields and operated at a steam pressure of 40lb psi with a speed of 8 knots. Her official number was 98774. She had originally been built as a ferry for the Imperial Tramway Company of Middlesbrough but on 11 May 1898 reverted to the ownership of Rennoldson's, who presumably acted as a broker for her sale to North Wales.

The ship was purchased by Lewis on behalf of the new company on 18 June 1898 and, renamed *Queen of the Conway*, made the long voyage round the coast to arrive safely at Bangor by the end of the month. The works outing to Trefriw is the only recorded trip of the 1898 season, but it seems likely that the ship would have undertaken other cruises in the Menai Strait and district while she awaited the completion of the necessary facilities at Llandudno.

The L&TSS Company were well aware of the rapid growth of Llandudno and also of the proposals which were afoot during 1897–98 to construct an electric tramway from Colwyn Bay to Llandudno town centre and thence, by way of newly laid-out Gloddaeth Avenue, to a terminus at West Shore. There was general optimism that the West Shore, overlooking the Conwy estuary and the mountains beyond, would develop rapidly to rival Llandudno's north-facing bay as a holiday and residential area, and that the proposed tramway could only speed the process.

The company immediately set about constructing a new pier almost opposite the end of the proposed Gloddaeth Avenue, on an area of foreshore leased from the Ecclesiastical Commissioners for a period of 21 years, at an annual rent of £10. The plans were drawn up by J.J. Webster Esq. of Westminster and resulted in a fairly narrow piled structure 360ft in length, which was ready in time for the 1899 season. It was variously referred to as West Shore Pier or Llandudno West Shore Jetty.

Queen of the Conway made her inaugural invitation cruise from the West Shore on the afternoon of Wednesday, 31 May 1899. Well laden with 'influential gentlemen' from Llandudno, the Mayor of Conwy, assorted councillors, members of the

The Llandudno & Trefriw Steamship Company's *Queen of the Conway*, which arrived on the river in 1899, was of a very different design to the St George Company's steamers. A former Tees ferry boat, she was double-ended and was fitted with sunken deck saloons fore and aft. This view of her pulling away from a pier clearly shows her pointed stern and deck awning.

press and 'a number of ladies', she set off upstream at 2 p.m. Because it was a neap tide and the steamer, which was still in ballast, drew 3ft 3in of water, the decision was made not to proceed beyond Tal-y-Cafn, where the guests were allowed 20 minutes ashore to view the new bridge. During the return downstream speeches were made, votes of thanks passed and 'For he's a jolly good fellow' and 'God bless the Prince of Wales' sung. Musical selections on the guitar and harp were 'admirably rendered by Mr & Mrs Tarleton', while the guests were served with light refreshments in the saloons. The catering was provided by the Grosvenor Hotel, Llandudno, and it was noted that 'Miss Berridge made a very capital superintendent over the comestibles'.[4] The ship was back alongside the jetty at 6.30 p.m. With her double-ended hull and upright funnel she was certainly no beauty, but with a passenger capacity of 257 and her superior under-cover accommodation, she seemed poised to provide a serious challenge to the St George's Company.

The steamer commenced public sailings shortly afterwards. The number of passengers embarking at the new West Shore Jetty was extremely encouraging and the L&TSS Company began to congratulate itself on discovering a winning formula. However, before the season was far advanced, the Board of Trade intervened and prohibited *Queen of the Conway* from operating from the jetty

Taken from the southern slopes of the Great Orme headland, this view of the embryonic housing development at West Shore, Llandudno, looks over the junction of Abbey Road and Great Ormes Road towards West Parade and the beach beyond. The sloping 360ft pile pier completed in 1899 for the *Queen of the Conway* is clearly visible. (Conwy Archive Service)

on the grounds that it lay outside the limits of her No. 5 passenger certificate, which restricted her to plying within 'smooth waters'. Her owners had made the basic and very expensive error of failing to notice that these limits, by which the St George's Company's steamers were also governed, had been set much closer to Deganwy than the point at which the new pier had been constructed.

Thus, at a stroke, the very basis on which the L&TSS Company had been formed was destroyed and the company was left with a new pier at which their ship could not call and a ship with no base. Having no other options, *Queen of the Conway* was compelled to start from Deganwy but, having no landing stage of her own there, was forced either to negotiate for use of the *St George's* stage or ferry people out to the steamer in small boats. The new ship's problems were exacerbated by the fact that she drew almost 3ft 6in – a full 2ft more than *St George* and *Prince George* – and was consequently unable to reach Trefriw as regularly. She frequently ran aground and for many days either side of neaps she was forced to terminate her sailings at Tal-y-Cafn. The Capts Roberts must have rubbed their hands in delight!

Despite these initial difficulties, the L&TSS Company persevered and some-how staggered through its first season and by May 1900 had applied to erect jetties at both Conwy and Deganwy. Conwy Corporation granted them a site near the Custom House but the set of the tides rendered it unsuitable and in May 1901 another application was submitted. The rival companies were

Queen of the Conway steaming downstream past Deganwy. The fact that she appears to be towing a boat suggests that the picture was taken in late 1899 or early 1900, after the ship had been banned from using her pier at west Shore, Llandudno, but before her new jetty at Deganwy had been completed.

summoned to a meeting of the Harbour Committee 'with a view to arriving at an arrangement as to their embarkation of passengers'.[5] When, quite understandably, the St George's Company failed to show enthusiasm for sharing their facilities with L&TSS Company, the committee recommended that the corporation should erect a new public landing stage at Conwy in time for the 1902 season. It must have caused great irritation to the long-established local company, which had built all its facilities at its own expense to hear that an interloping 'outside' company might have jetties provided from the public purse! In fact, although the council continued to discuss the idea of a public jetty for several more years, the L&TSS Company gained permission to construct their own jetty at Deganwy during 1901 or 1902, and at Conwy in 1903. Meanwhile an agreement was reached for both companies to use the St George's stage at Deganwy during 1900 and 1901, with each company's ships starting first on alternate days. Their Conwy stage was located just upstream of the St George's jetty and was of similar construction, with a substantial timber walkway and hinging bridge leading to the hull of a disused sailing flat, which acted as floating landing stage and coal hulk. *Queen of the Conway* started calling at Conwy in August 1903 and for the next 4 years provided spirited competition to the established St George's Company steamers on an identical route. Prior to 1902 *Queen of the Conway* had retreated each winter to lay up at Bangor but in October of that year was granted permission to construct 'a grid iron near Mr Crowe's shed on the Morfa'. Whether this was ever constructed is unclear, since from 1903 to 1907 she spent each winter laid up in a wooden cradle on the Conway foreshore just downstream of the St George's Company's yard near Twthill Point.

The master of *Queen of the Conway* was Capt. John Jones, known locally as John Shem, who lived at 27 Berry Street, Conwy. He was a well-known local character and remembered as 'a man of many parts'. He was a town councillor, a long-term member of the local army volunteers and a champion marksman. He served as a sergeant major during the First World War and a photo of him, his chest almost hidden by medals, hung for many years in the ante-room of Conwy Guild Hall. He was a skilled boatman and is remembered in his old age building a beautiful, clinker-built rowing boat in an old smithy yard at the top of his street. While in command of *Queen of the Conway* he always wore a full master's uniform, much to the amusement of the skippers of the St George's Company steamers, who were not inclined to such flamboyant gestures and generally limited their 'uniform' to a suit or jacket and a white-topped cap.

Due to her deep draught, *Queen of the Conway* was usually the last steamer to arrive at Trefriw and the first to leave, with the result that her passengers got less time ashore than those travelling with the St George's Company. Because she was also 13ft longer than her rivals, swinging in the river at Trefriw was also more difficult and time consuming and she generally moored in the deepest berth at the downstream end of the quay. Despite these precautions she frequently ran

THE STEAMERS OF THE

St. GEORGE'S S.S. Co., Ltd.

Will ply (weather and other causes permitting) on one of
the most beautiful Rivers in Wales, between

DEGANWY, CONWAY AND TREFRIW.

SEPTEMBER, 1900.

Date of Sailing.	From Deganwy.	From Conway.	Ret. from Trefriw. †
7 Friday	7 55 a.m.	8 10 a.m.	9 52 a.m.
8 Saturday	8 45 —	8 50 —	10 43 —
10 Monday	9 50 —	9 56 —	12 15 p.m.
11 Tuesday	10. 25 —	10 35 —	1 0 —
12 Wednesday	11 15 —	11 20 -	1 45 —
13 Thursday	12 0 noon	12 15 p.m.	2 23 —
14 Friday	12 35 p.m.	12 50 —	3 5 —

Fares : Fore End, 1 -; Cabin & Deck, 1 6; Return, 2 6.

† — Doubtful if Steamers will reach TREFRIW.
Fares according to distance.

THE TREFRIW STEAMER
"QUEEN of the CONWAY,"
Will leave DEGANWY STAGE,
Weather and other circumstances permitting, as under:

Date of Sailing. SEPT., 1900.	From Deganwy.	From Llandudno Train.	From Colwyn Bay Train.
7 Friday	8 0 a.m.	7 40 a.m.	—
8 Saturday	8 45 ,,	8 35 ,,	7 43 a.m.
10 Monday	9 55 ,,	9 40 ,,	8 35 ,,
11 Tuesday	10 25 ,,	10 15 ,, '	9 58 ,,
12 Wednesday	11 20 ,,	11 5 ,,	10 51 ,,
13 Thursday	12 5 p.m.	11 45 ,,	11 28 ,,
14 Friday	12 35 ,,	12 25 p.m.	12 10 p.m.

FARES TO TREFRIW.—Return, 2/6; Single, 1/6

For further particulars see detailed handbills and posters.
† Doubtful if Steamer will reach Trefriw. Fares according to distance.
The Llandudno and Trefriw S.S. Co., Ltd.,
Secretary, G. W. GRIFFITH,
602—   1, Leonard Terrace, Llandudno.

Newspaper advertisements for the rival steamer services in September 1900. Note that *Queen of the Conway* is operating from the St George's jetty at Deganwy but has not yet obtained landing rights at Conwy.

aground in the river. If this occurred on a flood tide she would simply wait until the tide rose sufficiently for her to float off and continue her journey, but on the ebb it was a different matter, as her passengers ran the risk of being stranded on board until the tide returned 12 hours later. Swift action was required, and one of the St George's steamers would be called alongside to take off enough passengers to allow her to refloat. Although the Capts Roberts must have derived a good deal of kudos and amusement from these rescues, they must also have proved irksome. Putting an already-crowded paddle steamer alongside a grounded vessel

The rival companies' jetties at Deganwy, *c*. 1903. To the left, *Queen of the Conway* and to the right *Prince George* are disembarking passengers at the end of their return sailings from Trefriw. St George's Harbour at Deganwy is in the centre of the photograph, while in the background the low line of The Cobb leads to the Conwy bridges on the extreme right.

Queen of the Conway's new jetty at Conwy was constructed in 1903 just upstream of the established St George's jetty.

Capt. John 'Shem' Jones of *Queen of the Conway* poses for the camera on the floating jetty at Deganwy. Note the advertising banners on the jetty and ship.

in a fast-flowing river on a falling tide was both inconvenient and potentially dangerous, and must have required excellent seamanship.

Although the advent of *Queen of the Conway* must have cut into its trade, especially from Deganwy, the St George Company continued to prosper, aided by the fact that the *North Wales Weekly News* made hardly any reference to the newcomer, whilst including regular advertisements and frequent flattering articles regarding the established company. By 1899 William Roberts was the company's manager and a James A. Pollitt the vice-chairman.

In August 1899, after a gap of 15 years, the Deganwy and Conwy Regatta was revived on a relatively small scale but proved such a success that it was expanded for 1900 and repeated for many years thereafter. With yacht racing in the estuary, rowing races, diving, swimming competitions and musical entertainments, these events proved a great success and attracted numerous steam and sailing yachts to the river, providing an animated spectacle. *St George, Prince George* and *Queen of the Conway* were placed at the disposal of the organising committee and, with their usual up-river trips suspended, were employed either as committee boats to take spectators to follow the yacht races or, occasionally, to tow becalmed boats

Captain Jones in conversation with a lady passenger on Deganwy jetty. To the modern eye the sartorial appearance of his uniform is somewhat offset by the two cigarettes, one in his mouth and another behind his ear. The body language on display makes the photo a fine candidate for a caption competition!

home when the races had to be abandoned due to lack of wind. In 1901, for example, it was noted that the *St George* would:

> ... ply up and down the river inside the Perch Point during the races ... The Committee intend to charge a shilling fare, and for that consideration visitors may remain on board throughout the afternoon and enjoy the music of the band which has been secured for the occasion.

On 3 August 1900 North Wales was struck by a particularly severe gale which caused all Trefriw sailings to be cancelled. At Conwy a mussel boat was smashed to pieces and a yacht sunk at her moorings while *St George* suffered damage to one of her paddle boxes as she bumped violently against the landing stage.

On 26 June 1901 the well-known local cargo steamer *W.S. Caine* was backing away from Conwy Quay with the intention of using the flood tide to swing her stern around before proceeding downstream on her next voyage to Nefyn. Unfortunately her stern got into a back eddy, refused to come round and the ship

With an ebb tide under her and *Prince George* hard on her heels, *Queen of the Conway* thunders under Tal-y-Cafn bridge on a return sailing from Trefriw. Note that her funnel is lowered and that the canvas awning over her aft deck is giving her passengers some protection from the black smoke and falling smuts. (Crawford Alexander)

Passengers stream ashore from the rival steamers at Trefriw. The shallower *Prince George* has arrived a few moments ahead of the larger *Queen of the Conway*, which is occupying the berth at the deeper, downstream end of the quay.

The Steamer at Trefriw on the Conway River.

Having swung round to point downstream, both steamers lay quietly at the quay while passengers begin to drift back on board in readiness for departure time. The horse-drawn cart in the foreground appears to be carrying a passenger's trunk to accommodation in the village. A variety of carriages were also available for hire from D. Roberts' Jubilee Central Stables to take visitors on tours of the local beauty spots or to return them to Conwy if they happened to miss the steamer.

drifted broadside on to the tide upstream past the custom house, where she became entangled in the small boat moorings. The proximity of her propeller to the steep river bank further hindered her movements and she was in imminent danger of colliding with the Conwy bridges when the little *Prince George* appeared on the scene. Bound upstream on one of his regular trips, Capt. Roberts noted the *Caine's* plight, quickly weighed up the options and, in the nick of time, managed to pass a rope and pull her bows round. A serious accident had narrowly been averted.

Throughout the early years of the century Conwy Council had been criticised in the local press for its lack of imagination and action regarding the development of the port which, it maintained, was 'sinking deeper into that slough which has held it down for many years, because of the lethargy of the representatives of the people'. At the beginning of 1902, however, the council took what was widely regarded as an encouraging first step towards reform, by appointing Capt. William Roberts as harbourmaster. An editorial in the *North Wales Weekly News* applauded the action and went on to state:

> Captain Roberts is, above all else, a gentleman by virtue of that innate grace which gives a man the right to the title. Disdaining ostentatious display, he is modest and retiring to a degree, yet is possessed of all the qualities necessary to the proper discharge of the duties of the office to which he has been appointed; honesty, fairness, experience, foresight and enthusiasm.

His fairness and neutrality were put to a severe test during his first few weeks in office when a heated debate broke out over proposals to introduce a steam ferry between Conwy and Deganwy. In March 1902 the St George's Company (of which Roberts was the manager) wrote to the council asking to be granted sole rights to run a steam boat between the two places for an initial period of 7 years. The boat, which it was estimated would cost about £350 to purchase, would operate to a published timetable and fares would be set at a 'reasonable and popular' rate.

This application provoked a strong letter from Mr George Griffiths of Llandudno, who wrote to remind the council that he had made a similar application 3 years previously, but had never received a response. It also provoked fury amongst the local boatmen on both sides of the river who, since time immemorial, had spent the winter months engaged in mussel fishing and their summers providing boat trips and a ferry service from Deganwy over to the Conwy Morfa. It was claimed that between fifty and sixty boatmen earned their living in this way, and that the introduction of a steam ferry would throw their families into poverty. One impassioned boatman wrote:

> Why does a company, consisting of merely a few persons, seek such an application with protection? I argue that if the application is granted they will gradually take full control of the river. They have monopolised all the up-river trade and, not content with that, they now seek to rob the boatmen of their daily bread in another way. I say, 'live and let live'.

Supporters of the scheme pointed out that the journey from Conwy to Deganwy by the none-too-frequent trains took 17 minutes while walking occupied at least half an hour. A steam ferry would be able to make the crossing in 5 minutes and the inhabitants of Deganwy would be encouraged to spend their money in

Conwy rather than Llandudno. It was also pointed out that when a stiff breeze was blowing, especially in wind-over-tide conditions, the rowing ferry was often suspended, as the boatmen were unwilling to expose their passengers to a thorough sousing from spray breaking over the boat, or to undertake the long pull in dangerous conditions which might result in the boat sinking. These problems would no longer arise if a larger steam ferry was provided.

The council pointed out that it was not within its powers to grant a monopoly to any single company and invited all prospective operators to produce Board of Trade certificates for their craft and apply for boatmen's licences in the normal way. Meanwhile, it proposed taking a poll of ratepayers to discover their attitudes to the proposed ferry. The arguments raged on throughout 1902, but no application was made by the St George's Company's. Perhaps Capt. Roberts was concerned about his personal conflict of interests, or his directors had concluded that the potential income was not worth the loss of goodwill from the local boatmen.

On 25 March 1903 the ferry finally came into being, operated by the steam launch *Eider Duck*. She embarked her first passengers at Conwy at 8.30 a.m., returning from Deganwy Beach at 9 a.m. and thereafter advertised a departure from each side hourly until dusk. The fare was 3*d* in each direction. *Eider Duck* was initially promoted by a Mr Arthur Hill of Deganwy, who passed the project on to Mr G.C. Holt of Victoria Cottage, Deganwy, before the boat entered service. *The North Wales Weekly News* of 20 March 1903 described her as:

A remarkably smart and swift little craft, propelled by steam power and capable of carrying 30 passengers. She will be under the charge of two experienced yachtsmen who are thoroughly well-acquainted with the river and will be known to many as having served on Mr Fletcher's steam yacht *Dorothy*.

The paper went on to congratulate the promoters on providing a much-needed public service and encouraged the local populace to 'generously patronise the new venture which, in addition to supplying a swift, sure and constant means of crossing to and from Deganwy, will provide a pleasant trip in the summer and enable folk to reach Llandudno with very little effort'.

Eider Duck ran over the Easter period and was then withdrawn until the week before Whitsun. At the beginning of July she had to be withdrawn for repairs, but Mr Holt continued the service using a motor launch named *Evelyn*. No further mention of the steam ferry has been discovered after the summer of 1903, so it must be presumed that the venture did not prove successful and that the local boatmen and their rowing boats prevailed. Indeed, despite the placing of a bell on the Morfa to call the ferry from Deganwy, by 1904 the papers were once again full of complaints regarding delays and pleas for more effective arrangements to be put in place!

NEW RIVER SERVICE
BETWEEN
Deganwy and Conway.

THE Fast Steam Launch "EIDER DUCK" will ply between the above-named places daily (weather and other circumstances permitting), from 25th March, 1903.

TIME OF SAILING.
Leaves Conway	....	....	8.30	a.m.
,,	Deganwy	..	..	9.0 ,,
,,	Conway	....	....	9.30 ,,
,,	Deganwy	..	..	10.0 ,,

And Sailing regularly until dusk from Deganwy and Conway at intervals of an hour.

FARE, 3d.

A newspaper advertisement for *Eider Duck*'s new ferry service, dated 20 March 1903.

The year 1903 also saw the arrival of a second competitor for the river trade to Trefriw. *The North Wales Weekly News* of 3 July noted that, 'A new steamer chartered by Mr George Griffiths made her first trip last week between Deganwy, Conway and Trefriw' but gave no further details. There is photographic evidence that during 1903 a small, wooden screw steamer named *Trefriw Belle* was definitely running on the river, so it seems probable that this was the vessel in question. In July 1904 Mr Griffiths applied to the council for permission to undertake Sunday sailings from Deganwy which, at the time, would have been a very controversial proposal. During the same year the Liverpool & North Wales SS Company had caused a tremendous furore in Llandudno by proposing to introduce Sunday steamers from Liverpool and, despite the criticism heaped upon them by local residents, it would seem that Griffiths felt it appropriate to follow their lead. The chapel-going Capts Roberts never ran Sunday trips during their own lifetimes and, together with the town council, strongly disapproved of Griffith's 'Sabbath Breaking' proposals. Permission was refused and the waters of the Conwy remained unruffled by Sunday sailings for many years to come.

Very little is known about the *Trefriw Belle*. She has not been located in the Beaumaris or other shipping registers, and both her dimensions and builder remain a mystery. One source suggests she may have been built in 1895 and was 60ft in length. Photographs show her to have been a pretty little vessel, constructed of wood with a curved stem and shapely transom stern over which her large rudder was hung. She had a single funnel, twin screws and the curved upper section of her boiler was clearly visible above her upper deck. Her passengers sat on rows of seats facing forward; her deck rails were covered in a fine wire mesh and large frames over her decks allowed awnings to unrolled to provide some protection from inclement weather. Her hull was painted white, with a dark-painted rubbing strake at deck level and a dark underbody.

Trefriw Belle was unique on the river in having her own postal cachet. A number of postcards have been discovered, all posted in 1903 or 1904, bearing the stamped message 'Arrival of the s. "Trefriw Belle"' or 'Per Passgr.s. "Trefriw Belle"' in purple ink. Her owners clearly did not issue official postcards of their ship, for all the cachets so far discovered are on cards showing Trefriw Quay with a variety of ships alongside.

It would seem that Mr Griffiths' charter lasted until at least the summer of 1904 (and most probably until 1906), after which she passed into the ownership of Capt. H.C. Edwards of the Post Office, Tywyn, Deganwy, who set up the Trefriw Belle Steamship Company, which operated her for the remainder of her time on the river, probably until 1912. Edwards also owned a bakery in Tywyn together with a sailing vessel called *Esther*, which at one time was engaged in the gravel dredging trade on the river. While operated by Mr Griffiths the *Trefriw Belle* seems to have sported a red funnel with black top and a narrow white band, while Capt. Edwards adopted a buff funnel with black top.

Faced with competition from both *Trefriw Belle* and *Queen of the Conway*, the St George's Company must have felt under severe pressure during the summer of 1903, but may have derived some comfort from the fact that passenger numbers continued to increase and all four ships usually sailed well laden. On 16 August, the day of the annual regatta, the company received a welcome boost when royalty decided to make the trip up river. Princess Louise of Schleswig-Holstein was

Passengers cross the decks of *St George* to board the already-crowded *Trefriw Belle*, while another large and smartly dressed group throngs the quay, awaiting their turn to board the paddle steamer. A combination of a small tide and her greater draught has meant that the *Trefriw Belle* has decided not to risk running aground by berthing alongside the quay itself.

ta. Per Passgr. s. "Trefriw-Belle."

Arrival of the s. "Trefriw-Belle"

Examples of *Trefriw Belle's* two known postal cachets with which postcards purchased on board were franked. (Geoff Ellerton/Crawford Alexander)

Conway Castle.

Trefriw Belle about to pass under the Conwy bridges on her way upstream to Trefriw. Note that her name is emblazoned in large letters on the canvas awning stretched over her aft deck.

spending a holiday in North Wales as guests of the Hon. Mr and Mrs Brodrick of Coed Coch, Abergele, who arranged for their party to travel to Deganwy station by train, whence they walked along the beach:

> ... which was thronged by spectators who were eagerly following the progress of the Conway regatta, while the river was crowded with yachts and steamers and small boats of every description, all mixed up in picturesque confusion. It was a glorious afternoon of brilliant sunshine and every train added scores of people to the already crowded scene. All the steamers, with one exception, were literally filled to overflowing. The exception, spick and span in her white paint and conspicuous for her graceful outlines, was the well-appointed steamer 'New St George', a large portion of the deck of which had been reserved for the accommodation of the distinguished party.

The party were greeted by the company chairman, Mr Pollitt, and another director, Mr Lees, before being introduced to Capt. Roberts. As soon as the royal visitor and her friends had seated themselves in the reserved area towards the stern, the steamer took on additional members of the public and crossed to Conwy where the few remaining places were filled and a large crowd had gathered to catch a glimpse of the celebrities.

It was reported that 'a sense of enjoyment too deep for words' came over all on board as *New St George* 'glided over the smooth surface of the waters' on her way to Tal-y-Cafn, where she moored briefly while two further distinguished guests joined the party and staff from Caer Rhun house brought provisions on board in order that the princess and her guests might take tea on deck. To the strains of appropriate music played by the Clifton family, *New St George* continued for another mile or two before turning homeward, touching briefly at Tal-y-Cafn once again, and landing the royal party at Conwy where the princess 'spoke a few gracious words to Capt. Roberts and Mr Pollitt'.

The royal trip provided the St George's Company with some marvellous promotional material and for some time thereafter the steamers were adorned with large banners proclaiming 'as patronised by HRH Princess Louise'!

Notes

1. Dorr, Julia C., 'A Week in Wales', in *Atlantic Monthly*, vol. 62, issue 371 (September 1888), and later in *The Flower of England's Face: Sketches of English Travel* (London & New York, 1895).
2. Editorial in *North Wales Weekly News*, 23 March 1906.
3. *Trefriw Mineral Springs and Guide to the Neighbourhood* (T.E. Jones: 1897).
4. Editorial in *North Wales Weekly News*, 2 June 1899.
5. Editorial in *North Wales Weekly News*, 10 May 1901.

6

The Edwardian Heyday, 1904–13

The summer of 1904 marked the beginning of a decade which was to see both the village of Trefriw and the river steamers services reach their zenith.

The major population centre and resort of Llandudno had continued to grow apace and was exceptionally well served during the summer months by frequent trains from the Midlands and North of England, as well as by the Liverpool & North Wales Steamship Company's large paddle steamers which landed thousands of day trippers at the pier.

Due to its proximity to Llandudno, Deganwy had grown into a minor resort in its own right and had now become the premier embarkation point for the river steamers. Its railway station, which was conveniently located only a few minutes' walk from the steamer jetties, was served by long-distance trains heading for Llandudno, as well as by 'steamer specials' which brought holiday makers on the short trip from Llandudno to arrive shortly before the departure of the steamers to Trefriw. These 'specials' must have been almost unique in having a timetable, which changed on a daily basis and was governed by the tides! Deganwy was also served by trains on the Conwy valley line, which enabled passengers to make one leg of their journey to Trefriw by steamer and the other by railway from Llanrwst station.

On a typical summer's day in 1904, the beach at Deganwy would have presented a truly animated appearance. About 2½ hours before high water the steamers, having been coaled and cleaned at Conwy, would arrive empty to moor at their respective jetties, each of which consisted of a small floating pon toon connected to the beach by a hinged, timber walkway. The St George's Company

P.C. 41733 Deganwy Station & Town

Deganwy station and town with a train from Llandudno Junction standing at the down platform.

may have felt slightly disadvantaged by the fact that their jetty was now the furthest downstream, while those of the interloping *Queen of the Conway* and *Trefriw Belle* were a little closer to the railway station and therefore more likely to attract passing trade.

Shortly after the arrival of the trains, crowds would pour along the beach and form long queues at each of the jetties. The three rival companies engaged in vigorous touting, and erected advertising banners at the entrance to their jetties, as well as on board the steamers themselves. 'All the way to Trefriw' was a common theme to which *Trefriw Belle* added, when the tides were right, a subsidiary banner reading 'or fares returned'. The St George's Company chose to go for 'The Old Established Company' to which they added 'St George, first away for Trefriw' or 'Plenty of room' as appropriate. *Queen of the Conway*, with her propensity to run aground, had to be more circumspect in her claims and was careful to display her slogan of 'To Trefriw Direct, all the way' only when Capt. Jones was certain there was enough water in the river!

Of the St George's Company's steamers, which had been moored side by side, *Prince George* was usually loaded first and, if up to capacity, would sail directly for Trefriw, leaving *St George* to collect passengers from Conwy. *Trefriw Belle* was usually next away and, since there is no evidence that she had her own stage at Conwy, probably went straight to Trefriw. *Queen of the Conway* was a little more complex. Because she had a ticket agent in Llandudno she carried more pre-booked passengers than the other steamers and was often full before leaving Deganwy, a situation which have caused much irritation to prospective passengers

Rival steamers at Deganwy sporting a variety of advertising banners, probably in 1905. Many details of *Trefriw Belle*'s deck layout are visible. Note the crew member leaning on the wheel just ahead of the large, curved engine room skylight and boiler casing. In the background *St George* and *Prince George* await their passengers.

waiting on her jetty at Conwy. The colourful spectacle of the four little steamers loading and departing from Deganwy beach within minutes of each other always generated a crowd of spectators and, during the spring of 1904, led to a number of minor accidents. Conwy Council had already expressed concern about *Queen of the Conway*'s jetty and pointed out 'the great danger that attended the use of this erection as a landing place', when a potentially serious accident took place on the St George's Company stage. A teenage boy had been watching the embarkation of passengers when he lost his footing and fell into the water. The tide was running fast and the boy was in imminent danger of drowning when Capt. Roberts, without a moment's hesitation, dived in and successfully rescued him.

At some stage around 1904 the hulk of *Caemes*, which formed the floating coal hulk and pier head of the Conwy stage, was replaced by one of Roberts' family's former sailing ships, the *Commerce*. Between 1892 and 1903 she had mostly been engaged in carrying cargoes of gravel, which were dredged from the River Conwy to Liverpool where they were used as aggregate in the major dock extension scheme which was then under way.

The year 1905 proved to be a bumper year for the river steamers. Excellent weather throughout the summer brought the crowds flocking to the neighbourhood, assisted perhaps by a vigorous advertising campaign initiated by Conwy Council. At Trefriw, shopkeepers and lodging houses were reported to be busy and the wells as popular as ever, even though the daily concerts and entertainments were 'of a very homely nature' consisting mostly of local vocalists and some 'minor competitions'. The steamers remained in operation until 5 October, their passenger figures having broken all previous records. The winter proved less kind.

At the end of November the coast was swept by gale-force winds and heavy rain. At Deganwy the promenade was undermined, shelters badly damaged and the railway closed to traffic until the displaced ballast could be replaced, while further up river at Tal-y-Cafn a substantial section of permanent way was washed away by the heavy rain and tidal surge.

The year 1905 was also when the 'Sabbath Breakers' finally got their way, and Sunday steamer excursions from Liverpool to Llandudno were introduced by the Liverpool & North Wales Steamship Company's famous paddle steamer *La Marguerite*. The Act which ensured that Welsh hostelries remained closed on Sundays did not, of course, apply at sea, and those 'who felt themselves unable to rise to the moral standard of the Welsh Sabbath'[1] were theoretically able to imbibe steadily from one pier head to the other. In Llandudno fears had been expressed of inebriated crowds flocking ashore from the 'floating grogshops', of scenes of disorder in the Happy Valley, and of respectable citizens having to remain indoors. In the event, complaints seemed to be limited to dangerous crushes at the gang-ways while the ship was filling up for her return journey, some 'exuberance of animal spirits which amused rather than offended'[2] and by the 'discordant rendition' of various hymns and popular songs!

In the Conwy valley a significant increase in the number of Sunday travellers and tourists had been noted, and the landlord of the Ferry Hotel at Tal-y-Cafn successfully applied for a Sunday licence. It is not recorded whether *Trefriw Belle* or *Queen of the Conway* attempted to cash in on this developments by attempting

Trefriw Belle (left) and *Prince George* at their Deganwy landing stages.

TREFRIW STEAMERS.

A typical busy summer's day at Trefriw Quay. From left to right, *St George*, *Prince George*, *Trefriw Belle* and *Queen of the Conway* have embarked their passengers and are about to set off in convoy, downstream to Conwy. With a large puff of smoke from her funnel, *Queen of the Conway* is just getting underway, while the wash from *Prince George*'s paddles shows that she is going gently astern in order to spring her bows off the quay.

to run Sunday sailings, but it is certain that *St George* and *Prince George* continued to spend the Sabbath moored firmly to their jetties while the Roberts family attended chapel.

Charles Fruen, who had swept on to the Trefriw scene with such panache back in 1896, returned to the village after a period of absence and took over the direct management of the Belle Vue Hotel. The tenant, Miss Wade, had found herself in severe financial difficulties and, under pressure from Fruen and his business associates Messrs White, Tewson and Burfield, had been forced to surrender her 80-year lease. Fruen announced his intention to 'lift the trade' and, early in 1906, went on to lay out his plans to improve the quay, the wells and other parts of the village.

Work at the quay went ahead swiftly. By the summer of 1906 the entrance had been widened, the long wall which created the difference in levels between the landing stages and the upper terrace had been rebuilt, and three broad sets of steps installed – two joining the upper and lower levels and a third leading up on to the road opposite the Belle Vue. Parts of the terrace and stairways were fitted with handsome terracotta balustrades. On the levelled and gravelled upper terrace Fruen intended to build a coach house and stables and create an area large enough for a coach-and-four to turn with ease, together with a new 'stand' for coaches and cabs, thereby easing the congestion which frequently occurred in the narrower parts of the village. He also planned to erect a splendid 80ft by 40ft cast-iron and glass winter garden pavilion, which would provide a new focus for high-class entertainment, and lay out the far end of the terrace to lawns and parterres.

It was claimed that the facilities at the wells had now fallen far below expected standards and that 'the portion of the premises in which the water is dispensed to the patients who swallow it at "one penny a dose" resembles the tap room of a working class tavern, from the high counter down to the sawdust on the floor'.[3] Fruen and his associates, claiming to have obtained a controlling interest, planned to rectify this by completely stripping and rebuilding the interior, adding new wings on either side of the existing building, installing additional baths and adding a glazed vestibule at the front. A spacious and elegant pump room would thus be created which, with its fine views over the vale below, would provide a pleasant meeting place for visitors, whether partakers of the healing waters or not.

Never one to hold back, Fruen also urged that a kerbed and gravelled pavement be added to Gower's Road, which led from the village to Llanrwst station, and made a number of improvements at his golf course in the Crafnant valley. The mock-Tudor pavilion was refurbished, a professional from north Berwick employed to oversee the season ahead, and a number of prizes donated with the aim of revitalising the tennis and croquet tournaments at the recreation grounds. Behind the scenes he was also planning to float a new company, with a capital of £30,000, to

Ferry Hotel, Tal-y-Cafn, R.S.O., North Wales.

Trefriw Belle and *Queen of the Conway* moored at the Ferry Hotel, Tal-y-Cafn. Located on the west bank of the river just upstream of the bridge, the hotel was the regular stopping point for all of the steamers when small tides prevented them from going all the way to Trefriw. The passengers are ashore enjoying refreshments at the hotel.

Prince George alongside Trefriw Quay, *c.* 1906. Although the quay is still very rough underfoot, a start has been made on Mr Fruen's improvements. In the background, the first section of the new terracotta balustrades has been completed, together with the improved flight of steps up to the main road in front of the Belle Vue Hotel. (Gill Harvey)

which he proposed to sell his interests in the Belle Vue Hotel, Ship Inn, the quay, golf links, recreation ground and the wells. He claimed that investors from as far afield as London and Wolverhampton – including Mr Pollitt, the Chairman of the St George's SS Company – had promised to take substantial numbers of shares but, significantly, Rev. Gower and others, who actually held a controlling interest in the wells and other local facilities, declined to become involved.

By August 1906 the season was in full swing. Although nothing further was heard of the plans for the grand, glazed pavilion, the newly terraced and bal-ustraded quay was much appreciated by the steamer passengers and Trefriw positively buzzed with activity. The recreation grounds were well patronised, the sports tournaments regained much of their former popularity and the range of entertainment was provided to meet all tastes. At the wells the main public rooms had been refurbished and, under the management of the Misses Williams of Cae Coch Farm, offerings included 'various eminent vocalists, Mr Owen with humorous songs' and the ever-popular blind harpist, Mr Francis. There were organ recitals and choir concerts at the Ebenezer Chapel, lectures at the public hall, and unspecified entertainments by the popular Mr Canning who proved 'as interesting and clever as in former years'![4]

There can be little doubt that Charles Fruen's energy and vision had a major impact on the village but, sadly, behind the scenes all was far from well. The first hint of troubles to come came in November 1906 when he was summoned to Conwy County Court, but failed to appear. At a repeat hearing held at Llandudno during December it emerged that he was in serious debt to a number of creditors but, claiming that his proposed company floatation would prove to be a panacea, was given a little more time to put matters right. This did not prove to be the case and by January 1908 he found himself in the bankruptcy court where a sorry and tangled tale of misjudgement and deception soon spilled out.

It emerged that Fruen had previously been declared bankrupt in Brighton during 1902 and that, despite declaring a surplus of over £23,000 on that occasion, not a penny had been paid to any of the creditors. At Trefriw his property ownership was extremely opaque, with some conveyed to him as a trustee of his syndicate with Messrs White, Tewson and Burfield, and other parts mortgaged back to individual partners. On some occasions he had claimed to be the owner of the Belle Vue Hotel and on others merely its weekly tenant, and when the bailiffs had arrived on behalf of the unpaid Cambrian Mineral Water Company and various food and furniture suppliers, this confusion had allowed him to pass off responsibility and avoid payment. Counsel on behalf of the creditors ridiculed Fruen's attempts to justify his behaviour and suggested that it was extremely fortunate that the public had not been taken in by his proposals to form a Trefriw Spa company, which had proved to be nothing more than a conspiracy to avoid paying his creditors. It was the end for Charles Fruen, who retreated to London leaving solicitors to sort out the tangled web of mortgages and local property ownership.

Hotel Belle Vue, Trefriw, North Wales.

The Belle Vue Hotel, *c.* 1905/6. The white extension which had been added in the 1890s is clearly visible, while beside the road to the left of the hotel is the Store House, home of one branch of the Roberts family. Careful scrutiny reveals that the steps leading down from the road to the quay have not yet received their terracotta handrails. To the bottom right the mast of one of the Roberts' trading vessels, most probably the *Gladys*, is visible at the quay.

Afloat, there were also some very significant changes as, for the first time since 1898, the St George's Company faced no competition on the river. It is not clear whether *Queen of the Conway* entered service at all during 1906 but, if so, she had certainly been withdrawn by the middle of the season. The reasons for her demise remain unclear but it is likely that she had failed her Board of Trade survey, and that the cost of the repairs required could not be justified by her income. Alternatively, her owners may have finally admitted that the limitations imposed by her deep draught made her fundamentally unsuitable for the river and that, due to tidal constraints, she was losing too many trips to be economic. Whatever the case, the 14-year-old ship was withdrawn from service and broken up sometime during 1906 or 1907. Her register was formally closed on 6 April 1908.

Her owners, however, had not quite finished with the river trade. In February 1907 a number of shareholders from Llandudno & Trefriw Steamship Company together with some new investors set up the Llandudno & Trefriw Motor Boat Company Ltd, with the express purpose of taking over most of the old company's assets and replacing the *Queen of the Conway* with a fast, shallow-draught motor boat costing £2,700. Included in the assets were the disused pier at West Shore Llandudno, established landing rights at Trefriw Quay, the landing stage at Deganwy and the Conwy stage, together with the coal hulk and the cradle on the foreshore where the steamer had been laid up during the winter. Three of the directors – Thomas Lewis, Richard Conway and Richard Dunphy – had been part of the old company, and were joined by Arthur Hewitt and W. Ellis Jones from Llandudno, Hugh Hughes from Conway and Francis Nunn from Colwyn Bay.

Queen of the Conway laid up on the beach at Conwy, *c.* 1906.

Their plan seemed both logical and well timed. While admitting that *Queen of the Conway*'s draught had always made her unsuitable for the river, they reasoned that a modern, 250-passenger motorboat designed to ensure that she would obtain the necessary Board of Trade certificates to operate from West Shore Pier should be capable of turning a handsome profit. With a shallow draught of 2ft and high speed she would be able to offer her passengers more time ashore at Trefriw than the rival steamers, as well as having far lower running costs and a complete absence of smells, smuts and heat. The timing was seen as ideal since Gloddaeth Avenue, which led from the centre of Llandudno to the West Shore, had just been adopted by the local council as a public highway and the much-delayed Llandudno & Colwyn Bay Electric Railway was finally nearing completion and due to open early in 1907. Its southern terminus would be within a few yards of the West Shore Pier and the trams should prove far cheaper and more convenient than travelling by train to Deganwy. The prospectus suggested that if only 400 of the 50,000 visitors visiting the area each week in summer travelled on the new boat, which would run 5 days a week over an 18-week season, then an income of £900 would be generated, giving a profit of £530 after expenses had been deducted. The capital of the new company would be £5,000 divided into 5,000 shares of £1 each, with shareholders in the old company receiving an appropriate allotment of deferred shares.

Sadly, the floatation did not go entirely to plan. Questions were raised by potential shareholders about the condition and maintenance costs of the West Shore Pier and whether the motorboat could guarantee a reliable service from such an exposed and tidal spot. Shares sold slowly, the tramway did not open until October 1907, and the company secretary fell ill. An announcement was made that the start of the new service would be deferred until 1907, but nothing further was heard of the scheme and the company was formally dissolved on 24 February 1911.

It would appear that *Trefriw Belle* was also absent from the river during 1906. As has been stated previously, this little vessel remains something of an enigma, and the reasons for her temporary absence can only be inferred from the few scraps of evidence which have been discovered. It will be recalled that she had originally come to the river under charter to a Mr George Griffiths, who operated her until she passed into the ownership of the Trefriw Belle Steamship Company, which was owned by Capt. H.C. Edwards of the Post Office, Tywyn.

Three pieces of evidence have survived in the archives which suggest a possible sequence of events. The first is a newspaper article dated 21 June 1907 which states categorically that the previous season had found the St George's Company steamers 'alone surviving' on the river. The second is a plan for a solid wrought-iron crankshaft for the *Trefriw Belle*, dated 25 April 1907 and discovered amongst the Dinorwic Quarry records. The final thread is a plan showing a proposed landing stage at Deganwy, requested by Capt. Edwards and dated early in 1907.

It therefore seems a strong possibility that *Trefriw Belle* operated for George Griffiths until 1906 when she broke her crankshaft and had to be withdrawn. A replacement crankshaft was ordered from the Dinorwic Company's foundry and in all probability fitted at Port Dinorwic, where we know the St George's Company also sent their ships for repair and where they retained a Mr Hugh Pritchard as their consulting engineer. With *Queen of the Conway* out of the way, Capt. Edwards may have perceived a gap in the market, purchased the ship (either before or after her repair) and applied to construct a new landing stage for her to use from the beginning of the 1907 season.

The unopposed 1906 season had run from 24 May until 6 October, for most of which *Prince George* had been skippered by William Roberts and *St George* by Robert Roberts. Their regular trips had been enlivened by a number of lucrative charters for works outings, including one to the *North Wales Weekly News* which had its offices on Conwy Quay and which continued to take every opportunity to sing the praises of the St George's Company. The year had also been marked by the arrival in Conway of John Crossfield, previously a senior partner in the noted yacht and boatbuilding firm Crossfield Brothers of Arnside in Westmorland. Crossfield set up a new boatbuilding yard, located on the Conwy foreshore adjacent to the St George's yard but immediately downstream of the town walls, which quickly built up an excellent reputation. One of his first boats was a 56ft racing yacht for a Mr James Spurr of Blackpool, after which he went on to design and build a wide variety of yachts, launches, working boats and 'Nobbies' – the distinctive local fishing boats. A harmonious working relationship was quickly established between the two

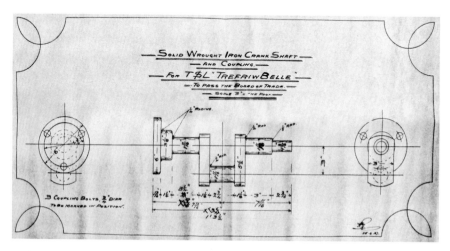

A plan of the replacement crankshaft and coupling made for the *Trefriw Belle* in the spring of 1907 by the Dinorwic Quarry Company and, in all probability, fitted at Port Dinorwic. (Gwynedd Archives)

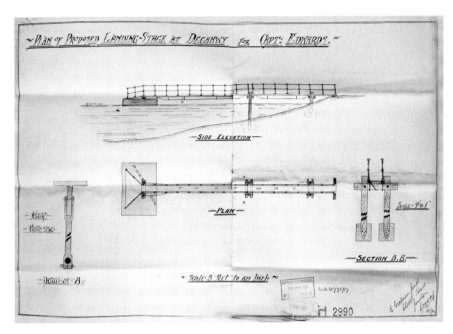

Plans showing Capt. Edward's proposed *Trefriw Belle* landing stage at Deganwy. (Conwy Archive Service)

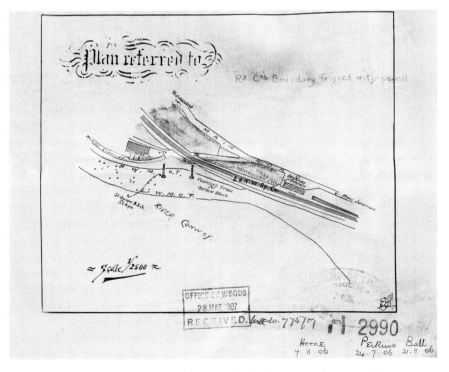

Plans showing Capt. Edward's proposed *Trefriw Belle* landing stage at Deganwy. (Conwy Archive Service)

neighbours with the St George's Company allowing Crossfield to use their covered slipways for the storage of his plank stock. Crossfields were shareholders in the St George's Company and the two concerns even shared an office in the old custom house at Porth Bach, which today houses the harbourmaster's office. One of John Crossfield's two sons, Vincent, was to play major role in the later history of the St George's Company and its steamers.

Buoyed up by their ever-increasing passenger figures, the demise of the rival *Queen of the Conway* and the breakdown of the *Trefriw Belle*, the St George's Company decided to look into building a third steamer in time for the season of 1907. Having considered a number of potential builders they settled on W.J. Yarwood & Sons of Northwich, a company which had built a formidable reputation for the construction of small tugs, workboats, barges, canal boats and passenger vessels at its inland Castle Dock yard on the River Weaver.

During the summer of 1906 Yarwood's had sent a team across to Conwy to make a close examination of *Prince George*, take careful measurements and discuss the company's precise requirements before submitting a tender for the new ship. The Capts Roberts required a ship which would have a higher speed and larger passenger capacity than her predecessor but would be of similar appearance and, critically, of the same shallow draught. Intriguingly, a surviving notebook which

The St George's Company's yard, double-bayed covered slipways and landing stage pictured sometime after 1907. The hinging section and floating pier head of the former *Queen of the Conway* stage have been removed, leaving only the piled section which was to remain in situ for many years. Crossfield's boatyard, established in 1906, is hidden from view on the other side of the Town Wall.

records Yarwood's visit[5] indicates that *Prince George*'s managing owners at that time were still recorded as Messrs P. & H. Lewis, proving that the timber merchants were indeed major shareholders in the St George's Company.

The production of such a specialised paddle steamer was not an easy brief but Yarwoods rose to the challenge and submitted a detailed specification dated 28 September 1906. Following further discussions with their clients a few minor alterations were agreed (including the reduction of both the proposed moulded breadth and depth by 1in each), detailed plans were drawn up and building commenced during the winter of 1906–07.

The finished ship, named *King George*, measured 79ft in length, 13ft 3in in the beam (excluding paddle boxes) and 4ft 9in from the side of her deck amidships to the bottom of the keel, with a gross tonnage of 44.81 tons. Her displacement at a mean draught of 2ft 1in was calculated as 41.14 tons and, fully laden with stores, coal for 6 hours' steaming and her full complement of passengers, would float in precisely the same depth of water – 2ft 10in – as *Prince George*. Her riveted steel hull had a straight stem and an elliptical counter stern and was specially stiffened and fitted with 12ft by 6in chafing plates along the turn of each bilge to allow for her need to dry out on each low tide. It is interesting to note that *King George* was slightly too large to be drawn right up the slipway and into the company's sheds at Conwy, and was therefore forced to spend her winters either moored to the pon toon or on a drying mooring upstream of the bridges.

Her streamlined paddle boxes were constructed of galvanised steel sheet, and the sponsons abaft the boxes cleverly sloped to ensure the best possible flow of water from the paddle wheels, which were fitted with curved, steel floats of a feathering design. The 2in-thick Kauri pine upper deck was adorned with teak companion ways, a wheel platform and, with its rows of forward facing seats, was capable of accommodating 280 passengers – precisely 100 more than the *Prince George*. Below decks there were small saloons forward and aft of the machinery spaces, two WCs, a store room, a chain locker in the bows and three watertight bulkheads.

Her 80ihp compound stem engine was of a rather unusual design in that while its 22in-diameter, low-pressure cylinder was positioned in the accepted manner in the bottom of the ship and drove diagonally upwards on to the crankshaft, the high pressure cylinder, which had a diameter of 10¾in and a stroke of 24in, was placed horizontally above and to one side of it. The engine was fitted with a surface condenser, the usual air, circulating and feed pumps, and a donkey pump capable of being used as a bilge, fire or fresh water pump. Her engine room was 23ft 9in in length and was illuminated by a small skylight, angled forward and positioned so that the cranks could be seen by the man at the wheel, who also controlled the speed and direction of the engine via appropriate levers. These consisted of a steam valve or throttle, a reversing lever and, very importantly, an auxiliary starting lever. Whenever the engine came to a halt it was important that the crank driven by the high pressure cylinder was either at the top or bottom of its rotation, meaning that the piston would be halfway through its stroke. If not, the engine could 'stick' and refuse to go ahead or astern, with dire consequences. In the event of this happening, the auxiliary starting lever would be used to admit high-pressure steam into the low-pressure cylinder, forcing the engine to turn. Steam came from a single steel, return tube marine boiler 6ft 6in long by 7ft diameter, with a single furnace and working pressure of 130psi. Her twin coal

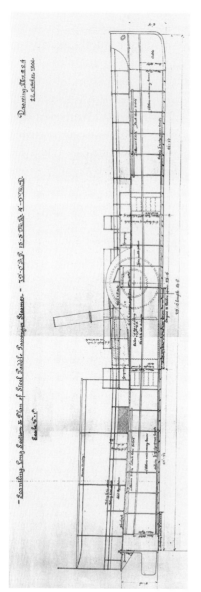
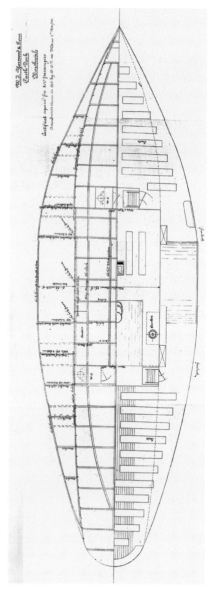

Profile and plan views of the new paddle steamer *King George* of 1907. (Gwynedd Archives)

bunkers were constructed of galvanised iron with circular hatches from the upper deck and together could hold 6 hours' supply of coal, making it essential to refuel at least every other day. Her service speed was 8 knots.

Like her predecessors, she had a single, well-raked, hinged funnel just abaft the paddle boxes, an awning over the aft deck, gilt-topped flag staffs at her bow and stern, but no mast. Her railings were of a standard design and in the bows was a short section of solid bulwark pierced by her hawse pipe and adorned with her name and some very elaborate, gilded scroll work. She was painted in the company's standard

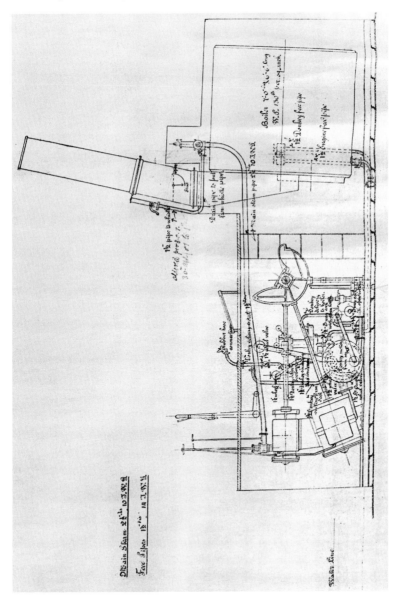

Profile view of the main engine and boiler layout of the *King George*. Note the unusual arrangement of one diagonal and one horizontal cylinder, and the way in which the engine controls project through the deck where they can be operated by the skipper at the wheel. (Gwynedd Archives)

livery of the time. The funnel was buff with a black top, the hull a light green with either a black or salmon under-body, the engine room casing buff and her railings in aluminium silver. All seats, rails and other woodwork was varnished. This livery lasted for much of the company's history, though photographs show that there were years when the hulls were painted a dark colour, probably black, and *Prince George's* distinctive, lattice-patterned rails were painted white.

Christened *King George* and with the official number 120787, the new ship was launched on 11 April 1907 and found her way into salt water for the first time on Friday 14 June when she left Eastham on the Mersey shortly before 10 a.m. and turned her bows westward for Conwy, where she arrived at 4 p.m. *The North Wales Weekly News* explained that:

> The weather being fairly fine the trip was a most enjoyable one and the proud skipper, Capt. Roberts, saluted and was saluted by everything with a funnel on the journey. The passengers on the Liverpool and Menai Strait steamers immediately recognised the vessel and its mission and raised round after round of encouraging cheers.

The following morning was spent making final adjustments and during the afternoon the company's directors and invited guest assembled for the official christening and trial trip. The newspaper continued:

> Those on board and upon the landing stage included, among others, Mr J.A. Pollitt (Chairman) and Mrs Pollitt, Mr Owen Rowland J.P., Mr A.S. Wood,

King George pulling away from the landing stage at Conwy on her way upstream. As built she appears to have been fitted with a very short-lived bell-topped funnel. Her name and some ornate scrollwork was emblazoned on the solid bulwark at the bow.

Mr. Cornelius Sever, Mr J.C. Griffiths (National Provincial Bank) and Mrs Griffiths, Mr Hugh Pritchard M.I. Mech. E. (of Portdinorwic and the company's consulting engineer) and Mrs Pritchard, Miss Bownes, Miss C. Lewis, Miss Gwen Lewis and Mrs Furness ...

The christening ceremony was happily performed by Mrs Pollitt. Having duly broken the bottle she said: 'I am very pleased to have the honour of christening this new steamer "King George", which will be a splendid addition to the present river fleet which comprises three steamers, well-built, substantial and up-to-date, namely "King George", "Prince George" and "St George". I hope the "King George" will carry us safely and give the same amount of pleasure to the thousands of passengers who take the trip up this beautiful Welsh Rhine, and I hope our friend Capt. Roberts and his colleagues will be able to make a record dividend for the shareholders of the well-known St George S.S. Co.' (cheering and prolonged applause).

This pleasing ceremony over, the 'King George's' powerful steam whistle warned those who were not going to proceed to Trefriw to retire, and with a beautifully flexible movement the handsome boat was quickly under way. The whole of the journey was performed in the smoothest possible manner and it was no exaggeration to say that the graceful appearance of the steamer is quite in keeping with the unsurpassable scenery associated with this delightful excursion ...

The journey down again, after a brief stay at Trefriw, was equally interesting and, despite unusual exertions on the part of the skipper of the 'Prince George' who steamed out of Trefriw a few seconds after Capt. Roberts, he hopelessly failed to close the gradually increasing gap between the two vessels. 'King George' was back at the landing stage shortly after 3 p.m. and it is gratifying to find that she has given such complete satisfaction to directors, crew and those members of the general public who had the privilege of being on board on the day of the first trip. Here's to the 'King George'!

King George, skippered by Capt. William Roberts, with 'Huw Black' Williams as engineer and Hugh Davies and Thomas Evans as deckhands, entered public service the next day. The *New St George*, no longer the newest ship in the fleet, reverted to her registered name of *Prince George*, and was referred to as such in all subsequent advertisements. With three well-matched ships in its old, established and well-known fleet, the St George's Company cannot have felt too perturbed by the re-entry of the little *Trefriw Belle* into the fray, and went on to enjoy a highly successful 1907 season.

This spirit of optimism also communicated itself to Trefriw where, following the trauma of Mr Fruen's bankruptcy, other influential parties regrouped and pressed ahead with improvements. A new company, with a Mr Charles Adamson as manager and secretary, was formed to take over the wells and pressed ahead with

King George still sporting her bell-topped funnel, with *St George* and *Prince George* outside her, loading passengers at Deganwy.

Engineer 'Huw Black' Williams was part of the crew which commissioned and delivered *King George* in 1907 and, apart from a very few years during the 1920s, remained with the ship throughout her working life. This photograph was taken at Conwy in 1933. (Doris Williams)

THE STEAMERS of the old established Company,
ST. GEORGE'S S.S. CO., LTD.,

Will ply (weather and other causes permitting) on one of the most beautiful Rivers in Wales,
between

Deganwy, Conway & Trefriw.

Please note the name of this Company's Steamers—"KING GEORGE,"
"PRINCE GEORGE," and ST. GEORGE," and that they start from the
St. George's Landing Stages at Deganwy and Conway.

JUNE, 1907.

Date of Sailing.	Steamer leave Deganwy.	Steamer leave Conway.	Steamer return from Trefriw.
1 Saturday	1 0 p.m.	1 10 p.m.	3 15 p.m.
3 Monday	3 25 ,,	3 30 ,,	5 15 ,, †
4 Tuesday	4 15 ,,	4 30 ,,	6 30 ,, †
5 Wednesday.....	5 40 ,,	5 50 ,,	7 40 ,,
8 Saturday	8 10 a.m.	8 20 noon.	9 55 a.m.
10 Monday	9 44 ,,	9 48 ,,	11 20 ,.
11 Tuesday.........	9 45 ,,	9 50 ,,	11 55 ,,
12 Wednesday.....	10 15 ,,	10 20 ,,	12 30 p.m.
13 Thursday	10 28 ,,	10 40 ,,	1 0 ,,
14 Friday..	11 18 ,,	11 25 ,,	1 25 ,,
15 Saturday	12 0 noon.	12 10 p.m.	2 5 ,,
17 Monday	1 10 p.m.	1 25 ,.	3 18 ,,
18 Tuesday.........	2 0 ,,	2 10 ,,	4 8 ,, †
19 Wednesday ...	3 10 ,,	3 25 ,,	5 12 ,, †
20 Thursday	4 10 ,,	4 20 ,,	6 25 ,, †
21 Friday...........	5 40 ,,	5 45 ,,	7 30 ,,
24 Monday	8 10 a.m.	8 20 a.m	10 0 a.m.
25 Tuesday.........	8 25 ,,	8 35 ,,	10 50 ,,
26 Wednesday ...	9 45 ,,	9 50 ,,	11 45 ,,
27 Thursday	10 15 ,,	10 20 ,,	12 40 p.m.
28 Friday...........	11 18 ,,	11 20 ,,	1 25 ,,
29 Saturday	12 0 noon.	12 5 p.m.	2 15 ,,

† Doubtful if Steamers reach Trefriw.   Fare according to distance.

Fares—Fore End, 1s.; Return, 2s.; After End, 1s. 6d.; Return, 2s. 6d.

CHILDREN HALF-FARE.

For further particulars apply to Messrs. P. & H. Lewis, Conway and Llanrwst ; Messrs. Roberts & Co.,
Quay, Conway ; Messrs. R. E. Jones & Bros., *Weekly News* Office, Conway and Colwyn Bay ; The
Hotel Belle Vue, Trefriw ; Mr. Slater, Photo Artist, Mostyn Street. Llandudno ; Mr. John Jones,
Glasgow House, Penmaenmawr ; Mrs. Tritton, Castle Hotel, Deganwy ; Mr. Tomkinson, *Indispensable*
Colwyn Bay : and all the principal Hotels in the neighbourhood.

For further information apply to the Manager, Capt. W. Roberts, Quay, Conway.

For the Convenience of Passengers, Luncheons and Teas will be ready on arrival at
Hotel Belle Vue, Trefriw.

SPECIAL NOTICE.—Tickets for THESE Steamers are NOT SOLD at
LLANDUDNO and other places, and can only be had on board the Steamers.

R. E. Jones & Bros., Printers, Conway.

A St George's SS Co. Ltd sailing bill for June 1907.

improvements to the pump room which were almost identical to Fruen's original proposals. The building of 1873/4 was greatly enlarged by the addition of two wings and a large entrance vestibule whose grey stone and stepped gables closely matched the original. Internally the large and airy pump room was completely remodelled to include two new fireplaces and an elegant bar from which health-seekers could purchase their recommended doses of the healing waters. Equipped with tables, chairs, newspapers and other requirements for relaxation, the space proved to be an ideal venue for indoor concerts. The large windows and glass vestibule gathered the sunshine and provided fine views over the tranquil valley below while, externally, the grounds were 'tastefully laid out to harmonise with their charming and pictur-esque surroundings'[6] and became a popular destination in their own right.

To the rear of the building a long, low extension to each side provided sepa-rate bathrooms for ladies and gentlemen. These were fitted with a range of new baths 'made of special materials to resist the strong actions of the waters and of the latest and most scientifically approved types'[7] and other 'hydropathic appli-ances' and were supervised by uniformed attendants. The pipes which brought the waters to the bathrooms and pump room from the caves above were also renewed in materials which would neither affect or be affected by the medicinal properties of the waters, and a modern bottling plant was installed.

The new Wells Company issued a splendid, hardback guidebook to the wells and surrounding area,[8] which contained numerous illustrations, together with much detail about the waters, their history, composition, uses and powers.

Trefriw Wells as reconstructed in 1907, showing the two new side wings with their stepped gables, the glazed vestibule and the long rear extension which housed the bathrooms.

An advertising card issued by the new Wells Company showing both interior and exterior features of the wells in precise detail. Note the original, heavily built bath house of 1863 on the hillside above the new buildings.

As before, the chalybeate waters were claimed to provide an effective cure for diseases of the skin, eyes, nervous and digestive systems, as well as 'mental affections, melancholia, brain fag, female complaints'[9] and much more. Patients were urged to consult their 'medical attendant' in order to select the best course of treatment for their complaint but, broadly, two options were recommended.

The first of these was to drink the waters regularly over a period of 6 weeks, building up from a dose of ½oz twice a day after meals in the first week to 1oz double doses three times a day in the third and fourth weeks, before reducing gradually to the initial small dose by the end of the treatment. These 'No. 1 waters' were dispensed from taps at the pump room bar at 2*d* per dose and drunk quickly from dark brown glasses in order to minimise the effects of sunlight, which quickly turned the waters discoloured and foul-tasting. For those unable to remain in Trefriw for the full 6-week treatment, the waters were also supplied for home consumption in boxes containing a dozen dark-brown 1oz glass bottles at a cost of 3*s* 6*d* per box. Patients were told very firmly that, before beginning a course of treatment 'the bowels should be attended to and any temporary derangement of the stomach rectified'!

The second option was to immerse oneself in the waters. The newly fitted baths came in a variety of designs – sitz, douche, foot, wave, etc – to suit every need and

The front cover of a hardback guidebook issued by the Wells Company in April 1908.

could be taken either hot or cold. Cold baths were recommended for muscular and nervous weakness and were said to impart a pleasant sensation and agreeable warmth to the skin, especially if followed by a brisk walk. Warm baths, which were heated to a temperature of 90–95°F, were recommended for kidney disease, rheumatism, sciatica and skin diseases. Whether taking a hot or cold bath, patients were urged to leave the water as soon as a 'general feeling of exhilaration and vigour' was detected, as longer emersion could lead to a feeling of depression and be 'productive of much harm'. Again, for those unable to visit the wells daily, the external or 'No. 2 water' could be provided in 2-gallon cans, enabling patients to sponge or soak affected limbs at home or buy sufficient quantities to fill a full-sized bath.

The popularity of the revitalised wells grew rapidly and more than fulfilled its promoters' dreams. By July open-air concerts featuring David Francis the blind harpist, Miss Blodwyn Jones (who appeared in Welsh costume) and many

An illustration of one of the boxes containing twelve bottles of water for internal use, available by post at 3s 9d.

A 2-gallon can of water intended for external use, costing 3s by post.

other 'vocalists of fame' were in full swing. The pump and bathrooms were in great demand, and bottled water was being dispatched daily – one record order exceeded 3,000 bottles and postcards showing the interior and exterior of the new pump room had become popular souvenirs.

The Rev. Gower – who one presumes had retained a financial interest in the wells – and his Improvement Committee gave every possible support to the new Wells Company. Additional seats were provided along the road from the village to the wells, the bridge near the woollen mill was given additional ornamentation and the Peniel Bridge was repainted. The Recreation Grounds passed into private hands.

In addition, a new pavilion was, at long last, erected on the steamer quay. Instead of Mr Fruen's grand iron and glass winter garden, the new pavilion took the more modest and practical form of a timber building, with a pitched, slate roof set against the back wall of the quay's upper terrace. At the same time the terracotta balustrades on the terrace and steps were completed and a flag staff erected. It would appear that all of this work was undertaken by the new company which had taken over the Belle Vue Hotel and let it to a Mr Michael Judge as their tenant. With as many as four crowded steamers arriving almost simultaneously at the quay, the Belle Vue had been finding it very difficult to cope with the huge demand for refreshments during the very short time the ships remained alongside. The facilities of the main hotel had been stretched to breaking point, but the addition of the new pavilion almost doubled the capacity and allowed teas and mineral waters to be dispensed in far more agreeable conditions.

All-in-all the season of 1908 proved to be exceptionally successful. During July and August the steamers ran with capacity loadings, Trefriw was crowded with visitors and almost every available room was let, the charabancs *Duchess of York* and *Princess Mary* were kept busy conveying sightseers on tours to Betws-y-Coed and Gwydir and Mr Evans of Crafnant House experienced heavy demand for the fleet of landaus, waggonettes and other vehicles which he offered for

Trefriw, The Quay and Denganwy Steamer

Trefriw Quay showing the improvements which were finally completed during 1908. The rebuilt walls and steps with their terracotta balustrades are clearly visible at the village end of the quay below the Belle Vue Hotel. The timber refreshment rooms and restaurant are in place and, next to them, a small hut with a banner which reads 'Trefriw Water' is presumably selling boxes of bottled water to day trippers who have insufficient time to walk to the Wells themselves. *Prince George* simmers quietly alongside the quay, awaiting her return passengers.

hire. The North Wales croquet and tennis tournaments at the recreation grounds were well supported and a new committee which had been formed to take over the lease of the Golf Club succeeded in refurbishing the pavilion and greens, while the Belle Vue Hotel Company provided some handsome new medals and trophies.

The only cloud on the horizon so far as the St George's Company was concerned, was a proposal to build a light railway up the west bank of the Conway. At the time the Aluminium Corporation Ltd were in the process of developing an enormous new aluminium works at the village of Dolgarrog, some 3 miles downstream from Trefriw, and had applied for permission to build an industrial light railway from the works to the coast at Llandudno Junction. Many people felt that, with the inevitable increase in population of Dolgarrog and district as workers flooded in to the new works, it would make great sense to open the proposed railway to passengers as well as industrial products. At an inquiry held in July 1908 the Light Railway Commissioners granted the application to apply for a light railway order on the condition that the line was extended as far as Trefriw and would be capable of carrying passengers. Initially known as the Abbey, Dolgarrog & Trefriw Light Railway and later as the Dolgarrog Light Railway, the proposals underwent various minor alterations until 1911, when the route was changed

A horse-drawn charabanc pauses outside the Belle Vue Hotel to collect passengers from one
of the steamers at the quay below for a tour to Betws-y-Coed, Gwydir or beyond. The large
noticeboard fixed to the tree is advertising the attractions of the Trefriw recreation grounds
and has a sale notice pasted to it. *Queen of the Conway* lies at the far end of the quay suggesting
that, although the card was posted in 1908, the photograph was taken in about 1905 before she
was withdrawn and the quay was improved.

completely. Now named the Conway Valley Light Railway, it was planned to take
the line from Conway via Gyffin and Dolgarrog to Trefriw and thence across the
valley, presumably following Gower's road, to terminate near the main line station at Llanrwst. In 1912 the plan were changed again, with the spur to Llanrwst
abandoned in favour of a continuation to Gwydir.

Any of these schemes would, of course, have posed a direct threat to the river
steamers and all were stiffly opposed by the St George's Company both in prin-
ciple and detail. As soon as the original proposed route was disclosed, a dispute
broke out over the navigational height under a bridge which would carry the
line across the river near Dolgarrog and which, at only 14ft 6in, would have
impeded the passage of the steamers on big tides. Their fears of navigation being
compromised and the light railway stealing away their trade preoccupied them
until 1914 when, with the outbreak of the First World War, all plans of a railway to
Trefriw faded away and were never heard of again.

Captain Edwards of the Trefriw Belle Steamship Company had clearly also
enjoyed a profitable 1908, for in September of that year he bought a second
steamer to partner the *Trefriw Belle* during the 1909 season. Named *Jubilee*, she had
been owned by Evan Griffith of Barmouth, who used her on regular sailings up
the Afon Mawddach to Penmaenpool Bridge and on short coastal cruises. *Jubilee*

had been built in 1896 by Cochran & Company of Birkenhead was presumably named in anticipation of Queen Victoria's Diamond Jubilee in 1897, and had replaced a smaller vessel of the same name. Cochrans are of some interest in themselves, carrying out ship building and engineering at Birkenhead from their formation in 1878 until 1899 when they moved to Annan in Dumfries & Galloway. There they began to specialise more and more in boiler making and survive to this day as one of Britain's few specialist boiler companies.

Constructed of pitch pine over elm frames and oak stem and stern posts, *Jubilee* measured 61ft in length with a beam of 12ft and a depth of 4.9ft. Her tonnage was 27 gross and 16 net. At her forward end the upper deck was flush with the gunwales and fitted with rows of seats. Amidships was a boiler and engine casing, surmounted by the steering position and a single funnel, the top of which was 13ft above water level. Aft it was possible to walk right round a small, plainly furnished 'half-saloon' let into the deck and entered by way of a sliding hatch and ladder. The top of the saloon was fitted with fixed seats while the side decks had small benches which could be folded up against the sides of the saloon. She was fitted with a single propeller driven by a 32ihp non-condensing engine, which would have meant that she made a gentle and distinctive chuffing noise as she steamed along. Her twin cylinders measured 7in and 14in in diameter with a stroke of 9in and were fed by a boiler with a working pressure of 100psi. Both engine and boiler were made by Cochran & Company.

If *Trefriw Belle*'s career on the river is something of an enigma, then *Jubilee*'s is a complete mystery! To date, not a single photograph has been discovered of her in

Jubilee at Penmaenpool on the Afon Mawddach where she operated between 1896 and 1908.

operation on the Conwy, which is all the more remarkable when one considers that the local press made repeated references between 1909 and 1911 to the spectacle of five steamers arriving in convoy at Trefriw Quay. One can only put the reason that no postcard photographer recorded the remarkable sight of *St George*, *Prince George*, *King George*, *Trefriw Belle* and *Jubilee* disgorging their hoards of passengers down to the fact that the market was already flooded with similar pictures of the quay and river. Equally, no reference to the *Jubilee* by name has yet been unearthed in the press or other records, leading historians to debate whether she ever actually came to the Conwy at all. However, her sale to Capt. Edwards, the frequent references in the press to five steamers operating on the river and an account of an accident which took place on Friday 11 August 1911 involving one of the steamers of the Trefriw Belle Company all confirm that she *was* there. One can only hope that further photographs and evidence will surface in due course.

Just before the 1909 season commenced the proprietors of Trefriw Quay set about removing a sandbank which had built up in the river and was making it difficult for the steamers to swing. On arrival it was their custom to put the passengers ashore and then turn the ship round, using ropes and a long pole so that her bows were facing downstream ready for a quick departure. With five ships alongside and all the berths full, there would be little room for manoeuvre and if one ship got stuck across the river there would be serious consequences for them all. The dredging operation was therefore greatly welcomed. The sand was taken ashore and spread on the quay, providing a beautifully smooth surface.

Despite the spirited competition on the river, the 1909 season proved another resounding success for all concerned. Indeed, after their last sailing took place on 16 September, the St George's Company were feeling sufficiently confident to order a replacement for their ageing *St George* of 1852. Influenced perhaps by the Llandudno & Trefriw Motor Boat Company's earlier proposals, the company made the bold decision to depart from the tried and tested combination of steam engines and paddle wheels and plump instead for a shallow draught, twin-screw motorboat. The intention was to design a boat which would be fast and shallow enough to reach Trefriw even on the smaller neap tides, which forced the paddle steamers to terminate at Tal-y-Cafn. It was assumed that she would be cheap to run and maintain and, being a motor vessel, could be started up at short notice to take the overflow when the two larger paddlers were filled to capacity.

The new boat was designed by Messrs John Crossfield and Hugh Pritchard, the company's consulting engineer from Port Dinorwic and was constructed at Crossfield's yard in Conway. The order was formally placed in January 1910 and by April building was well advanced. At the same time, a few yards away on the opposite of the town's medieval curtain wall, the faithful old *St George* was being dismantled in her owner's yard. It must have been a difficult and emotional task for the staff involved to break up a vessel which had been such an integral part of

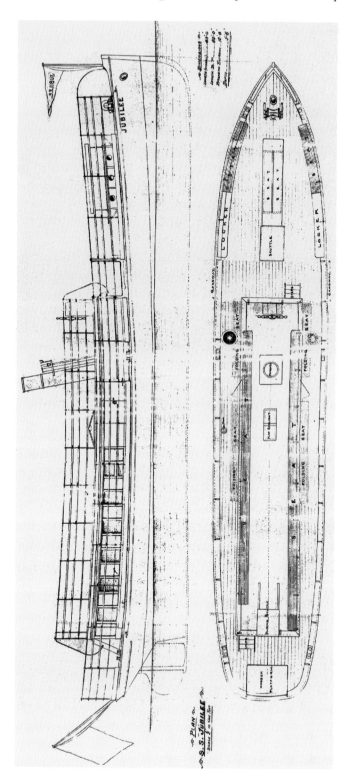

Builder's profile and plan views of the *Jubilee*. (Gwynedd Archives)

The daily convoy arrives at Trefriw in 1908 or 1909. Nearest the camera, *King George* has already turned and disembarked her passengers. *Trefriw Belle* and *St George* are just arriving while, further downstream, *Prince George* makes her approach.

Taken on the same day but a few moments later, *Trefriw Belle* has moved further up the quay to moor, *St George* is just completing her turn and *Prince George* is coming alongside the steps at the end of the quay. (Crawford Alexander)

St George swinging on arrival at Trefriw before disembarking her passengers. She has a bow rope ashore and is using the flooding tide to help her round. In the background *Trefriw Belle* is manoeuvring alongside the quay. Both ships are packed with capacity crowds of smartly dressed passengers. (Gwynedd Archives)

Prince George swinging at Trefriw. On this occasion the river flow has proved insufficient to turn her unaided, so a crew member at the stern is helping her round with a large quant pole. Note the quay improvements of 1908.

the local scene for 58 years, and to cut the final link with the pioneering days of the river trade to Trefriw.

Master Bertie Dunkerley, nephew of Mr J.A. Pollitt 'the genial Chairman of the company', launched the new boat on Thursday 23 June 1910 in front of a large crowd of well-wishers. The next day was spent undertaking trials, making final adjustments and, even though the boat was not quite finished, the official christening and trial trip took place on Saturday 25 June. With the usual large group of directors, shareholders and friends on board and John Crossfield at the helm, she set off up-river to Benarth Point where Mr C.M. Lees, the deputy chairman, explained to the guests that, since his wife was unavoidably absent, his mother would christen the vessel. Mrs Lees duly broke a bottle of champagne on the deck and christened the new vessel *St George (II)*. Refreshments were served and toasts made while *St George* motored upstream to Tal-y-Cafn where the guests were landed for a short stay. It was noted that the boat had made very good time and that, even with both engines at full speed, she was remarkably free from vibration. On the return trip she was given a noisy steam-whistle welcome by *Prince George* and *King George* before turning off Deganwy and returning to the Conway landing stage where she was greeted by an enthusiastic crowd.

St George (II) was a radical departure from anything previously seen on the river. Constructed of timber, she was 55.6ft long, 11.1ft wide and had a depth of 4.1ft. She was capable of floating in between 18in and 21in of water, depending

The stalwart *St George* was an integral part of the river scenery for 58 years from 1852 until she was dismantled on the company's Conwy slipway during the spring of 1910 and replaced by a motor vessel of the same name. Here she is setting off from Trefriw on yet another voyage downstream to Conwy and Deganwy.

on her load, and had a 'drop keel plate' which could be lowered when she was in deep water. She was fitted with two 30hp paraffin engines manufactured by Dixon Bros & Hutchinson Ltd of Woolston, Southampton, and supplied by Fairbanks of London. Each engine had four cylinders with a diameter of 4¾in, a stroke of 5in and drove through twin screws to give her a speed of 9 knots. Her official number was 120796 and she was certificated to carry 140 passengers. Outwardly she was extremely plain in appearance, with a slightly curved stem and a fashionable rounded stern which sloped in the opposite direction to those of the paddlers. Her upper deck was flush, apart from a short raised section over her 7.7ft engine room which extended to her full width and was pierced by four port holes. The helm and controls were positioned on this raised section, an awning was provided for the after deck but, as if to emphasise her pedigree as a modern motor vessel, she had no funnel.

It is apparent that the unfamiliar paraffin engines did not prove to be an unqualified success. At the end of July *St George (II)* was still undergoing trials and it was not until the middle of August 1910 that she actually entered regular passenger service. In 1911 the two paddle steamers opened the season on 26 May in time for the Whitsun holidays and, during the following week, were forced to terminate several trips at Tal-y-Cafn due to small tides. Early in July the local press optimistically reported that 'the new motor launch, which is now in thorough working order, is a fast vessel and will prove to be a decided acquisition to the fleet,' but, reading between the lines, it is clear that this was anything but true. The opposition was not slow to capitalise on the situation and on 15 September

The "St. George" leaving Conway.   Published by O. Evans, Photographer, Conway.

The new motor vessel *St George (II)* of 1910 passing Conwy on her way upstream to Trefriw.

William Roberts wrote an angry letter to Capt. Edwards stating: 'I am instructed by my directors to state that yesterday you made expressions to the public to the effect that your boats were the only ones that did not break down, thus implying that the boats of this company did so.' He also threatened legal action if the statement was repeated. Over the next few years her paraffin engines proved thoroughly cantankerous and she was frequently out of service. As her engineers struggled to get the better of her wilful machinery, they must have rued the day that the decision was made to change from steam to motor power.

The disappointment of the *St George (II)* aside, the 1911 season followed its usual routine. At Conwy, some excitement was provided by the Choral Society, which 'discoursed music from an illuminated steamer anchored in the river', and by a rather alarming accident which took place on 11 August as one of the Trefriw Belle Company's steamers was approaching her temporary landing stage. It seems that her skipper misjudged his approach and, as he swept around to face into the strong ebb tide, got carried in amongst the small craft moorings in the river. Two boats were sunk, several broken from their moorings and many others damaged. The steamers also faced some competition when, on 1 August, the London & North Western Railway introduced a motor coach service from Conwy to Llanrwst via Trefriw.

The following year, by contrast, was beset by heavy rain and gales and judged to be the worst season for 50 years. The steamers began on Whit Tuesday, 28 May, and the partisan local press, still clearly unsympathetic towards the Trefriw

Prince George departs from the Conwy stage, *c.* 1911. The bows of the motor vessel *St George (II)* can be seen protruding from behind the floating pier head.

Belle Company, urged intending passengers 'to scrutinise for the name of the St George's vessels before embarking' and eulogised both the quality of the three boats and the experience of William Roberts and the other skippers.

When the weather was fine the steamers were as crowded as ever but, sadly, this was the exception to the rule. On 8 June Trefriw was invaded by 3,000 employees of Messrs Bibby & Company of Liverpool, who travelled to and from Llanrwst in four special trains. Fields were rented, marquees erected and 100 local waiters recruited to serve the meals. Sports were held and entertainment provided by a brass band and a male-voice choir, but rain fell incessantly all day. Rain continued to fall throughout the summer and things reached a nadir at the beginning of August when the region was swept by the worst summer gales in living memory. Parts of Conway were flooded, many boats were damaged or wrecked, and the steamer service was suspended.

Things were further complicated between 21 and 27 June when some exceptional tides meant that the steamers were unable get even as far as Tal-y-Cafn and, in an unprecedented move, the service was cancelled altogether. In an attempt to claw back some profit, the steamers continued until 4 October when *King George* was laid up and *Prince George* was dispatched to Port Dinorwic for a major overhaul following what was described as 'topsy-turvy' and 'disastrous' season.

Full house at Deganwy. *Trefriw Belle* lies alongside her pon toon close to the beach while the three St George's Company's paddlers, *St George, King George* and *Prince George*, are moored abreast at jetty. In the background a trading vessel beats slowly upstream on the rising tide. (Crawford Alexander)

The St George's Company was able to survive the inevitable dip in profits, but it seems that Trefriw Belle Steamship Company was not. Although other factors may have been involved, it seems reasonable to assume that appalling weather and consequent loss of income must have contributed to Capt. Edwards' decision to withdraw his two steamers at the end of the season. Mysterious to the end, *Trefriw Belle* simply disappears from history and no record of her fate has yet been discovered. *Jubilee* was laid up in St George's Harbour at Deganwy and is thought to have had her machinery removed at some time during the First World War. Becoming steadily more derelict, she remained in the same berth for 9 years until, during 1921, she was cleared of a huge quantity of mud and moved to Crossfield's boatyard at Conway where she was converted into a storage hulk for two large motor yachts called *Llys Helig*. Her register was formally closed in May 1922.

The *Llys Heligs* were owned by W.E. Corlett, a Liverpool lawyer who had fallen in love with Conway during his time as a pupil at Conwy College. His first *Llys Helig*, a 35ft centreboard sloop built by Crossfields in 1909, was succeeded by a fine 54ft gaff ketch built in 1912 by A.M. Dickie of Tarbert. As he grew more wealthy his yachts increased in size and *Llys Helig (III)* was a second-hand, twin-screw yacht built by Rennie-Forrestt at Wivenhoe in 1913 and measuring 79.5ft overall. She was succeeded by *Llys Helig (IV)*, a splendid, brand new 107ft by 19.1ft by 10.3ft ocean-going vessel built by Thornycroft of Southampton which was delivered during 1922. During 1931 Corlett also acquired an even larger yacht,

The only known picture of *Jubilee* on the Conwy shows her laid up in a mud berth after her withdrawal from service in 1912. She is painted in the colours of the Trefriw Belle Steamship Company, but looking very neglected.

the 344-ton *Anna Marie*, which he renamed *Llys Helig (V)* before re-selling her almost immediately to a gentleman in London who renamed her *Northern Lights*. *Jubilee* served several of these yachts in turn and was used to store the anthracite, which was used to fire their galleys and heating systems, along with other items of ship's gear. Except when absent on their annual cruises, the successive yachts lay on moorings off Twthill Point with *Jubilee* alongside, and the ill-assorted pair became a familiar part of the local scenery. Following the death of Mr Corlett at the age of 94, *Llys Helig* was sold and left the river in 1960. *Jubilee* was towed up through the Conwy bridges for the last time and beached on the mudflats at the mouth of the Gyffin Brook, where she was eventually broken up.

During 1913 further concerns regarding the navigation arose when the Aluminium Corporation began to dig a canal from the river to their works at Dolgarrog. The St George's Company argued that the canal, which had a minimum depth of 2ft 9in and a rise of 4ft at high water on a 13ft tide, must inevitably abstract a significant proportion of the flooding tide and would therefore reduce the water level in the upper reaches. In addition, the river to the north and south of the point where the canal was being dug was already particularly shallow and the steamers often grounded on their way upstream. They asserted that, unless lock gates were fitted to the canal entrance, the reduced water levels would prevent the steamers from reaching Trefriw on many days, and that the company would suffer severe financial loss. Since many passengers who were staying in the village or had made

The hull of the *Jubilee* in use as a storage hulk for the yacht *Llys Helig (IV)* at Conwy sometime after 1922.

their outward journey by coach or rail were dependent on the steamers for their return journey, it was essential that a reliable timetable be maintained.

The Aluminium Corporation employed a consulting engineer who took soundings in the river, argued that there was plenty of water and attempted to blame any problems on silting at Trefriw. Captain Roberts pointed out that the soundings had been taken on a day when the river was swollen with rain water, and were therefore invalid. He also insisted that he had no difficulty in swinging the steamers on any tide when he was able to reach Trefriw. He unsuccessfully requested a Board of Trade enquiry but, since the canal was already being dug, the matter was something of a *fait accompli*. The lock gates were not provided, the river level dropped a little and, henceforth, the passage of the upper river on neap tides became slightly more difficult and the number of trips terminating at Tal-y-Cafn increased.

The company's other correspondence with the Board of Trade, although concerning a very serious subject, had a distinctly humorous tone. When the RMS *Titanic* had foundered in April 1912 following her infamous encounter with an iceberg, some 1,600 of her passengers and crew had drowned largely due to the lack of sufficient lifeboats. Following the inquest into the tragedy, new legislation had been passed requiring all passenger ships to carry additional lifeboats and lifesaving apparatus. The River Conway steamers, however, were scarcely bigger than lifeboats themselves and the directors wrote to the Board of Trade seeking an exemption. Their letter read:

> The channel used by these steamers is so narrow that expert steering is necessary to prevent vessels running on to the sandbanks on either side of the channel so that, should any untoward incident arise the vessel would immediately be grounded on a perfectly safe sandbank … from where the passengers could walk ashore when the tide receded or even before as the boats draw less than 3ft of water. A small boat would not be of any material use, besides being considerably inconvenient to place.

The Board of Trade sent an official to look into the matter and, after due consideration, conceded to Capt. Roberts' request. One small battle had been won and none of the river steamers were ever fitted with lifeboats.

Residents of Trefriw were saddened by the death, at the age of 81, of Rev. John Gower who, in addition to serving as their rector for the past 44 years, had been such a moving force in the development of the village. As chairman of the Development Committee and as a private investor, he had presided over the transformation of Trefriw from a sleepy 'lotus land' into a bustling and far-famed destination – it was perhaps fitting that he passed away before the horrors of the First World War changed things for ever.

With all opposition gone, and blessed by more favourable weather, the St George's Company enjoyed a successful 1913 season which extended from

11 June until 30 September. The river service returned to its calm and familiar rhythm and, with a maximum of three boats operating, Trefriw Quay was quieter than it had been for a decade. Although the village would never again witness the spectacle of five steamers arriving on the same tide, both the river trip and the attractions ashore remained as popular; the steamers were filled to capacity during the high season and Trefriw was positively crowded with health and pleasure seekers. Indeed, although nobody realised it at the time, the Edwardian summer of 1913 was to denote the high water mark for both the St George's Company and the delightful spa village.

Notes

1. Editorial in *North Wales Weekly News*, 21 July 1905.
2. Ibid.
3. Editorial in *North Wales Weekly News*, 16 April 1906.
4. Editorial in *North Wales Weekly News*, 10 August 1906.
5. Dorr, J., 'A Week in Wales', in *Atlantic Monthly*, vol. 62, issue 371 (September 1888) and later in *The Flower of England's Face: Sketches of English Travel* (London & New York, 1895).
6. *Trefriw Chalybeate Wells, North Wales: The Richest Iron Water Known* (Trefriw, 1908).
7. Ibid.
8. Ibid.
9. Ibid.

Waiting for the tide. Engineer 'Huw Black' Williams undertakes routine maintenance work on board *King George* as she lays alongside the Conwy landing stage at low water. Astern of her, *Prince George* can be seen moored to the lay-by piles.

Gradual Decline, 1914–40

The year 1914 dawned with the promise of another excellent season. *Prince George* and *King George*, having undergone their usual refits and trials, entered service at Whitsun and, under clear blue skies, carried heavy loads throughout June and July. *St George (II)* had proved so frustratingly unreliable that the decision was made not to commission her at all. Instead she was left on her slipway inside the company's double-bayed shed at Conwy where, as things turned out, she was to remain until 1920.

On the international stage, however, tensions were rising. Europe was divided into rival camps and defensive alliances, whose complex inter-relationships and burgeoning armed forces meant that the slightest spark might ignite a conflict. That spark came on 28 June when Austrian Archduke Franz Ferdinand and his wife were assassinated at Sarajevo. Events followed quickly. On 26 July Austria–Hungary declared war on Serbia, by the end of the month Russia had mobilised and on 3 August Germany declared war on France and demanded free passage through Belgium. Belgium refused and, on 4 August, Britain entered the war in her defence. The First World War had begun.

The wave of public alarm which followed the declaration of war was compounded by the withdrawal of many railway services during the initial mobilisation. With all vestiges of holiday spirit destroyed, visitors quickly deserted the North Wales resorts to return to their homes and the company's passenger figures experienced a catastrophic fall. All around the coast excursion steamer services – including that between Liverpool and Llandudno – were suspended and the steamers pressed into Admiralty service as minesweepers, patrol vessels and troopships.

On a damp day at Deganwy *King George* has already cast off and swung round to head upstream for Conwy and Trefriw while, hands on hips, *Prince George*'s skipper waits patiently for his last few passengers to arrive from the railway station. On board both of the steamers the passengers are huddled towards the stern under the shelter of the canvas awnings. On the beach, two children watch the fascinating, daily ritual of departure.

On the Conwy, however, things were rather different. The company's three ships were too small and specialised to be used at sea and were therefore never requisitioned. The patriotic fervour surrounding the departure of the first British troops to Europe was followed by a return to a sort of uneasy normality. North Wales was under no immediate threat of invasion or bombardment and, in the mistaken belief that 'it would all be over by Christmas', holidaymakers began drifting back to the area. On the Conwy, custom began to pick up again and the steamers were kept in service until the end of the season.

In the spring of 1915 the two paddlers appeared again, and were to do so each summer throughout the First World War. Although many local men (including several employees of the company) had been called up and the *North Wales Weekly News* contained regular, heart-rending casualty lists, the horrors of the war may have seemed somewhat remote to many and people still took holidays. Servicemen home on leave must have relished the calm of the beautiful Conwy valley, and the service continued on a satisfactory basis. The profit and loss accounts for the period 1913–18 show clearly that, interestingly, after an initial dip in 1915, income, profits and dividends rose steadily to far exceed their pre-war levels.

YEAR	INCOME	EXPENDITURE	NET PROFIT	DIVIDEND
1913	£1,230	£944	£286	8 per cent
1914	Unavailable	Unavailable	Unavailable	
1915	£863	£821	£42	5 per cent
1916	£1,192	£742	£450	10 per cent
1917	£1,549	£877	£672	15 per cent
1918	£1,998	£1,050	£948	20 per cent

At the beginning of the war the company had a share capital of £3,000, made up of sixty fully paid up shares of £50 each. A full list of shareholders has not been located, but we know that it included Miss Gwen Roberts of Vine Cottage, Trefriw (4); Messrs Roberts & Company (Comprising William, Robert Owen, Mrs Kate Whalley and Miss Winifred Roberts, who held 5½ between them, and Robert who was allocated ½); Mr P.G. Thorne of Warrington (2); Abraham Leach (2) and Ephraim Wood of Conwy (1), together with all of the directors.

The long-serving Mr Pollitt died during 1912 and Mr Charles Lees had succeeded him as chairman. The other directors were Capt. William Roberts (manager), Capt. Robert Owen Roberts, Mr W.M. Sever and Mr J.H. Dunkerley. The secretary was Mr J.W. Post. It is interesting to note that Robert, the third Captain Roberts, is not listed and seems by this time to have been far less active in the affairs of the company. Unfortunately Mr Lees died in 1913 and was replaced as chairman by Mr Sever. No new directors were added. Capt. W. Roberts and Mr Post received an annual salary of £10 each and the Chairman £7. In addition, Capt. William and Capt. Robert Owen received £2 5s 0d per week as their wages for skippering the *King George* and *Prince George* respectively.

The company's assets – comprising the three ships, landing stages and plant – were valued at £3,200 less 6 per cent depreciation in 1913 but only £1,767 less 10 per cent depreciation by 1918. Its registered office was listed as 'The Offices, The Quay, Conway' and it is interesting to note that from 1913 onwards the 's' was dropped from the company title, which was henceforth given as 'The St George S.S. Co. Ltd'.

During 1916 a rolling mill was added to the Dolgarrog aluminium works and production continued to grow. The Aluminium Corporation obtained permission to build a branch line to the works, crossing the river on the new Dolgarrog Bridge. Once again Capt. Roberts opposed the application on grounds that the new structure would further impede navigation, but his pleas fell on deaf ears. The new branch line opened on 17 December 1916 and was initially served by two locomotives, ten 12-ton wagons and two passenger carriages. The new Dolgarrog Halt was opened near the junction with the main line. Free morning and evening travel was allowed across the bridge until 1932 when the line reverted to

Prince George leads *King George* upstream towards Tal-y-Cafn and the dramatic mountains which form the backdrop to the west bank of the River Conwy.

freight only. Meanwhile, the new bridge provided another cause for the steamers to lower their funnels as they passed up and down the river. This task required two men and, with the steamer travelling fast with the tide under her, had to be carried out with split-second timing. Too soon and the passengers on deck would be enveloped in clouds of sooty smoke. Too late and the funnel would have struck the bridge with catastrophic results.

In September 1916 a new 21-year lease was signed with the Office of Woods for the continuing use of Deganwy pier at a rent of £5 per annum, along with permission to build a small extension, rendered necessary by increased silting, which was making it difficult for the steamers to get alongside on their return from Trefriw.

During the winter of 1916–17, *King George* was sent to Port Dinorwic for a major refit, arriving back in Conwy just in time for the start of the season.

As the country returned to a peacetime footing following the armistice of 1918, the river service continued on its familiar seasonal pattern and, initially at least, seemed to be continuing on the upward trajectory begun during the war years. At the end of the 1920 season gross receipts from passengers had reached £2,546, but unfortunately costs had also increased dramatically in comparison to the previous year. Coal rose from £60 to £114, wages and sailing expenses from £414 to £778 and material and repairs from £98 to £419. These additional outgoings saw the net profit reduced to £686, but a 20 per cent dividend was still declared.

Meanwhile Capt. William Roberts, who had been unwell for some time, concluded that he would no longer be able to take an active part in the company's affairs. At a directors' meeting on 19 April 1919 he formally relinquished the role

Immediately after the end of the First World War demand for steamer trips was extremely heavy. In this sequence of photos thought to have been taken in 1919, we see:

A long queue of passengers, many of whom will have arrived by train at Deganwy station, queuing at the entrance to the St George SS Company's landing stage. The small boat moored towards the Conwy Morfa shore is a survivor of those used by the army for training for beach landings during the war. (John Evans)

Passengers cross the landing stage to fill the decks of *Prince George* (outside) and *King George*. (John Evans)

Crowded to capacity, *King George* pulls away from the landing stage to follow her fleet-mate upstream. It is easy to see why, on days such as this, calls at Conwy often had to be abandoned and there was an urgent need for an 'overflow' boat which could be called up at short notice. (John Evans)

of manager and passed the reins to his cousin, Robert Owen, who also replaced him as skipper of *King George*. William had been at the helm of one or other of the company's steamers since 1891 and his retirement was a significant moment for the maritime community of Conwy. He went on to enjoy a 20-year retirement before his death on 26 January 1927 and is remembered in his old age enjoying his favourite occupation of hand-line fishing from a small boat in the river. *Prince George* was taken over by Capt. Robert Hughes, known locally as 'Bob Cyrnol' (Cyrnol being Welsh for colonel) on account of his long period (1903–14) in command of the sailing ship *Colonel Gamble*, previously owned by Robert Owen and wrecked off Port Colmon in 1914. He had also sailed in the *Agnes* (1896–98), *Pilgrim* (1898–1903) and *Tryfan* (1914–19).

The cranky motor vessel *St George (II)*, still on the slipway she had occupied since 1913, was put up for sale for £850 plus £50 to cover the costs of recommissioning. Several brokers and potential buyers were contacted but nobody showed any real interest in the eccentric vessel until September 1919 when enquiries were received from a P. N. Witter Esq. of Liverpool. Eventually, on 30 April 1920, she was sold for £600 to John Magee of Warrenpoint, County Down, under mortgage to the Belfast Banking Company. Taking such a mechanically unreliable vessel on the long crossing of the Irish Sea would not have been for the faint-hearted and one wonders whether she was towed across. Whatever the case, she arrived safely and was re-registered at Newry on 1 September 1920. Following the fitting of a more reliable diesel engine, she was based at Warrenpoint on Carlingford Lough,

Captain Robert Owen Roberts, who took over the management of the company in April 1919. The small boy in the photograph is his son, also named Robert Owen but known as RO (1902–67). RO did not take up a life at sea but worked on the railways. (Elsbeth Pears)

and served on the ferry crossing to Omeath as well as offering short cruises. She was not finally broken up until 1950.

For a few years after the war, the two remaining paddle steamers faced slight competition from a small motor boat carrying about twenty-four passengers, which was operated from Deganwy by a Mr Carl Parkinson. Local boatmen continued to offer short trips in the large rowing boats which were used on the Deganwy ferry in summer and for mussel fishing in winter. If the steamers were full, they would offer to take anyone left behind and would row gently upstream as far as the tide would carry them and return on the ebb. The St George's steamers prospered and in 1923 £700 was spent on a major refit to the *Prince George*.

On 24 July 1924, after a short illness, Capt. Robert Owen Roberts died. As the company's manager and senior skipper he left a yawning gap in the organisation, which led to some profound reorganisation. The St George's Steamship Company Ltd went into voluntary liquidation and its assets were sold to a new company of the same name. The bills of sale for the two paddlers were dated 29 August and on 6 September Vincent Crossfield, son of the boatbuilder John Crossfield, became the new company's manager. His sister, Isabella Mary, was appointed company secretary.

Robert Owen's death meant that, for the first time since the original company was formed, neither of the ships was commanded by a member of the family. Robert Hughes retained command of *Prince George* while the other new skippers, despite being called Roberts, were not related to the steamer-owning dynasty. *King George* was initially taken over by William Rolant Roberts – known as 'Willi Rolant' – of Deganwy. He had served as a naval reservist during the First World War

Captain Robert Owen Roberts with his
daughters Elinor and Gwen in a photo
taken shortly before his death. It is a family
story that the hedge by which they are
standing was supported by the deck rails
taken from the old paddle-steamer
St George when she was broken up in 1910.
(Elsbeth Pears)

and had then become skipper of the luxury yacht *Ena*, which was owned by
Mr Domingo De Larrinaga of the Liverpool shipping line. The De Larrinagas
kept a holiday property called 'Pendower' at West Shore Llandudno, and used
the yacht when they were in residence. After a few seasons Willi Rolant passed
command of *King George* to William Morris Roberts, one of the river pilots, who
remained with her until Robert Hughes took over in the mid-1930s.

The ships' engineers who laboured largely unseen down below, stoking the boilers and tending the engines, were also hugely respected local characters. John Owen
Bach (Small John Owen) spent many years on the *Prince George*, while 'Huw Black'
Williams went to Northwich in 1907 to commission the *King George* and served on
board for most of her working life. For a period in the 1920s he passed control to
Ned Palmer but, when ill health forced the latter to retire, 'Huw Black' took over
again and remained with the ship until her final sailing.

One of the new board's first priorities was to consider the under-capacity of
the steamers. Since 1920 it had, once again, been by no means uncommon for the
two steamers to fill up to their capacity at Deganwy and be forced to bypass the
Conwy call, leaving disappointed passengers on the landing stage. To address this
problem the board decided to acquire a large-capacity, shallow-draught motor
boat which could be called into service quickly on days when the steamers were
full, and would also be available for private charters. Motor-boat engines had
improved considerably since the days of the *St George (II)* and Vincent Crossfield
was confident that no technical problems would be encountered.

At the beginning of 1925 a suitable boat was located at Chester. Named *Princess
Mary* and built in 1920 for and by the Chester Boat Company, she had been

Your visit to N. Wales

is not complete without a Trip down the

Famous Conway River
The Rhine of Wales

THE ST. GEORGE STEAMSHIP CO. LTD.
PADDLE STEAMERS

"KING GEORGE"
"PRINCE GEORGE"

And the MOTOR LAUNCH
"PRINCESS MARY"

WILL SAIL (weather and other circumstances permitting) on one of the most beautiful rivers in Wales between

DEGANWY
CONWAY
TAL-Y-CAFN
TREFRIW

Passing DOLGARROG, the scene of the Welsh Dam Disaster, 1925.

Return Fare 3/-.   Single 2/-.
CHILDREN UNDER 12 YEARS HALF PRICE

Trains and Motor Buses, from Llandudno, Colwyn Bay, Rhyl, Penmaenmawr, Llanfairfechan, Bangor, etc., stop within 3 minutes walk of the Landing Stages at Conway, Deganwy Railway Station and Trefriw.

Bills of Sailing may be obtained from all Boarding Establishments, Hotels, Restaurants, Tobacconists, Pier Gates, Railway Stations, and the Kiosk on the Promenade, or from the Swimming Instructors at Llandudno, Rhos-on-Sea, Colwyn Bay or the Bathing Vans.

ASK FOR BILL OF SAILINGS, OR APPLY DIRECT TO THE

MANAGER - - V. CROSSFIELD
THE QUAY, CONWAY
Telegrams: "Crossfield." Phone 157.

NOTE.—The Motor Launch "PRINCESS MARY" MAY BE CHARTERED FOR PRIVATE PARTIES.

An advertisement taken from the new guidebook issued by the reformed St George's Steamship Company Ltd of 1924.

running seasonal pleasure trips on the Dee. Measuring 40ft by 9ft by 2ft, she was powered by an 18hp Thornycroft engine which gave her a service speed of 8½ knots. She was steered from amidships and had a Board of Trade certificate for seventy passengers, who were given some protection from the elements by a full length, permanent, polished wood awning. *Princess Mary* was quickly purchased and moved to Conwy in time for the beginning of the 1925 season.

In a taped interview Conwy mussel fisherman Mr Rowland Hughes recalled his first job on board the Trefriw steamers and threw interesting light on the working practices of the day. His uncle, Capt. Robert Hughes, had told him that, provided he could get permission to leave school early, he would guarantee him a job as trainee deckhand on board *King George* for 3 or 4 years and then take him trawling during the winters. Rowland Hughes joined the ship in about 1923, aged 12, while his pal Bobby Williams did the equivalent job on board *Prince George*. Mr Hughes recalled:

Well, our first job was in the morning, about seven o'clock, when we had to carry six hundredweight of coal on our backs from the shed, which was on the quay then, to the two steamers. Carry six each and then we had to wash down, hose down all the seats, and then we were allowed to go home for breakfast which took half an hour I suppose. Then we went back on the boat and cleaned all the seats up, cleaned all the brasses up, made the boat ship-shape ready for whenever we were working, because we had to work with the tide. So whenever the tide was right our boat was ready for it …

We used to go with the 'King' to Deganwy. The LMS [London, Scottish & Midland Railway] ran a special train for the Trefriw steamers. The tide was roughly twenty minutes or half an hour later each day, so the steamers ran half an hour or twenty minutes later each day. My job was to go to the signal box in Deganwy and, as the train came through, the chap in charge of the train, not the driver … he used to shout, 'Two hundred and thirty for Trefriw' and then he'd say to me, 'Two hundred and thirty, tell your uncle'. I would run down to Uncle Will and say 'there's two hundred and thirty, Uncle Will'. So he said 'Right oh, we'll have another steamer' … He used to blow on the old hooter, three blows and the 'Prince' had to come up or the spare boat 'Princess Mary' and we'd fill them. The other two boats would be full and all the fishermen in Conway would then go to the St George's stage and offer to perhaps hundreds of people, 'We'll take you up to Tal-y-Cafn', that's halfway up, 'We'll take ten in each boat'. And many and many a time [they] used to take them up to Tal-y-Cafn … used to charge a shilling each to go all the way to Tal-y-Cafn, give them an hour there and row them back. And that was rowing! … [The passengers] used to come to Llandudno with excursions and things and stay in all the big hotels there. That's why they had the special train, the Trefriw Special they used to call

The motor launch *Princess Mary* as new, from an article in *Motor Boat*, 23 July 1920.

it, coming all the way to Deganwy and dropping the people there. And then she would know within ten minutes when we were coming back … Remember there was no cars in them days.

The passengers were mostly 'fairly well-to-do … very, very nice and very, very well-spoken people' and Mr Hughes remembered them 'coming with a little pillow under their arm, so that they could put it on the seat, you know, to sit down … And my uncle would be very, very conscientious and made certain that there wasn't a speck of dirt going on their dresses.'

On board *King George* there were 'two huge, empty cabins, one for'ard and one aft', with room for about sixty people to shelter on rainy days, although, because there were only small portholes, they would miss the views completely. Others would huddle under the awning on the aft deck. Since Vincent Crossfield became manager, the ships gained all-day licences, and beers and teas were available in the saloons as soon as the ship had cast off. This had proved very popular, since the short stay at Trefriw still made it difficult for all the passengers to obtain refreshments ashore:

There was a hotel right by the landing stage where they used to go and have a cup of tea. Others would kind of run everywhere to try to get a cup of tea, but ninety percent of them didn't get one and that was the idea I think that they brought the bar on to the boat, so that people could have a cup of tea or coffee or a drink on the boat … because we had so many people grumbling. In Trefriw itself the tide only rises very, very little so by the time you were there and you were turned, people would start to embark again … so they had no time to go right to the top of Trefriw where the mills are now, you know, no time at all for that.

Despite the short time ashore, some people inevitably strayed too far from the steamer and missed the homeward sailing.

My uncle … always used to tell the people on our boat, 'Right, you are having twenty minutes ashore … but for every five minutes you are ashore I will blow my hooter.' Now, if we're ashore for twenty minutes he'd blow the hooter four times, now he'd say to them 'Now immediately my hooter's gone for the fourth time we are letting go, and we are going for Conway and you'll have to find your own way home.' I've seen a hundred and thirty, a hundred and forty people down in the offices trying to claim money, half fare, back. He would turn around and he'd call all the crew up and he'd say, 'Now boys, how many times did we use the old hooter, when did we let go to come back home?' and none of them ever had a penny back. He was very good and very honest about that, he made absolutely certain that they knew. After about ten minutes I should think they'd be on their way back to the boat because they'd heard two signals

On a sunny day at Deganwy passengers and crew relax on board *King George* while they await the arrival of a 'steamer special' train. (Eleanor Corkish)

by then, you see. They used to go all over the place. With the old hooter, you see, and with Trefriw being a small place, everybody knew ...

Other correspondents recall that the crew would also sell chocolates from a tray to passengers on deck and that the steamers were regularly joined at Deganwy by a husband, wife and daughter trio who, dressed in white and carrying a portable organ, would sing and play during the return voyage.

Because *Princess Mary* was the spare boat she did not have a full-time crew. Sometimes she would be skippered by Tom Evans or one of the other senior hands from the paddlers but, more often than not, if she was 'whistled up' from Deganwy, Vincent Crossfield and a couple of his joiners would stop what they were doing at the boat yard and take her across.

The year 1925 will also be remembered for the Dolgarrog Dam disaster. On Monday 2 November, after 2 weeks of heavy rain, a breach in a small gravity dam occurred at the Aluminium Corporation's Llyn Eigiau reservoir, high in the hills above Dolgarrog. Thousands of gallons of water were released which flowed down the course of the Porth Llwyd River to another small reservoir, the Coedty, which, unable to contain the extra water, collapsed as well, releasing an even greater quantity of water. As much as 350 million cubic metres of water, mixed with boulders and debris, swept down the mountainside through the hamlet of Porth Llwyd and into Dolgarrog, sweeping the church, houses and villagers away as it went. Sixteen people died and many more would have been killed but for the happy chance that many of them were in the local theatre watching a film that night.

As news of the disaster spread, and despite the exhortations of the police not to do so, sightseers from all over Wales and the Midlands poured into the area and on the following Sunday over 20,000 arrived, causing severe road congestion. Relief funds were set up to assist the many families made homeless and destitute by the disaster, and work pressed ahead to clear debris from the remains of the village. The events had a profound, emotional impact on the area.

The rush of water through Dolgarrog had, of course, carried silt and debris into the main channel of the Conway, and at the start of the 1926 season the steamers had to proceed with great care while they established a modified route through an already difficult section of the river.

The arrival of *Princess Mary* also enabled the season to start far earlier than previously. From 1926 onwards it became the practice to bring the launch out in late April to carry the smaller numbers anticipated until the two paddlers entered service at Whitsun. She opened the season on 29 April and her advertisements, rather ghoulishly, contained the additional line 'Passing Dolgarrog, the scene of the Welsh dam disaster, 1925'. Fares had now risen to 2s single and 3s return, or half that amount when she terminated at Tal-y-Cafn. Further details were to be had from Vincent Crossfield or from Messrs Edwards & Sons, Coal Merchants of Conwy.

King George at Trefriw during the early 1920s. The card is from the Pathe Frères Cinema Ltd, giving rise to the suspicion that it may be a still from a newsreel film made prior to 1925 when the company ceased trading. If so, what was the special occasion? It has even been suggested that the distinguished-looking gentleman on the left could be King George V or Lloyd George! For the moment, however, he remains unidentified.

On 26 April a national miners' strike was called, halting coal production. As attitudes hardened on both sides, the Trade Union Congress (TUC) called a General Strike in support of the miners, to begin at midnight on 3 May, and more than 1.7 million workers downed tools. After the TUC called off the action on 14 May the miners continued to strike until November when they too were forced to return to work with lower wages and longer hours.

During the strike coal supplies were diverted to urgent national needs and the government immediately forbade the bunkering of pleasure steamers. The railways too were badly affected, both by lack of coal and striking workers, and most trains to the seaside resorts were cancelled, along with the steamer service from Liverpool to Llandudno. With no coal and few passengers the two paddle steamers were laid up, leaving the economical *Princess Mary* to provide a one-boat service each day to Trefriw.

Although coal was still strictly rationed, the company was determined to maximize its summer earnings and on 26 June brought the two paddlers back into service, their boilers fired with wood and coke. These alternative fuels clearly proved adequate, for the three vessels remained in service for the rest of the season. The Liverpool–Llandudno service had resumed on 13 June and with rail services gradually returning to normal visitors began to flow back to the area. August Bank Holiday was reported to be as busy as normal and, in a preview of things to come, the number of motor vehicles crossing Conwy Bridge broke all records. The queues were the longest ever seen and the town centre was brought to a virtual halt.

It is easy to forget how rapid the growth of motor transport was in the late 1920s and early 1930s. The number of private cars had risen from 15,900 in 1905 and 20,000 in 1920 to a staggering 1 million by 1930. The famous 1930 Road Traffic Act abolished the 20mph speed limit, introduced the Highway Code, gave local councils the powers to control traffic and, in a very real sense, marked the beginning of the end for the river steamers.

The horse-drawn coaches, landaus, gigs and 'cars' which had served Trefriw so faithfully through the Victorian and Edwardian eras were now but a memory, and had been replaced by faster and more convenient motor bus services, often run in conjunction with the railways. A wide range of coach tours from the major resorts offered visitors the opportunity to see far more of North Wales in a day than had ever been possible before, while the growing band of private car owners could choose to go wherever and whenever they wanted.

By contrast, the constantly changing departure times of the Trefriw steamers began to seem inconvenient and constraining, while the short time ashore prevented passengers from exploring the village and visiting the wells or woollen mill. The public's enthusiasm for the river trip began to wane and the steamers' passenger figures started an inexorable decline.

In Trefriw itself, however, things were far from static. During 1928 a fresh source of medicinal waters had been discovered issuing from an old mine entrance directly behind the Belle Vue Hotel. The waters were rich in iron, sulphur and silicates and promised to have similar healing effects to those at the existing spa. At this point a Mr Carel Hoefftcke and his wife appeared on the scene and went into business with the hotel. Hoefftcke had come from Holland, obtained his naturalisation papers and settled in Thames Ditton back in 1915. Although not medically qualified, he had built up a business designing and manufacturing medical appliances. As early as 1908 he had patented, 'An apparatus for facilitating the putting on of India-rubber gloves', but went on to specialise in leg splints, hip appliances and traction devices. He was the author of a book entitled *The Ambulatory Treatment of Fractures and Diseased Joints* and by 1930 had an office in the prestigious Harley Street, London.

The Belle Vue Hotel was taken over by a London syndicate, which included Hoefftcke, and a number of significant developments took place. The long, six-gabled extension on the north side of the hotel was converted into a 'nursing wing' with special facilities where 'sufferers of rheumatoid arthritis or osteo arthritis, who have been bed-ridden for months or years and want to walk again without pain, can avail themselves of the Hoefftcke ambulatory extension treatment under medical supervision'.[2] On the quay, the old mock-Tudor pavilion from the golf course was rebuilt and a brand new, single-storey building erected containing both bath and treatment rooms. Across the front was a covered veranda and bar where the healing waters were served from taps. Named 'The Belle Vue Spa',

Bound upstream, *King George* passes under the Conwy bridges. (PSPS Archive)

it was officially opened by Sir Arbuthnot Lane, representing the London syndicate, on 26 April 1930. In his speech, Sir Arbuthnot alluded to the fact that Trefriw was 'under a cloud and in a back alley' and hoped that the new complex, marketed as the 'Bellevue Spa and Hotel', would make it once again 'one of the most popular and useful places in the country'.[3]

The new developments received the wholehearted support of the local council. Early in May, Hoefftcke hosted a large meeting at the hotel 'to consider ways and means of restoring the village to its once-enjoyed fame and attractiveness to tourists'. The outcome was the formation of a Publicity Committee which was tasked with raising public awareness of what were regarded as 'not only the strongest waters in Europe, but in the whole world'. A new guidebook was published containing advertisements for local guest houses and businesses, details of the village and its transport links, and emphasising the benefits of the new Bellevue Spa and Hotel.

The proprietors of the old-established Trefriw Wells were unimpressed with the council's support for the newcomers, especially that the new guidebook, which made no mention of the original spa, was titled *Trefriw Spa, The Pearl of Ancient Gwynedd*. They attempted to retain custom by building a small kiosk on the quay from which steamer passengers could purchase doses of bottled chalybeate water during their short stay. They also issued a small guidebook of their own which began with the pointed statement 'Trefriw Wells is not connected in any

A sign of things to come. Motor cars replace the more familiar horse-drawn carriages outside the Trefriw Wells pump room and baths

way, either directly or indirectly, with any Hotel or establishment in the district, and the waters can only be obtained direct from Trefriw Wells'.

The Trefriw Publicity Committee, encouraged by a respectable profit during its first year in existence, published a new edition of its guidebook annually until the war. The Belle Vue Spa and Hotel seem to have prospered but Trefriw, rather than a destination in itself, had become a place to pause while a brief visit was made to the woollen mill or wells during a longer coach or motor-car tour. In a glance back to its glory days, a memorial window to the late Rev. John Gower was opened in the parish church during the summer of 1932, while the two little paddlers and the motor launch continued to maintain the steadily declining river service. It was also during 1932 that, grasping at any straw to boost passenger numbers, the company finally abandoned the three Capt. Roberts' religious principles and introduced Sunday sailings. This caused great distress to 'Huw Black' Williams and other chapel-going members of the crew, but since the ships were their livelihoods, they had little choice but to co-operate.

It is believed that by 1933 passenger figures had fallen to such an extent that the Vincent Crossfield and the board decided that a three-ship service could no

The buildings of the new Belle Vue Spa on Trefriw Quay, viewed from the Belle Vue Hotel.
The terracotta balustrades of 1906–08 are intact but the former 'stand' for horse-drawn
carriages has been converted into a lawn. (Karen Black)

The official opening of the new Belle Vue Spa, 26 April 1930. (Karen Black)

TREFRIW
SPA.

✺✺✺✺✺

𝔗𝔥𝔢 𝔓𝔢𝔞𝔯𝔩 𝔬𝔣 𝔄𝔫𝔠𝔦𝔢𝔫𝔱 𝔊𝔴𝔶𝔫𝔢𝔡𝔡.

✺✺✺✺✺✺✺

SUPPLEMENTARY
GUIDE,
1934.

Bellevue Spa & Hotel, Trefriw

Bellevue Hotel and Nursing Wing

The Bellevue Spa sulphur-iron water (ferrous-sulphate), described by medical men as the purest & most highly concentrated in the world, is collected from an ancient Roman mine & bottled according to medical advice, so as to prevent any air coming in contact with the iron water.

For home spa treatment a seven weeks course of the Bellevue Spa waters can be sent direct to the patient.

Sufferers from Rheumatoid Arthritis or Osteo Arthritis, who have been bed-ridden for months or years & want to walk again without pain, can avail themselves of the Hoefftcke Ambulatory Extension Treatment. Special facilities are provided for those requiring this treatment in the nursing wing under medical supervision.

This treatment has been favourably commented upon by many eminent medical men in their books and also in the medical papers. (See "The Medical Press & Circular", April 27 1932, pp. 345-351, "The Ambulatory Treatment of Fractures and Diseased Joints by the Hoefftcke Extension Splint" ; also August 2 1933, "The Ambulatory Treatment and Manipulation, with Extension for Diseased Joints" by Carel A. Hoefftcke 7, Harley Street, London, W.1. and Bellevue Spa, Trefriw.)

For reprints and further particulars apply :-
The Secretary, Bellevue Spa, Trefriw, North Wales.

The front and back covers of a 1934 guidebook describing Carel Hoefftcke's new Belle Vue Spa and the rebranded hotel with its 'hospital wing'. (Karen Black)

longer be justified. As the oldest ship in the fleet and the one requiring the great-est maintenance, the pretty *Prince George* of 1891 was therefore not commissioned, leaving *King George* and *Princess Mary* to carry on alone.

The chances of disposing of such an elderly and specialised steamer to anyone other than the scrap merchant seemed unlikely, but a surviving memorandum dated 26 September 1935[4] shows that the company was quick to grasp at any possibility. Addressed to S. Dawson Ware, Esq., c/o Messrs M&M Needham of Coleman Street, London, it read:

Dear Sir,
The Harbour Authority at Deganwy has handed your letter over to us regard-ing transport of coal by river to Trefriw.

We have a shallow draft paddle steamer for sale which has been out of service for a few years owing to slackness in trade, which we would sell cheap.

This could be made to carry cargo at very little cost. She was built specially shallow for this river. She would draw 4ft 6' with a cargo of 25 tons. We would be pleased to show you over her at any time.

The maximum draft to go up the river on spring tides is 7ft. and on 24ft tides 4ft 6'.

Yours faithfully,
St George Steamship Co. Ltd.

Whilst the precise nature of Mr Ware's plans remain obscure, it is intriguing to think that 66 years after the demise of *St Winifred*'s packet service back in 1869, someone should consider re-introducing a river-borne cargo service to Trefriw. Had it happened it would indeed have been a case of the wheel turning full circle! Unfortunately the sale did not go ahead and at some stage *Prince George* was removed from her normal slipway in Conwy, towed up river and placed on the company's heavy, drying mooring in the shelter of Cymryd Point. With the top section of her funnel and most of her deck gear removed she was left there, slowly deteriorating, to await her fate.

The joint capacity of *King George* and *Princess Mary* proved suitable for the availa-ble custom, and over the next 4 years they continued to follow their familiar routine, passing their silent, erstwhile fleet mate on every trip. On 7 January 1939, as war clouds gathered once more over Europe, the last link with the 'old days' was finally broken when Capt. Robert Roberts died at the age of 79. Living in his house on the corner of Berry and Chapel Streets, Conway, he had enjoyed a long retirement and was affectionately remembered as having a perpetual smile.

The declaration of war on 3 September 1939 was followed by a period remembered as the 'Phoney War' due to the relative lack of military operations by the Western

Allies against the German Reich. Pleasure steamers all around the British coast were once again called up to serve the flag but, as in 1914, the Conwy steamers were unaffected and ran until the end of the season. For *Prince George*, however, the war meant the end. With the rising demand for scrap metal she was sold for £80 to a Rhyl firm of scrap metal merchants and broken up on the foreshore at the Conway end of the Marine Walk, within sight of the St George's jetty. The work took place during the winter of 1939 and the last pieces were removed in January 1940. Vincent Crossfield recorded his regret that she had gone, but explained that she had been out of use for so long that she would have been too expensive to restore and that, with the steady fall in demand for the river trips, the company had no further use for her.

By the spring of 1940 the 'Phoney War' was over and reality had begun to bite. Air raid precautions and blackouts had been imposed in the Conwy valley, evacuees from Liverpool and further afield were beginning to stream into the area and petrol shortages meant a sharp decline in the use of private cars and motor coaches. On mainland Europe the Battle of France began in earnest on 10 May, but back in Conwy there was a determination that the Whitsun holidays should proceed as normally as possible. The railway companies announced plans to issue cut-price tickets spread over the holiday period and both *King George* and *Princess Mary* were brought into service. In the event, the government cancelled the Whitsun holiday at short notice and asked people not to travel due to alarming developments in Europe where the Allied armies were being pushed back rapidly towards the Channel ports. Operation Dynamo, the evacuation from Dunkirk between 27 May and 4 June, was followed by the Battle of Britain and the start of major bombing raids, but throughout the period the two boats continued to operate.

King George, with 'Bob Cyrnol' Hughes at the helm and 'Huw Black' Williams in the engine room, remained free from any government restrictions until

Looking extremely forlorn, and with the top of her funnel removed, *Prince George* lies on her heavy moorings off Cymryd Point awaiting her fate. (Lindsay Gordon, Princes Arms Hotel)

Deckhand Cyril 'Mulligans' Davies, Capt. 'Bob Cyrnol' Hughes and engineer 'Huw Black' Williams on board *King George*. (Eleanor Corkish)

During August 1935 engineer 'Huw Black' Williams poses with his grand-daughter Eleanor on the deck of the old *Bluebell*, which acted as the floating pier head and storage hulk at the Conwy landing stage. He died in 1945 at the age of 81. (Eleanor Corkish)

mid-August 1940 and brought a welcome splash of colour and normality to the river. The *North Wales Weekly News* carried an article praising the rural delights of a trip on the paddler and the fact that the censor had not seen fit to restrict the publication of sailing bills; ironically this appeared on 29 August, the morning after 160 German aircraft had made their first major bombing raid on Liverpool. The raids continued for the following three nights and it is almost certainly during this period that *King George* made her last sailing. 'Huw Black' and other crew members recalled that they were loading passengers at Deganwy when a German bomber, returning from a raid on Liverpool, was pursued low overhead by RAF fighters. Alerted by the incident, the authorities decided that it was too dangerous to allow sailings to continue, and the ship was withdrawn immediately.

Thus, stripped of their portable gear and prepared for a long lay-up, *King George* and *Princess Mary* were sent up river and beached at Benarth to await developments.

Notes

1. Mr Rowland Hughes, 'Conway Mussel Picking and Pleasure Boats', Gwynedd Archives, Caernarfon, XM/T/434.
2. Trefriw Spa, *The Pearl of Ancient Gwynedd*, Trefriw Spa Publicity Committee, Supplementary Guide (1934).
3. *North Wales Weekly News*, 1 May 1930.
4. Conway Archives, CX90/2.

FINEST SCEN... ...N NORTH WALES

The Steamers of the St. George S.S. Co. Ltd.
"KING GEORGE" & M.L. "PRINCESS MARY"
Will ply Daily, Sundays included (Weather and other causes permitting)
on one of the most Beautiful Rivers in Wales, between

Deganwy, Conway and Trefriw

JULY, 1939				
Date of Sailing.	Train from Llandudno.	Boat leaves Deganwy.	Boat leaves Conway.	Boat leaves Trefriw.
21 Friday	1 10 p.m.	1 35 p.m.	1 45 p.m.	3 50 p.m.
22 Saturday	2 0 ,,	2 30 ,,	2 40 ,,	4 40 ,,
23 Sunday	3 20 ,,	3 35 ,,	3 45 ,,	5 35 ,,
24 Monday	4 25 ,,	4 40 ,,	4 50 ,,	6 40 ,, *
25 Tuesday	5 25 ,,	5 45 ,,	5 55 ,,	7 45 ,, *
28 Friday	8 5 a.m.	8 15 a.m.	8 25 a.m.	10 15 a.m.
29 Saturday	8 45 ,,	8 55 ,,	9 5 ,,	11 5 ,,
31 Monday	10 0 ,,	10 15 ,,	10 25 ,,	12 25 p.m.
AUGUST, 1939				
1 Tuesday	10 40 a.m.	10 55 a.m.	11 5 a.m.	1 5 p.m.
2 Wed.	11 15 ,,	11 30 ,,	11 40 ,,	1 35 ,,
3 Thursday	11 35 ,,	12 0 noon	12 10 p.m.	2 10 ,,
4 Friday	12 12 p.m.	12 35 p.m.	12 45 ,,	2 40 x
5 Saturday	12 45 ,,	1 5 ,,	1 15 ,,	3 10 ,,
6 Sunday	12 50 ,,	1 45 ,,	1 55 ,,	3 45 ,,
7 Monday	2 0 ,,	2 25 ,,	2 35 ,,	4 25 ,,
8 Tuesday	2 55 ,,	3 15 ,,	3 25 ,,	5 15 ,, *
9 Wed.	4 0 ,,	4 25 ,,	4 35 ,,	6 25 ,, *
10 Thursday	5 25 ,,	5 40 ,,	5 50 ,,	7 40 ,, *
14 Monday	8 43 a.m.	9 20 a.m.	9 30 a.m.	11 30 a.m.
15 Tuesday	9 35 ,,	10 0 ,,	10 10 ,,	12 20 p.m.
16 Wed.	10 40 ,,	10 55 ,,	11 5 ,,	1 10 ,,

Evening Trip to View Illuminations.—Aa S.S. King George. Fare 1/-.
* Doubtful if Steamer reaches Trefriw.   † Talycafn only.
Fares : Single 2/- ; Return 3/-.   Children under 12 Half Price.
Steamer takes approximately 1 hour and 20 minutes each way.

x A Concession will be granted to holders of L.M.S. 10/6 Holiday Contract Tickets on x
Return Fare. Buses and Trains from Llandudno, Colwyn Bay, Bangor, Penmaen
mawr & Rhyl, etc., stop within 3 minutes' walk of the Landing Stages at Conway
and Deganwy (near the Station). For further information apply to the Manager :
V. CROSSFIELD, THE QUAY, CONWAY. Tel. 157

R. E. Jones & Bros., Ltd., Printers, Conway

A sailing bill for *King George* and *Princess Mary* covering the last days of peace in July and August 1939. Despite the fact that she had been laid up for several years, a sketch of *Prince George* still heads the bill.

A happy crowd throngs the deck of *King George* at Trefriw shortly before the outbreak of war while local children look on. (Vaughan Roberts)

King George moored at Deganwy towards the end of her career.

Capt. 'Bob Cyrnol' Hughes tends *King George*'s ropes alongside Trefriw Quay while engineer 'Huw Black' Williams stands at the wheel. (Doris Williams)

King George approaching Tal-y-Cafn bridge on her way downstream from Trefriw to Conwy.

A little further downstream, with Tal-y-Cafn bridge astern, *King George* sweeps round the deep-water channel on the outside of the bend beneath Bodnant Hall.

Heading downstream, *King George* keeps close to the east bank in order to avoid one of the river's many sandbanks.

King George leaving Deganwy, 20 August 1939.

King George preparing for her final season in service on Whit Monday, 13 May 1940. Too large to fit on the company's covered slipway, she has been placed 'on the blocks' at Benarth Beach for bottom painting. Her waterline has been drawn in and a start has been made on applying the anti-fouling paint. (Malcolm McRonald)

Almost the end. Taken on a gloomy day from the road above Trefriw Quay, this evocative photograph shows valuable detail of *King George*'s deck layout and the primitive, un-railed gangplank. The four crew members are clustered around the steering position and paddlebox while passengers shelter beneath the deck awning. The picture is believed to have been taken in 1940. (Lindsay Gordon, Princes Arms Hotel)

The last crew of a Conwy paddle steamer? Captain 'Bob Cyrnol' Hughes and engineer 'Huw Black' Williams stand at the wheel, with deckhand Bob Widnes. The gentleman on the left has not yet been identified. The picture is believed to have been taken in the summer of 1940, possibly on *King George*'s very last trip. (John Evans)

8

The Priest, the Scrapman
and the Motor Boats, from 1941

At Trefriw the BelleVue Spa and Hotel closed its doors and Carel Hoefftcke, whose wife had died in 1939, left the area. Between 1941 and 1945 the hotel was taken over by the Merchant Marine Service Association and was used as a retirement home for elderly seamen and their wives who had been evacuated from the association's Mariner's Park welfare village at Wallasey. The twenty-nine who died during their stay in the Conwy valley were buried in the graveyard high above the village, where a fitting memorial may be seen to this day. The Trefriw Wells remained open and continued to advertise in the press but, with the river service suspended and the tourist trade gone, both the quay and the village were quieter than they had been for over a century.

By the summer of 1942 the St George's Steamship Company Ltd, watching its assets slowly deteriorate on a mud bank, had concluded that there was little realistic possibility of trading profitably after the war and had placed itself into voluntary liquidation. Logic suggests that *King George* should have been sold and cut up as a contribution to the wartime scrap metal drive but instead, in the most unlikely of transactions, she was sold on 30 August 1942 to Father Sylvester Baron, the Catholic parish priest of St Mary's Church, Rhyl. *Princess Mary* and the landing rights at Trefriw Quay also seem to have been included and colourful rumours circulated that an order of nuns were somehow also involved in the deal.

One may reasonably enquire why a Catholic priest and a group of nuns should wish to purchase an elderly paddle steamer in the middle of a world war! Father Baron had something of a reputation for becoming involved in various eccentric business ventures, often in partnership with some of his relatives

Father Sylvester Baron, the parish priest of St Mary's Church, Rhyl, who purchased the paddle steamer *King George* on 30 August 1942.

in Lancashire, and it seems that his excursion into ship owning was one such. Realising that the paddler would probably be scrapped – and motivated by sentiment, an eye for a profit, or a mixture of both – he had stepped in to buy her in the hope of reviving the Trefriw service once hostilities had ceased.

The rumour that some nuns were involved in the purchase seems to have arisen from Fr Baron's close connections with the Sisters of St Mary of Namur (who had a convent in his home town of Rhyl together with the arrival, in June 1940, of the Nuns of St Mary's Convent Lowestoft), who had been evacuated to a large house called Bryn Mair on Morfa Drive, Conwy. These various connections seem to have become conflated but, in reality, neither the Catholic Church nor the nuns actually had any direct connection with the paddler.

It is possible that *Princess Mary* may have found some intermittent employment on the estuary in connection with the construction of Mulberry harbour units on the Conwy Morfa, but for most of the war she lay beside *King George*, beached and idle. Fr Baron never used either vessel and by the time VE Day arrived in May 1945, both were in very poor condition. In the summer of 1945 a Bolton businessman named George Crompton was on holiday in Conwy when he spotted the two boats deteriorating in their lay-up berths and began to make enquiries. Crompton was another small-scale entrepreneur and it is quite probable that he already knew Fr Baron through previous business ventures or may even have been related by marriage. A former motor engineer, he had dabbled in journalism, groceries, timber and haulage and, at the time of his visit to Conwy, was also a dairy proprietor.

By January 1946 Crompton had purchased *King George*, *Princess Mary* and some land at Trefriw Quay from Fr Baron and by April had registered the St George Steamship Company (1946) Ltd, with himself and his wife as sole directors.

He employed Vincent Crossfield as manager and announced his intention of reintroducing the Trefriw sailings during the summer, as well as obtaining an additional boat to run longer, open-water trips around Puffin Island. The town council granted him the tenancy of the old company's jetty and store rooms in the basement of town wall tower at Conwy on condition that he demolish the hulk of the *Bluebell*, which had formed the floating pier head and which was now lying derelict beside the Marine Walk. *Bluebell* was a former Fleetwood sailing trawler which had landed her catch at Conway for many years before taking the place of the old *Commerce* at the head of the Conwy jetty. For the sum of £1 per annum they also gave him permission to keep *King George* in the lay-up berth at Benarth Beach near the mouth of the Gyffin stream, which she had occupied throughout the war.

It soon became apparent that Mr Crompton's skills did not extend to ship surveying, for *King George* was found to need a new boiler and other extensive repairs before she could obtain her passenger certificates. Mr Crompton could not justify such major expenditure, so the ship was left to deteriorate on Benarth Beach.

It seems that *Princess Mary* was refitted and operated on the river during 1946 and 1947, although local boatmen recall that she was in poor condition and proved unreliable. Mr Crompton also applied for a licence for a motor boat named *Mermaid*, possibly for his intended Puffin Island trips, and owned a boat called *Staka* which was skippered by Ifor Polin.

Although he had the experienced Vincent Crossfield as his manager, George Crompton's attempts to break into the local river trade during 1946 must have been hampered by his lack of local and maritime knowledge, as well as by the fact that he was faced with severe competition. The immediate post-war years were characterised by the proliferation of small motor boats on the river. Owned or operated by local boatmen, many of these were employed in fishing or mussel gathering throughout the winter months, but during the summer were painted up and used to carry up to twelve passengers on short river trips. A full list of these and other boats known to have operated on the river between the end of the war and the present day appears as appendix 3.

As can be seen, amongst the many twelve-seat launches were a number of larger boats, capable of carrying substantial numbers of passengers. In 1946 Ben Craven and Jack Roberts went into partnership to market their combined fleet of launches as the Red Motor Boats and reintroduced a regular service to Trefriw. The sailings were usually undertaken by their largest boat, the *Sunbeam I*, which had been built at Crossfield's yard during the 1930s and could be distinguished by her distinctive 'fiddle' stem post. *Sunbeam II*; another Crossfield-built boat, *Prince* which had come from Liverpool; and *Satellite* which had been built at Bond's yard at Rock Ferry and was purchased by Craven in 1934, all took their turn at various times, or went in convoy if the demand was sufficient.

Craven & Roberts' largest boat, *Sunbeam I*, loading passengers at Conwy. The old steamer landing stages with their floating pier heads have been replaced by a much smaller timber walkway extending to the low-tide mark. Behind *Sunbeam* are two other local launches, *Violet May* (with the portholes) and *Collingwood*. In the distance the bows of the old river steamer *Jubilee* can be seen poking out behind the motor yacht *Llys Helig* at her mooring off Twthill Point.

Craven & Roberts' *Satellite* on her mooring off Conwy.

The Trefriw trips were offered daily throughout the summer months, including Sundays, and the timetable was identical to that offered by the St George SS Company before the war, except that Deganwy had been abandoned and all trips now started from a small landing stage extending from the beach at Conwy. On small tides the boats turned back before reaching Trefriw or terminated at Tal-y-Cafn where passengers were given time ashore to visit the hotel. The full round trip took approximately 3 hours and the 1946 fares were 3s single and 5s return. The Red Motor Boats also offered frequent, shorter trips on the estuary and quickly established themselves as a successful and popular part of the Conwy scene.

Faced with such professional and organised opposition, George Crompton struggled to make significant inroads into the river trade. During 1946 he became embroiled in various disputes with the council when he was accused of erecting advertising boards on the town wall without permission and of failing to break up the old *Bluebell* hulk, which was still lying derelict beside the Marine Walk. Early in 1947 he caused further irritation by erecting a sawmill and parking heavy lorries on the quay without permission. In October 1947 the Ministry of Agriculture and Fisheries, whose mussel purification tanks were situated just above Benarth Beach where the mussel boats landed their catches, wrote to complain that the *King George* was 'practically derelict and in grave danger of breaking up'. They requested that Mr Crompton be required to move her to a location where any disintegration would pose no danger to navigation.

With debts mounting, Mr Crompton bowed to the inevitable and put *Princess Mary* up for sale. By 1948 or 1949 she was reported to be operating on the River Ouse at Goole and sometime later moved to York where she was owned by Hill's boatyard and carried sixty-four passengers on river cruises. In 1972 her original TVO engine was replaced with a new Perkins 4236 diesel by Turners Marine Services of Malton. In 1978 she was sold to French Brothers at Runnymede on the River Thames and remained with them until 1984 when she was purchased by the Mirfield Boat Yard in West Yorkshire and provided cruises and a river bus service on the Calder & Hebble Navigation between Mirfield and Brighouse. In 1990 she moved again, this time to the Sheffield & South Yorkshire Navigation, where she ran public and charter sailings from Sheffield Basin. She ran successfully for about 10 years before her owners, the Sheffield Canal Company, became locked in dispute with the British Waterways Board (BWB) over access and mooring rights while the Sheffield Basin was being redeveloped and eventually went bankrupt. In July 2002 she was purchased for £2,700 from the receivers by a local businessman called Alan Hynes who had plans to restore her. However, *Princess Mary* lay virtually abandoned in the basin until BWB, fearing that she would sink, towed her down the canal and moored her in the reeds just below No.3 Lock on the Tinsley Flight. Out of the public eye, her wheel was stolen, she was extensively vandalised and eventually sank in 2004. When BWB attempted to pump her out, her caulking came out, planks split and she sank again. Eventually, in 2007, her wreck was hauled from the canal using a hydraulic grab and her shattered remains taken away. Her engine and gearbox remain in the mud to this day as a sad reminder of the last survivor of the St George's Steamship Company's Conwy fleet.

In July 1948 Conwy Council served Mr Crompton with an order for the removal of *King George* from Benarth Beach, only to discover that he had sold the ship to a Mr Duncalf for breaking up. Mr Duncalf, having been told to remove the ship and reinstate the site within three months, seems to have subcontracted the work to Messrs J. & A. Higginbottom of Conwy and by June 1949 the harbourmaster was able to report that the dismantling 'was proceeding slowly'. His optimism was short-lived, for by August the work had ceased again and in March 1950 'the position of the hulk upon the beach was as last reported'. It would appear that the various scrap merchants involved (who included Michael Niedweski and Tom Rowlands), having removed all the valuable non-ferrous metals from the ship, may have underestimated the difficulty of breaking up her tough metal hull and prevaricated for as long as possible. Under continued pressure from the council, however, the work slowly proceeded and the last parts of the old ship were finally removed from Benarth Beach during 1951. Her brass

Princess Mary operating a water-bus service between Mirfield and Brighouse on the Calder & Hebble Navigation, 1994.

Princess Mary abandoned and waterlogged on the Tinsley Flight, Sheffield, on 1 June 2006.
(Andy Heath)

The sad end of the *Princess Mary*, 16 May 2007. Her wooden canopy floats in the foreground
while, under the canal bridge, the bows of her sunken hull stick forlornly out of the water.
Within days her remains had been dragged from the canal and the last survivor of the
St George's Steamship Company had finally gone. (Malcolm Fielding)

steam whistle, and possibly her bell, were retained by the company who bought the metal, and may well survive in Conwy to this day.

His disastrous venture into the river trade left George Crompton with considerable debts and it is said that he was forced to sell his grocery and dairy businesses in order to pay off his creditors. At Conwy the former St George's Company's yard reverted to council ownership and the old landing stage, together with the double-bayed shed with its slipways and workshop facilities, was demolished in 1950. The pon toon which had formed the pier head of the company's Deganwy jetty lingered on for some years, moored beside the Marine Walk. Out in the river near Twthill Point, the hull of the *Jubilee* continued to be used as a storage hulk for the *Llys Helig* until 1960 when the yacht left the river and the old steamer was finally broken up. The last direct link with the golden age of the Conwy River steamers had finally gone.

King George being broken up on Benarth Beach at the mouth of the Gyffin stream during 1949 or 1950. The photographer was aiming to record the Conwy mussel fishermen landing their catches on the beach before taking them up to the purification tanks, which were located just above the beach, but has accidentally recorded the death throes of the old paddle steamer. The forward part of her hull has already been cut back as far as the engine room bulkhead and the curve of her boiler, funnel uptake, engine control levers and the hub of her port paddle wheel can all be seen. (L. Groom/C. Hughes)

CONWAY FROM MARINE WALK.   W.3575.

The last days of the old river steamer *Jubilee* moored as a storage hulk alongside the splendid motor yacht *Llys Helig* off Marine Walk, Conwy, during the late 1950s.

In Trefriw the end of the war brought a gradual return to normality. The Trefriw Wells continued to trade, the Belle Vue Hotel was returned to its owners, and the woollen mill remained a key attraction to visitors passing through the village on motor tours. The Belle Vue Spa on the quay, however, never re-opened but was sold and converted into a private house.

The *Sunbeam I* and the Red Motor Boats offered regular sailings to Trefriw throughout the 1950s, and even found it worthwhile to publish their own illustrated guide to the river trip, in much the same style as those sold on board the old paddle steamers. As the decade wore on, however, it was noted that visitors to Conwy tended to spend less time in the town and preferred a short trip around the estuary rather than the 3-hour return trip to Trefriw. The number of up-river trips was therefore gradually reduced until, at the end of the 1959 season, *Sunbeam I* was sold and the timetabled service to Trefriw withdrawn altogether. Although little sentiment was expressed at the time, this marked the end of 112 years of scheduled passenger sailings on the River Conwy. By a curious and appropriate coincidence, the famous Trefriw Wells also closed its doors to the public in 1959, bringing to a close a long tradition of health-seekers arriving by water to take the waters.

Following the demise of Craven & Roberts' timetabled Red Motor Boat service, other local boats continued to offer occasional sailings to Trefriw. In 1964 the introduction of Rollie Hughes' brand new, 125-passenger *Princess Christine*, built by A.M. Dickie & Sons of Bangor, spelled the end for many of the twelve-seat launches, but did see a slight revival in up-river sailings. *Princess Christine* often ran a 2-hour afternoon trip to Tal-y-Cafn or just beyond, landing for half an hour

SAILINGS

By the Motor Launches "Sunbeam," & Red Motor Boats

BETWEEN

CONWAY & TREFRIW

Twelve Miles of Beautiful Scenery up the Conway Valley passing Tal-y-Cafn and Dolgarrog.

July, August, and September, 1952

JULY

Day		Leaves Conway	Leaves Trefriw	
Tuesday	1	4.40 p.m.	6.20 p.m.	D
Wednesday	2	5.40 ,,	7.20 ,,	D
Thursday	3	6.40 ,,	8.20 ,,	D
Saturday	5	8.30 a.m.	10. 5 a.m.	
Sunday	6	9.20 ,,	11.00 ,,	
Monday	7	10.15 ,,	12. 5 p.m.	
Tuesday	8	11. 0 ,,	12.50 ,,	
Wednesday	9	11.40 ,,	1.35 ,,	
Thursday	10	12.35 p.m.	2.25 ,,	
Friday	11	1.20 ,,	3.15 ,,	
Saturday	12	2.10 ,,	4.00 ,,	
Sunday	13	3.00 ,,	4.55 ,,	
Monday	14	3.55 ,,	5.45 ,,	
Tuesday	15	4.55 ,,	6.40 ,,	D
Wednesday	16	6. 5 ,,	7.50 ,,	D
Thursday	17	7. 0 ,,	8.50 ,,	D
Saturday	19	8.50 a.m.	10.30 a.m.	
Sunday	20	9.35 ,,	11.20 ,,	
Monday	21	10.10 ,,	12. 5 p.m.	
Tuesday	22	10.55 ,,	12.45 ,,	
Wednesday	23	11.25 ,,	1.15 ,,	
Thursday	24	12. 5 p.m.	1.50 ,,	
Friday	25	12.35 ,,	2.25 ,,	
Saturday	26	1. 5 ,,	2.55 ,,	
Sunday	27	1.40 ,,	3.20 ,,	
Monday	28	2.15 ,,	3.55 ,,	
Tuesday	29	2.55 ,,	4.35 ,,	D
Wednesday	30	3.40 ,,	5.25 ,,	D
Thursda	31	4.50 ,,	6.30 ,,	D

AUGUST

Day		Leaves Conway	Leaves Trefriw	
Friday	1	6.00 p.m.	7.45 p.m.	D
Monday	4	9.15 a.m.	10.55 a.m.	
Tuesday	5	10. 0 ,,	11.50 ,,	
Wednesday	6	10.50 ,,	12.40 p.m.	
Thursday	7	11.25 ,,	1.25 ,,	
Friday	8	12.10 p.m.	2.10 ,,	
Saturday	9	1. 0 ,,	2.55 ,,	
Sunday	10	1.50 ,,	3.40 ,,	
Monday	11	2.25 ,,	4.20 ,,	
Tuesday	12	3.15 ,,	5. 5 ,,	
Wednesday	13	4.15 ,,	5.55 ,,	D
Thursday	14	5.30 ,,	7.10 ,,	D
Friday	15	6.40 ,,	8.20 ,,	D
Sunday	17	8.45 a.m.	10.15 a.m.	
Monday	18	9.25 ,,	11. 5 ,,	
Tuesday	19	10.10 ,,	11.50 ,,	
Wednesday	20	10.35 ,,	12.20 p.m.	
Thursday	21	11. 0 ,,	12.50 ,,	
Friday	22	11.30 ,,	1.25 ,,	
Saturday	23	12. 0 p.m.	1.55 ,,	
Sunday	24	12.35 ,,	2.20 ,,	
Monday	25	1. 0 ,,	2.55 ,,	
Tuesday	26	1.35 ,,	3.20 ,,	
Wednesday	27	2.10 ,,	3.55 ,,	
Thursday	28	3. 5 ,,	4.50 ,,	D
Friday	29	4.15 ,,	5.50 ,,	D
Saturday	30	5.40 ,,	7.20 ,,	D

SEPTEMBER

Day		Leaves Conway	Leaves Trefriw	
Tuesday	2	9. 5 a.m.	10.45 a.m.	
Wednesday	3	9.50 ,,	11.35 ,,	
Thursday	4	10.30 ,,	12.20 p.m.	
Friday	5	11. 5 ,,	1. 5 ,,	
Saturday	6	11.45 ,,	1.45 ,,	
Sunday	7	12.35 p.m.	2.30 ,,	
Monday	8	1. 5 ,,	3. 5 ,,	
Tuesday	9	1.50 ,,	3.45 ,,	
Wednesday	10	2.40 ,,	4.20 ,,	
Thursday	11	3.35 ,,	5.15 ,,	D
Friday	12	4.45 ,,	6.25 ,,	D
Tuesday	16	9. 5 a.m.	10.45 a.m.	
Wednesday	17	9.35 ,,	11.25 ,,	
Thursday	18	10.10 ,,	11.55 ,,	
Friday	19	10.35 ,,	12.30 p.m.	
Saturday	20	11. 5 ,,	12.55 ,,	
Sunday	21	11.30 ,,	1.25 ,,	
Monday	22	12. 0 p.m.	1.55 ,,	
Tuesday	23	12.30 ,,	2.20 ,,	
Wednesday	24	1. 5 ,,	2.55 ,,	
Thursday	25	1.45 ,,	3.35 ,,	
Friday	26	2.40 ,,	4.25 ,,	

D—Doubtful if boat reaches Trefriw.

Weather and circumstances permitting

RETURN FARE, 5/-;   SINGLE, 3/-.

Private Parties and Special Trips can be arranged ; also River Trips at any time of the day by applying to the Proprietors, Messrs. BEN CRAVEN and JOHN ROBERTS, Berry Street, Conway, or 'Phone Conway 3157 or 3108,

R. E. JONES & BROS. LTD., PRINTERS, CONWAY

A poster for Craven & Roberts' Red Motor Boat service to Trefriw, 1952.

at the Ferry Hotel. Evening trips were also popular, but there were sometimes difficulties getting the passengers out of the bar, which meant that a late passage down the dark and unlit river on a falling tide tested the skipper's nerves to the extreme! Just occasionally, if the tide was right, *Princess Christine* would go all the way to Trefriw and, although slight variations in local memories make it hard to be precise, probably made her last call there in about 1965. Thus, the last ever boat to land passengers at Trefriw Quay slipped away without note or ceremony, and almost twelve colourful decades of river history drew to a close.

Since then, the upper reaches of the river have silted considerably, making it impossible for any but the smallest of boats to reach Trefriw Quay. *Princess Christine*

Conwy, *c.* 1960. The Hughes' family's twelve-seat launch *Collingwood* is beached in the foreground and *Satellite* is alongside the landing stage. Note the A55 bridge of 1958 which masked the view of Telford's 1826 suspension bridge. The new bridge was itself superseded in 1961 by the Conwy Tunnel, which today carries the A55 Expressway under the estuary.

or her larger running mate *Queen Victoria*, which run regular short estuary cruises from Conwy, still make occasional afternoon trips as far as Tal-y-Cafn but no longer land, as the Ferry Hotel has long since been demolished and replaced with a housing development and the landing place is now on private land.

The beauty and tranquillity of Trefriw are undiminished, its climate and surroundings as agreeable as ever and much remains to remind the present-day visitor of its Victorian and Edwardian heyday. The fascinating water-powered Trefriw Woollen Mill still stands at the foot of the Fairy Falls with its picturesque walks and iron bridges, and provide the village with its major tourist attraction. Close by, the original iron-arch frames the entrance to the remodelled recreation grounds, while Gower's Road continues to provide a pleasant shortcut across the floodplain to Llanrwst station. The scenic walks to Llyn Crafnant, Llyn Geirionydd and elsewhere in the mountains behind the village are still accessible, and a range of helpful leaflets and guided walks have been produced by the active local historical society. One can even stay the night at Crafnant House, the Ship Inn or one of the other 'boarding establishments' which were advertised in the village guidebooks at the turn of the twentieth century.

Following a period of dereliction the Trefriw Wells were purchased in 1972 by a Mr and Mrs Ineson, who converted the pump room into a private house, while preserving the historic features of the site. In 1987 a North Sea diver named Tony Rowlands bought the site from the Inesons and set about restoring the

DID YOU KNOW ?
THAT THE
PRINCESS CHRISTINE
sails on the beautiful
CONWY RIVER
on morning, afternoon and evening cruises daily
Boat usually departs 11.30 a.m. - 2.30 p.m. & 7.15 p.m.

For Particulars of which trip is available
RING **CONWY 2284** (DAY or NIGHT)
or Full Particulars are on Notice Board at the jetty in Conwy
Don't miss these enjoyable trips with the most beautiful scenery in the whole of Wales

Pawsons, The Colwyn Bay Press

A *Princess Christine* poster, 1964.

buildings to their former glory. The main pump room was returned to something resembling its original configuration, with replacement fireplaces and fittings. Most significantly, Mr Rowlands began bottling the waters once again, sold them through Harrods and health fairs and developed a new method of packaging individual doses in sachets. The business proved such a success that in 2003 he was able to sell it to Nelsons UK Ltd, who have been marketing the waters under the brand name Spatone ever since. Until 2011 the wonderfully preserved

Rollie Hughes' *Princess Christine* was the last ever boat to land passengers at Trefriw Quay.
(Malcolm McRonald Collection)

Viewed from the western end of Conwy quay, *Queen Victoria* awaits passengers for an
afternoon trip on 25 August 2009. The yachts drawn up on the foreshore beside the town wall
on the left are on the site of the St George Steamship Company's former Wing Gate Yard and
landing stage.

wells were open to visitors and it was possible to take an audio-tour of the caves, the 1863 bath house and grounds and to enjoy the museum, gift shop and café housed within the pump room while the busy bottling plant throbbed away in the background. By 2011 the demand for Spatone was so great that Nelsons required more of the building for production and packaging and closed the site to the public. While it is a delight to know that Trefriw's healing waters are more popular than they have ever been, it is regrettable that it is no longer possible to visit this enchanting site or view the wonderful collection of historic artefacts and archives which gave such a fascinating insight into the history of the wells and its links with the river trade. The buildings are, however, clearly visible from the road.

At Trefriw Quay – the very heart of this history – much of the Victorian infra-structure survives. On the terrace above the road the imposing Belle Vue Hotel is still very much open for business, although renamed the Princes Arms Hotel in 1969. Updated to the best of modern standards by its present proprietors, Lindsay

Trefriw Wells as they appear today.

The Princes Arms Hotel, formerly the Belle Vue, is still a popular and busy hotel. Note the terracotta balustrades on the steps leading down to the overgrown quay.

and Anne Gordon, it retains most of its original features, and to take breakfast in the former ballroom, while gazing out over the quay and floodplain below, is to be transported back in time. Next door stands the Roberts family's original Store House, now a private house named 'Arosfa'. Between the 1970s and 1990s the quay itself almost disappeared from view. Although the former Belle Vue Spa continued to be used as a private house, the terraces were overtaken by a dense tangle of vegetation while substantial trees sprouted from the quay wall, hiding the site from the river. The current owners, however, have undertaken a great deal of clearance and the spa building, the remains of the former Crafnant golf pavilion, the stone stairways and the terracotta balustrades have emerged once again from the undergrowth. Although the quay is private land, the view much favoured by Victorian postcard photographers can still be obtained from a nearby public footpath; it is not too difficult to imagine the distant sound of a steam whistle and the rhythmic beat of paddle wheels as one of the little pleasure steamers approached her destination after yet another trip up the beautiful River Conwy.

Trefriw Quay in 2009. The balustrades along the upper terrace, the buildings of the former Belle Vue Spa and the pavilion from the old Crafnant Golf Club can be glimpsed through the trees. The line of the quay is clear, but the spit of land in the foreground has grown considerably since Edwardian times, and the former steamer berths are badly silted up.

The same view in the heyday of the steamers. *King George* is at the quay and *Prince George* is just arriving.

Appendix 1

Sketch Map of Conwy Showing the Location of Key Sites Related to the River Steamers

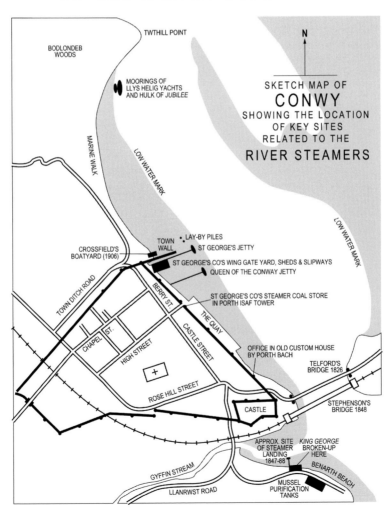

Appendix 2

Fleet List

NAME	BUILT ACQUIRED DISPLACED SCRAPPED	OFFICIAL NUMBER	BUILDER Type	LENGTH In feet	BREADTH In feet	DEPTH In feet	GROSS TONNAGE	MACHINERY	REMARKS
Inland Navigation Co (c.1847–1864), St George's Steamship Co. (c.1864–1888), St George's Steamship Co Ltd (1889–1924), St George Steamship Co. Ltd (reformed) (1924–1942), St George Steamship 1946 Co. Ltd (1946–1948)									
ST WINIFRED	? c.1847 c.1864 ?		Possibly J. Williams of Trefriw or Isaac Watt Boulton of Ashton under Lyme. ?						In service 1851.
ST GEORGE (I)	1852 1852 1910 1910	120789	Isaac Watt Boulton Ashton Under Lyme Iron paddle steamer	72.3	10.2	4.2	20.65	Diagonal, direct acting, surface condensing. Two cylinders, each 10in diameter x 17½in stroke, 7hp.	Registered Beaumaris. May origi- nally have had oscillating engines and have been lengthened and re-engined. Re-boilered 1902, steel boiler by H. Branch of Runcorn. 65psi, 8 knots, 120 passengers.
PRINCE GEORGE (also known as *NEW ST GEORGE* until 1907)	1891 1891 1939 1939	102788	William Thomas & Sons, Amlwch, Anglesey Steel paddle steamer	72.2	12.15	3.71	23.53	Diagonal, direct-acting, compound, condensing. Two cylinders of 11in & 20in diameter x 24in stroke by De Winton & Co. Caernarfon.	Known as *NEW ST GEORGE* 1891–1907, but never registered as such. Registered Beaumaris. 1 steel, multi-tubular boiler by De Winton, 85psi, 10 knots.

NAME	BUILT ACQUIRED DISPLACED SCRAPPED	OFFICIAL NUMBER	BUILDER Type	LENGTH In feet	BREADTH In feet	DEPTH In feet	GROSS TONNAGE	MACHINERY	REMARKS
KING GEORGE	1907 1907 1942 1950/51	120787	W.J. Yarwood & sons, Castle Dock, Northwich Steel paddle steamer	79.6	13.25	4.75	44.81	Diagonal/horizontal, direct acting, compound, condensing. Two cylinders of 10¾in & 22in diameter by 24in stroke, 80iph by W.J. Yarwood	Registered Beaumaris. 1 steel, multi-tubular boiler 130psi by Yarwood. 280 passengers.
ST GEORGE (II)	1910 1910 1920 C1950	120796	John Crossfield, Conway Wooden motor vessel	55.6	11.1	4.1	18.85	Two reciprocating, direct acting, vertical inverted petrol/paraffin engines. Four cylinders, 4¾in diameter by 5in stroke, 30hp by Dixon Bros & Hutchinson, Southampton.	Registered Beaumaris. Transferred to Newry 1 September 1920. Twin-screw motor vessel. Laid up 1913–1920. 80 passengers.
PRINCESS MARY	1920 1925 1942/1948 2007		Chester Boat Company Wooden motor launch	40	9	2		18hp Thornycroft.	Built for service at Chester. Operated by St George Steamship (1946) Co. Ltd 1946–47. Subsequently operated at Goole, York, on the Thames, at Mirfield and Sheffield. Abandoned and sank 2004, disintegrated 2007. 70 passengers.

NAME	BUILT ACQUIRED DISPLACED SCRAPPED	OFFICIAL NUMBER	BUILDER Type	LENGTH In feet	BREADTH In feet	DEPTH In feet	GROSS TONNAGE	MACHINERY	REMARKS
The Llandudno & Trefriw Steamship Co. Ltd									
QUEEN OF THE CONWAY	1891 1898 1906 1906/7	98774	J.P. Rennoldson & Sons, South Shields Steel paddle steamer	85.0	14.15	5.7	76.93	Side lever, surface condensing. One cylinder 22in diameter by 40in stroke, 20hp by J.P. Rennoldson & Sons, South Shields.	Formerly *Queen of the Tees*, registered at Middlesbrough. Re-registered Beaumaris 1898. Register closed 1908 Single steel boiler by J. Eltringham & Co., South Shields, 40psi, 8 knots, 285 passengers.
Mr George Griffiths (on Charter 1903 – c. 1906) Trefriw Belle Steamship Company (Capt. H.C. Edwards of Deganwy 1907–1912)									
TREFRIW BELLE	? 1903–7 1912 ?		? Wooden screw steamer					Twin screw	
JUBILEE	1896 1909 1912 1957		Cochran & Co., Birkenhead Wooden screw steamer	61.0	12.0	4.9	27	Single, vertical, reciprocating, non-condensing. Two cylinders 7in and 14in in diameter by 9in stroke, 32iph by Cochran & Co., Birkenhead.	Built for Evan Griffiths to operate between Barmouth and Penmaenpool and on sea cruises. Laid up at Deganwy in 1912 and became derelict. Refitted 1921 as storage hulk for yacht *Llys Helig* at Conway. Single steel boiler, 100psi also by Cochran & Co.

Appendix 3

Small Passenger Boats Known to have Operated on the Conwy from the 1930s to the Present Day

Compiled by retired boatmen Clifford Hughes and Ken Hughes of Berry Street, Conwy

NAME	SKIPPER	PASSGRS.	DETAILS
Operated by the Craven Family/Craven & Roberts 'Red Launches' (Ben Craven & Jack Roberts)			
Prince	Edward 'Tich' Hughes	40+	Built in Liverpool. Sold 1960
Satellite	Des Craven	30+	Built by Bonds at Rock Ferry. Acquired 1934. Sold June 1983 for use in Rhos-on-Sea and Colwyn Bay. Used for fishing in winter during the Second World War it was involved with construction of the Mulberry harbours
Sylvia	Sam Hughes (known as Sam Bach Quay)	12	Owned by B. Craven
Della	Ron Craven		
Sunbeam 1	Sam Craven / Douglas Roberts	80+	Built by Crossfields. Sold 1959 for service on the Thames
Sunbeam 2			Built by Crossfields. Sold 1957
Dawn			
Dotteral			Ran 1945 only, then sold
Un-named ex parachute lifeboat	Bob Craven	12	Double-ended craft designed by Uffa Fox to be dropped from aircraft to the aid of distressed seamen or airmen in the water
Operated by Rimmer Hughes Family			
Alice 1	Will Rimmer	12	William Hughes of 29 Berry Street had her in 1952. Varnished
Alice 2	Ken Rimmer	30+	Ex-sailing boat which came from Blackpool. Later fitted with a bow cabin and new engine
Sandra	Robert Rimmer	12	
Glendoveer	Jolin Rimmer	12	
Myra	Will Rimmer	12	
Mytilys		12	Workboat
Patsy	Evan Hughes 1944		Henry Beatson owner in 1944. Tender
Operated by Roberts Family			
Billyo	Clifford Hughes	12	
Conqueror	J.M. Roberts	12	
Violet May	Clifford Hughes	12	Thomas Owen skipper in 1945. Had short cabin with port holes
Non Pareil	Various	12	

NAME	SKIPPER	PASSGRS.	DETAILS
Sea Spray	Billy Roberts	12	Rowland Hughes was owner on 1 June 1948
Operated by Hughes Family			
Collingwood	Ifan Hughes	12	Owned by Mr H. Beetson in 1952
Black Bess	Robert 'Caddy' Hughes	40+	
Maid of Conwy	Robert 'Caddy' Hughes	12	Fibreglass hull, fitted out by Crossfields *c.* 1960
Operated by Roland 'Rollie' Hughes / Bryn Hughes			
Mermaid		12	Owned by Robert Rimmer & Rollie Hughes. Only remained on river for 1 year
Christine	Family	40+	
Princess Christine		125	Built 1964 by Dickies of Bangor. Still working
Anne		12	Varnished
Queen Victoria		94	Built 1987. 30GRT. Still working
Others			
Michelle	John Foulks	12	
Seabird	Trevor Jones	12	
Valma	Bobby 'Widnes' Williams	12	
Cariad	Llew & Hiw Jones	12	Porth Bach Family
Staka	Ifor Polin	12	Owned by Mr Crompton
Princess Mary		40–50	Owned by Mr Crompton, sold 1947/8
Gwylan	Johny Roberts	12	
Saucy Sal	Malcolm Wright	100+	Varnished
Neptune	Glyn Gregory	100+	
Garry	Evan Hughes	12	Ex-lifeboat
Kim	John 'Dumphy' Roberts	12	Ex-naval boat
Seaspray	J. Roberts	12	Painted blue

Appendix 4

The Trip Described

For many passengers the pleasures of a trip up the River Conway were enhanced by the availability of a small guidebook describing the scenery and sites of interest along the way. These guides were often referred to as *Jones's River Guides* or *Jones's Guide to the River Conway* after their publisher, R.E. Jones & Bros. of the *Weekly News* office in Conwy. The full title was *The Conway River Guide or A trip up the River by Steamer or Pleasure Boat*, implying that they could be purchased ashore as well as on board the steamers. Four editions appeared, with the cover designs updated from time to time. The text by J.R. Furness remained broadly unaltered, with only minor amendments to bring the notes up to date. Frustratingly, none of the guides are dated and one must work out their approximate ages from tiny clues within the text.

In 1925 or shortly thereafter the reformed company issued an entirely new and redesigned guidebook entitled *The St George Steamship Co. Ltd's Official Souvenir and Guide of the River Conway, The Rhine of Wales*. This was published by the British Publishing Company Ltd at the Crypt House Press, Gloucester and London, and appears to have remained available until 1940.

After the Second World War, Craven & Roberts returned to R.E. Jones & Bros. to print and publish an updated guide entitled *River Trip to Trefriw, Illustrated Guide*. This was sold on board *Sunbeam* and the other Red Motor Boats until the service ceased in 1959.

What follows are reproductions of four guidebook covers and the text of the fourth edition which was published between 1922 and 1924.

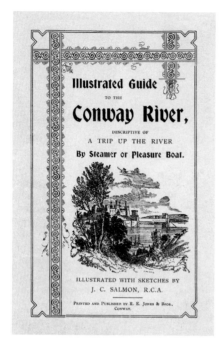

Third edition, c. 1900.

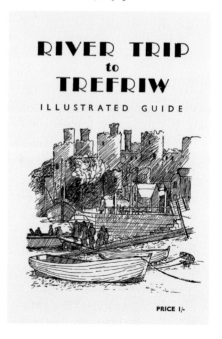

Fourth edition, c. 1923.

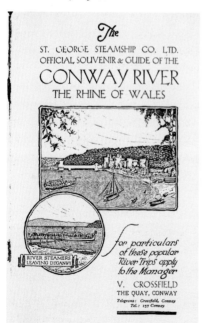

The new look river guide issued by the re-formed St George Steamship Company Ltd under Vincent Crossfield's management, c. 1925.

The guidebook issued during the time of Craven & Roberts' Red Motor Boats service to Trefriw, 1946–59.

**The
Conway River Guide**

Or
A Trip Up The River
By Steamer Or Pleasure Boat

With
Notes By The Way
By The Late J. R. Furness
Profusely Illustrated With Sketches By
J. C. Salmon, R.C.A.
Fourth Edition
Conway:
Printed And Published By R. E. Jones & Bros., Weekly
News Office

In journeying from one place to another there is a natural desire to know something of the country through which we are travelling, and the points of interest to be noted by the way; and as there is a demand for a description of the Conway Valley, I will briefly endeavour to describe this beautiful Vale with the object of showing the stranger how to make the journey in a day, and, with as little fatigue as possible, see the chief points of interest as he journeys along.

Remembering the lines of John Critchley Prince, one is instinctively drawn to the district which has impressed him so deeply; and, during the progress of the journey, we appreciate to the full the beautiful discriptive lines:—

'I lay me down to rest awhile,
　Upon thy banks, sweet Conway!
While summer evening's golden smile Sleeps on thy waves, sweet Conway!
　I lay me down beside thy stream,
To revel in the realms of dream,
　Or mourn o'er many a ruined scheme
Far from thy banks, sweet Conway'

During the season there are pleasure steamers plying daily (as weather and tide permits) between Conway (calling at Deganwy) and Trefriw, a picturesque little village some nine miles up the river. The visitor should, in the first place, visit that quaint old town, Conway; previously ascertaining at what hour the steamers leave the Quay for their daily sail, and arranging to be in Conway an hour-and-a-half earlier, so that the Church, the Castle, and Plas Mawr may be visited, and the town seen. In the old Churchyard is pointed out the grave which Wordsworth has immortalised with that beautiful and touching child-story entitled 'We are Seven' (written in 1798). There is no slab or stone to mark the spot, but the grave is near the sundial, at the tower end, on the South side of the Church. Here are a few of the verses:–

I met a little cottage girl;
   She was eight years old she said:
Her hair was thick with many a curl

That clustered round her head.

'Sisters and brothers, little maid,
   How many may you be?'

'How many? Seven in all,' she said,
   And wondering, looked at me.

'And where are they? I pray you tell,'
She answered:'
Seven are we; And two of us at Conway dwell,
And two are gone to sea.

Two of us in the churchyard lie,
   My sister and my brother; And, in the churchyard cottage, I

Dwell near them with my mother.'

'You say that two at Conway dwell,
   And two are gone to sea;
Yet ye are seven!—I pray you toll,
   Sweet maid, how this may be.'

'Their graves are green, and may be seen,'
   The little maid replied; 'Twelve steps or more from my mother's door,

And they are side by side.

My stockings there I sometimes knit,
    My kerchief there I hem;
And there upon the ground I sit,

And sing a song to them.

And often after sunset, Sir,
    When it is light and fair,
I take my little porringer,
    And eat my supper there.'

'How many are you then,' said I,
    'If they two are in heaven?'
Quick was the little maid's reply, 'O, master! we are seven.'

'But they are dead; those two are dead!
    Their spirits are in heaven?'
    'Twas throwing words away; for still The little maid would have her will.
And said: 'Nay, we are seven!'

From the walls of the Castle, or from the turret of Plas Mawr, a fine view of Conway Bay is obtained:—

'Lo! yonder is thy 'Mother-Sea,'
    Whose arms embrace thee, Conway!
And glorious must that mother be.
    Whose arms embrace thee, Conway!
The clouds will take thee up in rain, And
pour thee on the earth again, To wander
through each vale and plain That blooms
around thee, Conway!'

This run through the town is for those whose time is limited; in the ordinary way, a day or more may be agreeably passed in and around Conway.

Whilst looking round the town, the steamer has crossed to Deganwy, from which place the journey up the river commences. Leaving Deganwy, and looking across the river, you have the Conway Morfa in the immediate foreground – famous as a camping-ground for Territorials, for golf-links, &c. On the further side of the

Morfa is the Conway Town Mountain (about 800 ft. above sea), one of the favourite summer-walks. Near the summit are the remains of early British settlements; the foundations of the round houses of that period may be distinctly traced; splendid views, inland and out to sea, are obtained from the top; the Coast of Ireland, the Isle of Man, and the Cumberland Mountains being occasionally seen.

On the other side of the river, there is the peculiar hill above Deganwy, on which was once a stronghold of considerable importance. This was destroyed by lightning in 810; it was rebuilt, and finally destroyed by Edward I – of England. Taliesin, the celebrated Welsh bard, who lived in the sixth century, was for some time a prisoner in Deganwy Castle, when Maelgwyn Gwynedd, the Welsh chief, attracted by his bardic productions, at once ordered his release. Many of his compositions are mentioned in the 'Archaeology of Wales'. There is a tradition that Taliesin, when a babe, was found among the reeds of the Conway. Portions of the foundation walls of the stronghold at Deganwy may yet be seen.

Approaching the town of Conway, is extremely picturesque, – on the right is the well-wooded slope named 'Twthill' and the grounds of Bodlondeb, the residence of Albert Wood, Esq., J.P., and the mountain, sea, and river-views from this point are unrivalled. The Castle, standing boldly in front of a thickly-wooded background – the modern Bridges, the Quay, busy with shipping and boats – the cottages and town walls, make up a picture not easily forgotten. – It is worthy of note that the wall near the Pier is embattled on both sides, on account of it being exposed to attack, on either side; it originally ran farther out into the river and was terminated by a tower.

Prior to the days of the Suspension Bridge and the Embankment until early in the nineteenth century, the traffic was carried on by means of ferry-boats- The Rev. R. Williams, B.A., in 'History of Aberconwy', as the town was then called, says:– 'The Ferry at Aberconwy was retained as Royal property, and an Order was issued by Edward II for repairing the boat, or building a new one, for the use of which the inhabitants were to pay eight marks. The Ferries (Conway and Talycafn) were subsequently rented by the Corporation. The proprietor of the Marl Estates owned the one at Aberconwy, and was indemnified for the loss sustained by the erection of the bridge. On Christmas Day, 1806, owing to rough weather, the boat conveying the Irish mail, with eight passengers, the coachman, guard, and a boy, fifteen in number, including the boatmen, was upset, and only two escaped.' Many narrow escapes in the waters of the estuary and acts of bravery could be recorded. In the days when smuggling was rife, and pirates abounded, the river would, in consequence of its innumerable channels and rapids, afford facilities for the landing of contraband goods- Once within the river the smugglers; would soon get clear away, whilst the pursuers would be hampered by sandbanks and whirlpools.

The river has a rise of from twenty-seven to thirty feet. The geographical position of Conway is Lat. 53°20' N., Long. 3°47' W.

Immediately in front we have Telford's graceful Suspension Bridge, erected in 1826; the L.& N.W. Railway Company's Tubular Bridge, erected 1846-8, the principal engineers being Stephenson and Fairbairn (this bridge is four hundred feet long, each tube weighing one thousand three hundred tons, costing £150,000). The centre bridge was designed and erected (in 1893-4) by T. B. Farrington, C.E., for the purpose of conveying water mains for the Conway and Colwyn Bay water supply.

When the last Tube of the Railway Bridge was raised, the following colloquy took place between Mr. Stephenson and another eminent engineer:—Mr. Stephenson: 'Hallo What is the matter with you, Mr. ——? You seem out of sorts?' Mr ——: 'I am a martyr to nervous headaches, and must go up to town to be cupped.' Mr. Stephenson: 'Cupped! pooh! pooh! nonsense! lessen the supplies, eat less at meals; it is always better to damp the fire than blow off steam.'

As the bridges are approached we obtain a fine view of the Castle, which stands like an undaunted sentinel on the right.

'And this, despite the hand of Time, Still
   rears his hoary head sublime'.

Dismantled, ruined, rugged, bold—

Majestic as in days of old,
   Proud Conway's walls will stand'

or, as beautifully described by J. C. Prince:–

'Yon Castle's clustered turrets frown,
   Beside thy bank, sweet Conway!
And send their feudal shadows down
Upon thy face, sweet Conway!
Their ancient reign of strength is o'er,
Then regal splendours are no more, But
thou hast yet the charms of yore—
   Upon thy banks, sweet Conway!'

Passing underneath the bridges, there is the beautifully wooded hill of Benarth, with its picturesque house among the trees, near the summit. The house is best seen on looking round as we approach Cymryd point, which is immediately in front of us. From this point the river was formerly crossed by a ford and stepping-stones, reaching the opposite bank about half-a-mile above Glan Conway (or Llansant-ffraid-Glan-Conwy), which village is on our left. This is one of the several places claiming to be the birthplace of Gibson, the sculptor.

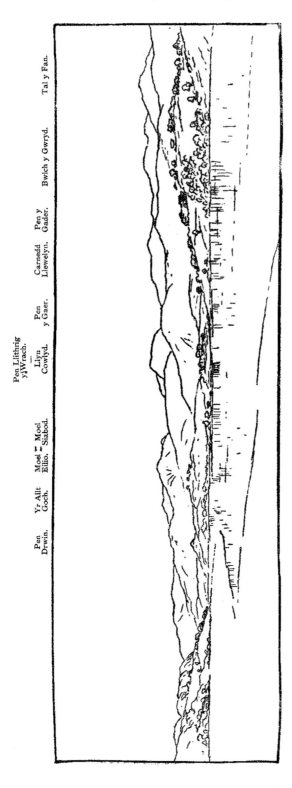

Pen Llithrig
y Wrach.

Pen
Drwin.

Yr Allt
Goch.

Moel
Eilio.

Moel
Siabod.

Llyn
Cowlyd.

Pen
y Gaer.

Carnedd
Llewelyn.

Pen y
Gader.

Bwlch y Gwryd.

Tal y Fan.

A sketch of the mountains to the west of the River Conwy as seen from the deck of the steamer passing upstream from Cymryd Point towards Tal-y-Cafn. The sketch appeared in almost every edition of *Jones's River Guide* and survived in a modified form into the Red Motor Boats era.

On the front of Salem Chapel House, about a mile to the south of the village, the following inscription is seen:–

    Yn y Ty Hwn, yn 1789,
  Y Ganwyd John Gibson, R.A.,
    Y Mynor-gerfiwr Enwog,
      Bu Farw yn Rhufain,
    Ionr. 27. 1866: yn 77
  Oed.

Which translated is thus:–

    In this house, in 1789,
  Was born John Gibson, R.A.,
    The noted Sculptor,
    Who died at Rome,
  Jany 27, 1866, aged 77.

On investigation it is found that John Gibson was born in 1790 (and not in 1789, as stated in the above inscription). He was baptised in Conway, the register containing the following entry:–

'1790, June 19th.—Baptised, John, son of William Gibson, of the parish of Gyffin, by Jane Roberts, wife.'

His friends subscribed for a bust in marble, which occupies a niche in the church. On the list of subscribers the name of the Prince of Wales appears. The following inscription is on a tablet below the bust:–

JOHN GIBSON,

Sculptor, Born of humble

pare, ts, near Conway, 1790,

Died at Rome, 1866. By the force of

natural genius and unremitting industry

He became one of the first Sculptors in Europe;

A Member of the Royal Academy of Arts in London,

of the Academy of St. Luke in Rome, and of other distinguished

foreign institutions.

His works will perpetuate his fame. Here, in his native place, a few loving friends have raised this memorial, as a tribute of affectionate regard for the unpretending simplicity and truthfulness of his life.

Hugh Hughes was another eminent artist associated with this district; he was a painter and wood-engraver (called the Welsh Bewick). He lived for some years at Glan Conway, where, in a; quiet farmhouse known as Meddiant, on the banks of the river, between the village and Hendrewaelod, he engraved most of his incomparable blocks for the 'Beauties of Cambria' (a subscription-work now very scarce), published in 1823, a copy of which Mr. T. H. Thomas, R.C.A., presented to the Royal Cambrian Academy of Art, and is now treasured at Plas Mawr, Conway. The artist was born in Carmarthen in 1796, and died in 1828. On the left of Glan Conway is the estate and house called Brynsteddfod. A field, on the river side of this estate, called *Cae'r* or *Acre Eisteddfod*, was formerly used as a meeting-place by the Druids, which custom gave the estate its present name.

Caesar, in his 'Gallic War,' thus describes Druidism:– "They are ministers of sacred things, and have the charge of sacrifices, both public and private. A great number of young men resort to them for the purpose of instruction in the system, and they are held in the highest reverence. Over the Druids one presides, to whom they pay the highest regard.

'They hold a meeting at a certain time of the year. Hither assemble all who have a litigation, and submit themselves to determination and sentence.

'Druids do not commonly engage in war, neither do they pay taxes like the rest of the community.

'It is especially the object of the Druids to inculcate this, – that souls do not perish, but, after death, pass into other bodies, and they consider that by this belief, more than anything else, men may be led to cast away the fear of death, and to become courageous.'

Eisteddfod is from the Welsh *eistedd* (meaning to sit in company), and this name is specially applied to the national festivals which are annually held in this country, with the object of encouraging literature, the arts and sciences, music and poetry. These meetings occupy several days; the competitions are usually open, and competent judges are appointed, who award the prizes. These festivals have been held in Wales over one thousand years.

Before the *Eisteddfod* proper is held, there is a meeting of a council of bards (called the Gorsedd), to which bards, minstrels, and others, go in high procession, when the public proclamation (in Welsh and English) of the *Eisteddfod* takes place. In a retired spot in the grounds of Brynsteddfod there is carefully preserved the stone which was used as a seat by the Chief Druid on these occasions; it is placed on a pedestal, on which is inscribed:– 'This was one of the Eisteddfod stones, and of great antiquity, used as a seat by the Chief Druid, when sitting in High Council. It has been preserved for ages in this field, giving it the name of Acre.'

The grounds of Brynsteddfod are strictly private. A stone, which was similarly used, is lovingly preserved in the outer court-yard at Plas Mawr, Conway, bearing undoubted marks of the glacial period. *The Conway & North Wales Weekly News*, in an article on the occasion of the visit of the Queen of Roumania to Conway, in September, 1890, says:– 'In the court-yard of Plas Mawr the Royal party were shown the ancient bardic stone, which, has, more than once, been used at the National Eisteddfod – The Queen then stood on the stone, saying 'that having so recently (just seven days previously) been admitted a Bard, she considered that, as 'Carmen Sylva' (her bardic name) she was justified in standing for a brief moment on the stone."

In the Churchyard at Glan Conway, a few tomb-stones bear date early in the sixteenth century. In front of Glan Conway station, and near the waiter when the tide is up, are two large pieces of rock; this is the site of the old Chapel of Saint Ffraid, from which this village took its name, Llansantffraid, meaning the Church of Saint Ffraid. As there are several other places of this name, the Railway Company call their station here 'Glan Conway.' Not far from here is one of the largest oak trees in North Wales; it is decayed in the trunk, and within the space nine persons have been at one time, with room left for a round table; the trunk is nearly thirty feet in circumference. Having rounded Cymryd Point, a fine stretch of distant mountains reminds me once more of J.C. Prince:–

'There are vast mountains stern and drear,
　Upon thy banks, sweet Conway! And broken fountains grand and clear
Upon thy banks, sweet Conway!
And there are wild woods rich and green, And broad lands, sunny and serene,
And many a happy home between,
Upon thy banks, sweet Conway!'

A few minutes after rounding Cymryd Point we are opposite (on the right) the snug little farm called Tyddyn Cynal, the Welsh home of the late Mr. H. Clarence Whaite, R.W.S., once President of the Royal Cambrian Academy of Art, &c.

There is a very pretty legend connected with this place, which says that Fairies used to dance in the large field to the left of the house on moonlight nights in summer-time, and, in proof of this, the large fairy-circles are pointed to by super-stitious people. The rings may be seen from the steamer.

Attention must be now turned to the opposite side of the river, where, in a field, there is a very large Cromlech. Looking at the far side of the field, and running the eye along the hedgerow (from the side of the river upwards) half-way along the wood, the eye will readily find this silent relic of the past. It is placed on five pillars, about three feet six inches from the ground. At one side are two other upright stones about eight feet high; the large stone is from three to four feet thick, thirteen feet long, and seven in width. The approximate weight is about twenty tons. Cromlechs are supposed to be Druidical altars or sepulchres upon which human sacrifices have been made. Above this on the left is the farm Meddiant, already referred to in connection with Hugh Hughes; and, almost immediately afterwards, low down, the house of Hendrewaelod. There is a large outbuilding connected with this house, which is called the Chapel, but it was formerly a tithe-barn. Many such buildings were so used up to about the year 1836 to store the produce which came as tithes from the various farms, the tenth of everything produced being due in that respect. There is a story about a farmer, who, on the birth of his tenth child, feeling the burden of nine quite sufficient, carried his tenth to the tithe-barn, as its due, which, however, to the delight of the mother, was returned.

A mile or so further on is a fine mansion, Bodnant Hall, built by the late Mr. H. D. Pochin, J.P., F.S.C., some time M.P. for Stafford, surrounded by its far-famed beautiful grounds. The Hall (now the home of Lord and Lady Aberconway) overlooks a fine reach of river, extending as far as Talycafn. The substantial bridge crossing the river at this place was built by Alfred Thorne, and opened in 1897, when the old ferry-boat was discontinued. The large round knoll (Castell y Bryn) immediately above, and a little on the right of the cottages of the Ferry, on the Carnarvonshire side, is said to be the site of a great Roman fortress.

A quarter of a mile further on, the river gradually narrowing, are 'The Arrows', a series of dangerous hidden rocks, impassable by the steamer during neap tides. Then, on the right, is seen the old salmon-trap on the Caerhun Estate, and, a little further on the same side, hidden partly by the giant yew trees by which it is surrounded, is the old Church of Caerhun, to which many a pilgrimage is made. In the midst of a clump of trees, situated between the river and the Church, some interesting remains have been discovered of the Roman City, Conovium. Lord Lytton's 'Harold: The Last of the Saxons', gives some interesting facts concerning the occupation of Castell-y-Biyn and Conovium by the Romans at the time of the Battle of Hastings

The ground on the right of the river, for two miles or more, is the site of one of the last battles between the armies of Prince Llewelyn and Edward the First, in 1282, which terminated at Cymryd Point, opposite Glan Conway. This battle furnished Mr H. Measham, R.C.A., with a subject for his famous picture, exhibited at the National Eisteddfod, Rhyl, in 1892, where it was awarded the silver medal and a prize of £20.

There is a strong contrast between those turbulent times and these we now enjoy:–

'Oh ! for a pure and tranquil life
　Upon thy banks, sweet Conway!

Afar from towns of sin and strife, Upon thy banks, sweet Conway!
With one unchanged companion nigh.
To watch me with affection's eye,
How calmly could I live and die
   Upon thy banks, sweet Conway!'

Two miles further on, in the distance on the right, the village of Tal-y-bont,
and, a little above, the cottages of Llanbedr are seen.

These villages are backed by a range of mountains, conspicuous amongst which
is seen Tal-y-Fan (2,000 ft.), Pen Llithrig (or 'Slippery Mountain'), Moel Siabod
(2,860 ft.), Carnedd Llewelyn (next to Snowdon in height, 3,482 ft.), and a host of
others. At the summit of one, Pen-y-gaer (the head fort), above Llanbedr, a British
fortress once stood, the position being well selected for defence. The foundations may still be traced of these ancient earth-works. Another feature connected
with this primitive stronghold may not be overlooked. At some distance from the
'trenches' there are innumerable stones set into the ground in irregular order round
the fort, leaving from three to five feet above the surface. The object was to break
the ranks of an advancing army, and create disorder and render retreat difficult.

A little above Tal-y-bont, on the Carnarvonshire side, is the large plain where
the camp of the army under Prince Llewelyn was situated in 1282. During heavy
floods, this plain, as far as the eye can reach, is under water to the depth of some
feet. High up on the hills to the right are the beautiful falls of Porthllwyd, and
below them the Aluminium Corporation's great works at Dolgarrog. From this
point the river narrows very fast. Dolgarrog Station is on our left. We glide under
the Aluminium Corporation's and Cowlyd Water Board's bridges, until the wide
river becomes a stream of beautiful bends and reedy banks.

The scenery, from here to Trefriw, is of great beauty, and is seen to fullest advantage from the little steamer.

'I've seen the Thames' vast waters flow,
   They're not like thine, sweet Conway!
I've seen the Seine meandering go,
   Yet not like thine, sweet Conway!
And, save the blue and storied Rhine
No waters may compare with thine,
For Nature's beauties all combine –
   Upon thy banks, sweet Conway!'

Included in the lakes amongst these mountains are Llyn Dulyn, from which
Llandudno draws its supply; Llyn Eigiau; Llyn Cowlyd, which supplies Conway
and Colwyn Bay; Llyn Crafnant; Llyn Geirionydd, and others.

On the Denbighshire side of the river is the mountain, Forth Hywel Goch (The Ferry of Red Howell), rising almost abruptly from the river. At the other end of this mountain is a spur called Cadair Ifan Goch – from Ifan the Bard, who went there for inspiration. The view from the summit is one of the finest in the valley. Tradition says that a giant who lived hereabout used to stand with one foot upon the top of this hill and the other on the hills above Dolgarrog, whilst he washed himself in the river.

When all is still and clear, and with favourable light, the surrounding scenery reflected in the river near Trefriw forcibly recalls those lines by Scott:–

'And deep in her bosom, how grand was the scene;
  O'er mountains inverted the blue waters curled,
  And rocked them on skies of a far nether world.'

It is interesting to see with what skill the ever-genial Captain (Robert Roberts) pilots the boat to its destination, which is reached in due course.

Having visited the well-known Belle Vue Hotel (close to landing-stage) for refreshments, the visitor may wind-up his day by a visit to the now world-famous Chalybeate Wells (one mile), which date from Roman times, and which have made Trefriw Spa the 'Mecca' of so many health-seeking invalids and antiquarians. Or, one may proceed through the village to the first stream which crosses the road under a single-arch bridge. Before crossing the bridge there is a narrow road on the right, with a sign-post at the corner pointing to the Fairy Falls, two minutes' walk from the main road. Half-an-hour will bring you to Llewelyn's old Church (Llanrhychwyn), on the same hillside, a little relic of pre-Anglo-Norman times, which should not be missed.

If, from this point, you would like a ramble over the mountains, there is a pleasant walk (about two miles) to Crafnant Lake, with boats and good trout-fishing, and over the mountains to Capel Curig, then down to Bettws-y-Coed, and home by train. If, after seeing the Fairy Falls, you prefer to go forward, return to⋆ the main road, and after a walk of a mile and a half you reach Gwydir Castle, adjoining the main road. Visitors are allowed to go through under the guidance of the housekeeper. Gwydir Castle is one of the ancient seats of the Wynne family, and now the property of Lady Tankerville. Apart from historic interest attached to the Castle, it is filled with one of the finest collections of carved oak to be met with in the Principality, if not in the British Isles. The ornamental plaster-work of the ceilings and walls have been copied from those so well-known at Plas Mawr. (⋆A large portion of the castle was recently destroyed by fire)

Leaving Gwydir, the walk can be continued over Inigo Jones' Bridge to Llanrwst, where the Church is interesting and readily accessible. The Gwydir Castle connected with this Church, built by Sir Richard Wynn, in 1633, from a design by Inigo

Jones, it contains some remarkable old brasses and other curious relics. The remainder of our day may easily be put in at this quaint old market town, whence there is a good service of homeward-bound trains and 'buses in the evening.

Time permitting most visitors will, however, prefer to continue their journey to the celebrated mountain village of Bettws-y-Coed (four miles), which may be approached by a pleasant river-side path, starting from the Gwydir end of the old bridge. Buses also ply between Llanrwst and Bettws during summer.

The chief points of interest at Bettws-y-Coed are the Swallow Falls, Miner's Bridge, and Pont-y-Pair Bridge on the Llugwy, and the Fairy Glen and Conway Falls on the upper reaches of the Conway, just above the confluence of that river and the Lledr, and within easy reach of the village, *via* Waterloo Bridge.

Bettws-y-Coed and the beautiful Lledr Valley (well called the 'Trossachs of Wales') have always been the happy hunting ground of artists. David Cox's celebrated painting, once the subject of famous litigation, still hangs in the lounge of the Royal Oak Hotel. Many of Leader's most notable landscapes were done in the Lledr Valley, and among other artists who have helped to spread the fame of this district are Creswick, Muller, Bond, Whittaker, Topham, and Tayler.

If the journey cannot be continued beyond Trefriw, the return may be made by steamer, on foot, or by 'bus to Cbnway (nine miles) past Tal-y-bont and Caerhun, turning off at that point to see the old Church, the yew trees and Roman remains. From the Church there is a field-path, through the woods, to Talycafn Station, or the walk can be continued either by Ty'n-y-Groes or Roewen to Conway, by which time,

'The sun is down, the birds are still, Upon thy banks, sweet Conway!
   The mist is creeping up the hill, Upon thy banks, sweet Conway!
The waning of another day
Will see me musing far away,
But still. I hope again to stray
   Upon thy banks, sweet Conway!'

Sources & Bibliography

Archives

Formerly in the Ancaster Estate Records at Grimsthrope Castle, Lincolnshire. Now in the Gwynedd Archives, Caernarfon:
Trefriw Wharfage Book 1857–1876 contained in 'L. Willoughby's Book'

Bangor University Library:
Trefriw Quay Book 1817–1829 (Bangor 26049)
Trefriw Quay Book 1826–1835 (Bangor 10390)
Trefriw Quay Book 1835–1847 (Bangor 7057)
Trefriw Wharfage Book 1855–1826 (Bangor 7058)

Bodleian Library, Oxford:
Bradshaw's General Railway and Steam Navigation Guides from 1847

Cheshire Record Office, Chester:
Records of W.J. Yarwood, shipbuilders of Castle Dock Northwich. DDX 289. Including Vessel Register 1902–1965 (DDX 289/5) and Offset Book 1906–1931 (DDX 289/6)

Gwynedd Archives:
Ships Registers for the Ports of Beaumaris and Caernarfon
St George Steamship Co. Ltd records:
Letter Book 1911–1915 (XM/1669/1)
Letter from Capt Roberts to Capt. Edwards (XM 1669/1/85)
Correspondence File (XM/1669/75 and XM/1669/1/54)
Sailing Bills and advertisements (XM/1669/1/85 and 86)
Annual Reports and Statements of Accounts for 1913 and 1915–1920 (XM 1669/1/79 to 84)

Taped interview with Mr Rowland Hughes, Conwy, Mussel fishing and Pleasure boats (XM/T/434)

Bundle of twenty-two blueprints and tracings together with the builder's specification of the paddle steamer *King George* within the Dinorwic Quarryrecords (DO3473)

Two plans and full builder's specification of the steamer *Jubilee* within the Dinorwic Quarry records (DO3556)
Plan of replacement crankshaft for steamer *Trefriw Belle* within the Dinorwic Quarry records (DO3470)

National Archives, Kew:
Memorandum of Association of the Llandudno & Trefriw Motor Boat Company, 1907. BT31/11837/91961 and 67
Memorandum of Association of the Trefriw Chalybeate Wells & Baths Company Ltd, 1879. BT31/1863/7341

Newspapers

Chester Chronicle
Llandudno Advertiser
Llandudno Directory
North Wales Chronicle
North Wales Pioneer
North Wales Weekly News and Visitors' Chronicle
The Original Llandudno Directory

Articles

Clammer, R., 'A Welsh St. George', *Paddle Wheels*, No.84, Summer 1981
Clammer, R., 'Conwy River Steamers', *Waterways World*, November 1980
Davies, I.E., 'The Floating Traders of Oak and Iron', *North Wales Weekly News*, 16 December 1976
Dickens. C. (ed.), 'The Narrative of an Uneventful Voyage', *All the Year Round, a Weekly Journal*, Vol. 13, 1875
Dorr, J., 'A Week in Wales', *The Atlantic Monthly*, Vol. 62 Issue 371, September 1888, and later in *The Flower of England's Face; Sketches of English Travel*, London & New York, 1895
Evans, J.R., 'The Trefriw River Steamers', *Transactions of the Aberconwy Historical Society*, 1989
Garner, R., 'Holiday Excursions of a Naturalist', London, 1867
Hayward, J., 'The Vale of Conway Spa', *The British Journal of Homeopathy*, Vol. 23, 1864
Richards, R., 'Up the River Conway to Llanrwst', *Miscellaneous Poems & Pen-and-Ink Sketches*, North Wales Chronicle Office, Bangor, 1868
Thomas, C., 'The Shipping Trade of the River Conway in the Early Nineteenth Century', *Transactions of the Caernarvonshire Historical society*, Vol.33, 1972

Guide Books

A Guide to Trefriw, Llanrwst and Betws-y-Coed, Rees & Evans' Cambrian Series, published Caernarfon, June 1872
A Handbook for Travellers in North Wales (3rd edition), John Murray, London, 1868
Historic Conway & Sunny Deganwy, c. 1932
Baddeley & Ward's North Wales Guide, 1895
Black's Picturesque Guide to North Wales (5th edition), Adam & Charles Black, Edinburgh; and Catherall & Pritchard, Chester, 1874

Conway River Guide, or A Trip up the River by Steamer or Pleasure Boat, 3rd & 4th editions of the guide sold on board the steamers. Text by J.R. Furness, illustrations by J.C. Salmon, printed and published by R.E. Jones & Bros at the Weekly News office, Conway. Undated but *c.* 1920

Gossiping Guide to Wales, part II, by A. Roberts and E. Woodall, published by Woodall, Minshall, Thomas & co. of Oswestry & Wrexham, 1908.

Guide to Trefriw & The Vale of Conway Spa, J.M. Hayward, 2nd edition 1872, 3rd edition 1881

North Wales (Part 1), by Baddeley & Ward, Thorough Guide Series, Thomas Nelson & Sons, 1909

Red Guides, Ward Lock, various dates

River Trip to Trefriw: Illustrated Guide. Text by Asa Davis, illustrations by Eryl Jones, printed and published by R.E. Jones Ltd, Conway, *c.* 1954–59. Sold on board Craven & Roberts' Red Motor Boats

The Llandudno Visitor's Handbook with Historical Notices of the Neighbourhood, R. Parry, published in Llandudno, 1855

The St. George Steamship Co. Ltd Official Illustrated Souvenir & Descriptive Guide of Trips on the Conway River, the Rhine of Wales, British Publishing company, *c.* 1925–30

Trefriw Chalybeate Wells, N. Wales, the Richest Iron Waters Known, published on behalf of the Wells, April 1908

Trefriw: It's Chalybeate Wells, Lakes & Walks, Abel Heywood & Sons Guide Books, 1910

Trefriw Mineral Springs with Guide to the Neighbourhood, T.E. Jones, 1897

Trefriw Spa: The Pearl of Ancient Gwynedd, Trefriw, Spa Publicity committee, 1934. (Guidebook to the Belle Vue Spa of 1930)

Trefriw Wells, published by the Wells Company under the patronage of Trefriw Council, *c.* 1930

Other Printed Books

Alexander, C., Dovey, M. & Ellerton, G., *British Pleasure Steamer Cachets*, TPO & Seapost Society, 2011

Baughan, P.E., *A Regional History of the Railways of Great Britain: Vol 11, North and Mid Wales*, David & Charles, 1980

Bennett, A.R., *The Chronicles of Boulton's Sidings*, David & Charles, 1971 (reprint of 1st edition, 1927)

Clegg, V., *The Belle Vue Hotel*, pamphlet produced by the author as a gift to the hotel's proprietors, 1998

Davies, H.R., *A Review of the Records of the Conway and Menai Ferries*, University of Wales Press, Cardiff, 1966

Duckworth, C.L.D. & Langmuir, G.E., *West Coast Steamers*, T. Stephenson & Sons Ltd, 1953 and 1956

Ellis-Williams, M., *Bangor, Port of Beaumaris*, Gwynedd Archives, 1988

Ellis, T., *Trefriw: An Illustrated Miscellany of Literature*, Trefriw Historical Society, 2011

Ellis, T., *Artists in the Conwy valley, 1770–1940*, Trefriw Historical Society, 2011

Greenwood, R.H. & Hawks, F.W., *The Saint George Steam Packet Company*, World Ship Society, 1995

Harman, R.G., *The Conway Valley Railway*, Branch Line Handbook No. 17, 1963

Hope, B., *A Commodious Yard: The Story of William Thomas & sons, Shipbuilders of Amlwch*, Gwasg Careg Gwalch, 2005

Jones, M., *Hanes Trefriw / The History of Trefriw as it used to be and as it is now*, W.J. Roberts, Llanrwst, 1879. Translated by Tony Ellis and published by the Trefriw Historical Society, 2009

Lewis, S., *A Topographical Dictionary of Wales*, S. Lewis & Co., London, 1833 (later editions 1844 & 1849)

Lloyd, L., *De Winton's of Caernarfon*, published by the author, 1994

MacArthur, W., *The River Conway*, Cassell, 1952

McRonald, M., *Passenger Sailings on the River Conwy and a Route Description*, produced by the author for the Coastal Cruising Association to mark its charter sailings on board the *Queen Victoria* to Tal-y-Cafn on 3 August 1996, 15 August 1988, and 10 August 2002

McRonald, R. *Saint George Steam Packet Co.* 2002. Pamphlet published by the author

McNeill, D.B., *Irish Passenger Steamship Services: Vol. 2 The South of Ireland*, David & Charles, 1971

Miller, N., *The Lancashire Nobby*, Amberley, 2009

Napier, J. & Richards, A.J., *The River Conwy, Source to Sea*, Gwasg Carreg Gwalch, 2011

Pattinson, E.M., *The Spirit of Conwy: Vols 1&2*, Landmark Publishing, 1993

Senior, M., *The Crossing of the Conwy*, Gwasg Carreg Gwalch, 1996

Senior, M., *The Conwy valley and its Long History*, Gwasg Carreg Gwalch, 1984

Shepherd, J., *The Liverpool and North Wales Steamship Company*, Ships in Focus Publications, 2006

Thornley, F.C., *Steamers of North Wales*, T. Stephenson & Sons Ltd, 1952 & 1962

Turner, K., *Trams Beside the Seaside: The Story of the Llandudno & Colwyn Bay Electric Railway*, Gwasg Carreg Gwalch, 2004

Wynne-Jones, I., *Betws-y-Coed and the Conway Valley*, John Jones Ltd., 1974

Further Reading

The Trefriw Historical Society (Cymdeithas Hanesyddol Trefriw) has produced a fascinating series of picture and history books, all edited by one of their members, Tony Ellis. Produced electronically and printed in small editions, they are updated regularly as new material becomes available. Included among the titles are:

A Postcard from Trefriw
A Postcard from the Conwy valley, 1900–1930
Hanes Trefriw: A translation of Morris Jones' original Welsh language history of Trefriw, published in 1879 and translated by Tony Ellis, 2009
Trefriw: An Illustrated Miscellany of Literature
Artists in the Conwy valley 1770–1940
The Train to Trefriw: A history of the various proposals to put Trefriw on the railway map, as chronicled in extracts from the London Gazette, *1845–1912*

Websites

www.postcardnostalgia.co.uk/trefiw has a well-indexed and excellent selection of local postcard views

Index

n.b. Heavy Type indicates an illustration;
Ship names in italics
ss = steamship
ps = paddle steamer

mv = motor vessel
ml = motor launch